W9-BKB-828

Here are some reviews of Simpson's bestselling titles:

"Simpson writes with a light, engaging style that will appeal to readers put off by the ponderous and sometimes impenetrable prose of some technical manuals."

—Business Software

On **Understanding dBASE II**: "Simpson's step-by-step tutorial method is easy to follow and the layout of the book helps enormously. If you have need for dBASE II, you have need for **Understanding dBASE II**."

—United Press International

". . . even experienced dBASE programmers can benefit from reading **Understanding dBASE II**. Its concise explanations and clear examples can provide insights that often escape long-time users and can help a programmer with basic principles he may have forgotten or never adequately understood."

—Digital Review

Advanced Techniques in dBASE III "is the best choice for experienced dBASE III programmers."

—Data Based Advisor

Understanding
dBASE III PLUS

Academic Edition

Understanding
dBASE III PLUS™
Academic Edition

Alan Simpson

San Francisco · Paris · Düsseldorf · Soest

Acquisitions Editor: Dianne King
Developmental Editor: Eric Stone
Copy Editor: Kathleen D. Lattinville
Technical Editor: Michael Gross
Production Editor: Carolina Montilla
Word Processors: Deborah Maizels and Winnie Kelly
Chapter Art and Layout: Lucie Živny
Typesetter: Len Gilbert
Cover Designer: Thomas Ingalls + Associates
Cover Photographer: David Bishop
dBASE and dBASE III PLUS are registered trademarks of Ashton-Tate Corp.

SYBEX is a registered trademark of SYBEX Inc.

TRADEMARKS: SYBEX has attempted throughout this book to distinguish proprietary trademarks from descriptive terms by following the capitalization style used by the manufacturer.

SYBEX is not affiliated with any manufacturer.

Every effort has been made to supply complete and accurate information. However, SYBEX assumes no responsibility for its use, nor for any infringement of the intellectual property rights of third parties which would result from such use.

The text of this book is printed on recycled paper

Copyright ©1990 SYBEX Inc., 2021 Challenger Drive #100, Alameda, CA 94501. World rights reserved. No part of this publication may be stored in a retrieval system, transmitted, or reproduced in any way, including but not limited to photocopy, photograph, magnetic or other record, without the prior agreement and written permission of the publisher.

Library of Congress Card Number: 90-70869
ISBN: 0-89588-729-0
Manufactured in the United States of America
10 9 8 7 6 5 4 3 2

To Susan and Ashley

ACKNOWLEDGMENTS

Many thanks to everyone at SYBEX who helped nurse the original edition of this book from the idea stage to your hands: Carole Alden, Acquisitions Editor; Karl Ray, Managing Editor; Barbara Graves, Editor; David Clark, Word Processor; Brenda Walker, Typesetter; and Jon Strickland, Proofreader.

I would like to thank Jannie Dresser, Indexer, and Nick Wolfinger, Technical Support.

For this newer *Academic Edition*, I wish to thank Eric Stone, Developmental Editor; Kathleen Lattinville, Copy Editor; Michael Gross, Technical Editor; Carolina Montilla, Production Editor; Deborah Maizels and Winnie Kelly, Word Processors; Len Gilbert, Typesetter; and Lucie Živny, Artist.

Also, I want to thank Bill and Cynthia Gladstone, my long-time literary agents and new family.

Special thanks to Susan for being patient while I disappeared for long hours to pound the keyboard.

CONTENTS

Introduction

C H A P T E R   O N E

Understanding Databases

C H A P T E R   T W O

Building a Database

C H A P T E R　　T H R E E

Searching the Database

C H A P T E R　　F O U R

Sorting the Database

CHAPTER FIVE

Editing and Modifying Databases

CHAPTER SIX

Creating and Printing Formatted Reports

C H A P T E R S E V E N

Designing Custom Screen Displays

C H A P T E R E I G H T

Managing Numbers and Dates

C H A P T E R   N I N E

Managing Multiple Data Files

C H A P T E R   T E N

File Maintenance and Performance

C H A P T E R E L E V E N

Understanding Memory Variables

C H A P T E R T W E L V E

Creating Command Files

C H A P T E R T H I R T E E N

Making Decisions

C H A P T E R   F O U R T E E N

Designing and Developing Programs

C H A P T E R   F I F T E E N

Debugging Techniques

C H A P T E R S I X T E E N

A Complete Mailing System

C H A P T E R S E V E N T E E N

Some Useful Tips

A P P E N D I X   A

Interfacing with Other Software Systems

A P P E N D I X   B

The Applications Generator

APPENDIX C

dBASE III PLUS Vocabulary

APPENDIX D

Converting dBASE II Files to dBASE III PLUS Files

EXERCISES

INTRODUCTION

dBASE III PLUS is the third major version of the classic dBASE database management system for microcomputers. Like its predecessors, dBASE II and dBASE III, dBASE III PLUS is a powerful and flexible system for storing, organizing, analyzing, and retrieving information on a microcomputer.

dBASE III PLUS, however, has two major advantages over its predecessors. The first is a much improved interface between you, the user, and your information. Unlike earlier versions, the new PLUS allows you to interact with your data through *menu selections* rather than through programming-like commands. These menus free you from memorizing commands and rules of syntax, and thereby allow you to interact with your data with fewer trips to the technical manuals.

dBASE III PLUS is also more powerful than any of its predecessors. Even the advanced dBASE III applications developer or professional programmer will appreciate new commands, functions, and debugging capabilities added to the programming language. Although this book is designed for the novice rather than for the professional, later chapters will touch upon some of these more advanced features.

WHO THIS BOOK IS FOR

This book is written for the absolute beginner. However, the reader who has some experience with either dBASE II or dBASE III will gain from this book an understanding of the new PLUS features.

To encourage rapid learning and complete mastery, we'll focus on practical examples of what dBASE III PLUS can do for you. When you see how easy it is to put its power to practical work, you'll probably find that the more advanced capabilities are much simpler than you expected.

Those of you with previous dBASE experience will probably rush through the first few chapters. The newcomers to the dBASE world should take the time to try the various examples presented in each chapter.

THE STRUCTURE OF THIS BOOK

The first ten chapters of this book discuss the many tasks that you can perform using dBASE III PLUS with no programming whatsoever. Many readers will no doubt find this information sufficient for their business needs.

Chapters 11 through 15 discuss programming with the dBASE language, using simple examples that eventually culminate in a complete, fully-automated mailing system in Chapter 16. Chapter 17 is a "catch-all" chapter of tips and tricks. This chapter also includes brief discussions of networking and RunTime +.

Appendix A discusses techniques for interfacing dBASE III PLUS data with other software systems. Appendix B discusses the dBASE III PLUS Applications Generator. Appendix C is a dictionary of the dBASE III PLUS vocabulary, and Appendix D shows how to transfer data from dBASE II to dBASE III PLUS.

ABOUT THE ACADEMIC EDITION

This *Academic Edition* of *Understanding dBASE III PLUS* offers one additional feature over the "regular" edition of the book—student exercises. These are provided to give you extra practice with the new skills you learn, and to challenge you to apply those skills to new and different situations. Rather than tell you step by step what to do, the exercises give you a goal or project to accomplish on your own.

The exercises begin on page 407. Most likely, you will be using this book as part of an introductory course on dBASE III PLUS, in which case your instructor will determine exactly how and when you will complete the exercises. Or, your instructor may provide alternative exercises in the form of handouts, depending on how he or she has planned the course.

INSTALLATION AND CONFIGURATION

Before you can use dBASE III PLUS to follow the examples in this book, you'll need to be sure that dBASE III PLUS is properly installed on your computer. If you are using this book as part of a course on dBASE III PLUS, chances are dBASE III PLUS has already been installed on the computer used in the classroom or computer lab. Therefore, you need not be concerned about this.

However, if you plan on using your personal computer (or one where you work), then you will need to be sure that dBASE III PLUS is installed on that computer. It's important to realize that dBASE III PLUS, like all computer programs, is not "built in" to your computer. It is an entirely optional software product that can be purchased in most computer or software stores, or through advertisements placed in many computer magazines.

Once you acquire a copy of the dBASE III PLUS program, you will need to refer to the *Getting Started* manual that comes with that package for installation instructions.

Note that installation procedures are different for computers with two floppy-disk drives, hard disks, and networked computers. Also, make sure to copy the CONFIG.SYS file from the dBASE III PLUS System Disk #1 to your boot-up disk, as described in the *Getting Started* manual.

Note: The *Getting Started* manual mistakenly states that the CONFIG.SYS file should contain these commands:

FILES =
20 BUFFERS = 15

The correct contents of the CONFIG.SYS file are

FILES = 20
BUFFERS = 15

If error messages appear on your screen as soon as you boot your computer, you must correct these commands in your CONFIG .SYS file.

NEW FEATURES OF dBASE III PLUS

For those of you who are already familiar with dBASE II or dBASE III, we'll summarize some of the new features of the PLUS version. If you're a newcomer to dBASE, don't worry about understanding the features that seem quite advanced. We'll start at square one in Chapter 1 and discuss the basics. This book assumes that every reader is a beginning user of these new PLUS features:

■

Pull-Down Menus: Rather than displaying a dot prompt and waiting for you to figure out what to do next, the new dBASE III PLUS displays a menu of options. Through the menus you can use virtually all of the dBASE capabilities, including many that are new to the PLUS version, without typing a single command. You can also remove the menus from the screen temporarily if you prefer the original dot-prompt method of entering commands.

■

Networking: The dBASE Administrator, which comes with your dBASE III PLUS package, allows you to run dBASE III PLUS on the IBM PC Network and the Novell Advanced NetWare/86. The *Getting Started* manual includes complete instructions for installing the dBASE Administrator, and setting up a CONFIG.SYS file for a Local Area Network (LAN) of computers. There are also new commands in the dBASE III PLUS programming language for use with networks.

■

Improved Custom Screens: A built-in Screen Painter makes it easy to create custom screens in dBASE III PLUS by simply "drawing" them. Screens can contain multiple pages, so you no longer need to write programs to handle multiple screens.

Applications Generator: An *applications generator* (or *program generator*) is a program that writes programs. Program generators were once expensive add-ons to programming languages. dBASE III PLUS comes with a built-in Applications Generator that can help you to customize dBASE applications more quickly.

New Commands and Functions: For the advanced programmer, dBASE III PLUS offers the ability to save and recall Queries, the ability to combine FOR and WHILE commands in a single condition, and the ability to use numeric functions for absolute value, modulo, highest number, and lowest number. HISTORY, SUSPEND, and RESUME commands are new debugging tools. With dBASE III PLUS commands, you can call assembly-language subroutines, and scan the keyboard for a keypress without halting program execution. If you are primarily interested in these more advanced programming topics, you will probably be better served by a more advanced book that focuses on dBASE programming, such as my own *dBASE III PLUS Programmer's Reference Guide*, also published by SYBEX. It's available in most bookstores.

Understanding Databases

W hat is a database? While *database management* sounds so technical, it's as ordinary as driving a car. Think, for instance, of a shoe box full of index cards with names and addresses for a mailing list. The shoe box and its contents are a database. Every time you juggle the index cards to get them in alphabetical order, you are *managing* the database. The average office file cabinet is a database too. It doesn't do anything; it just holds information. If you open a drawer and look up the Johnson account, you are searching a database, a way of managing it.

You typically keep your everyday databases in some order, either by alphabet, by date, or perhaps by zip code. You do so to *structure* your database, so that it is easier for you to work with. We human database managers do not like messy file cabinets. Ditto for computers. If you want to change the order of an alphabetical file, you might want to be able to say a magic word and have them instantly rearranged by zip code. Too bad you can't. Unfortunately, the task could take you hours of tedious labor. But with a computer, and the right magic word, the rearrangement can take place in seconds. But before we can discuss the magic words of dBASE III PLUS, we need to discuss a computer's view of a database.

In the computer world, a database is like a shoe-box file with a very rigid structure. While the shoe box is filled with index cards, a computer database is filled with *records*. And while each index card in the shoe box may contain several written lines of information, a record in a database contains *fields* of information. That is, a shoe box contains cards, each of which has several lines of information

John Q. Smith
123 A St.
San Diego, CA 92122

(619)455-1212

Figure 1.1: Index Card Record

on it. A database contains records, each of which has several fields within it. Take a look at the index card in Figure 1.1.

It has four lines of information on it:

    NAME
    ADDRESS
    CITY, STATE, ZIP
    PHONE NUMBER

This single index card represents one record in a computer database. Each of the lines roughly represents one field of information in the database.

There is a very important difference between human database managers and computer database management systems. As people, we can tell what each line on the index card represents. That is, you know who this card refers to, his first and last name, as well as his address, city, state, zip code, and phone number. You know this simply by looking at the context of the information. You can tell that (619) 455-1212 is not a last name. Although this is obvious to people, it is not at all clear to a computer. A computer can't tell a phone number from a last name from a meat loaf. Unfortunately, the computer doesn't understand anything about information based on its context. Thus, you have to structure a database rigidly so the computer does not mistake a name for a phone number, and you must be pretty explicit. Computers may be fast, but they are definitely not smart.

How do you structure a database with dBASE III PLUS? First you have to decide exactly what you want to store. To do so, you have to break down the information on the index card into meaningful units of information. In the above example, one card holds a name, address, city, state, zip, and phone number. You will want each record in your database to hold the same information. Recall that a given record in a database refers to one index card in a shoe box, and that each field in a record refers to one piece of information on a given card. Hence, in this database, you would want each record to contain these fields:

    NAME, ADDRESS, CITY, STATE, ZIP, PHONE

Notice that there are six fields in this record. Let me warn you here of the most common mistake that people make when structuring databases. On the index card in Figure 1.1, you see four written lines: one containing the name, one containing the address, one containing the city, state and zip, and the other containing a phone number. Looking at the card, you might be tempted to structure the database with these four fields:

   NAME, ADDRESS, CSZ, PHONE

The CSZ field would contain the city, state and zip. This is misleading in reference to computer databases because if you ever wanted to sort your data file by zip code, you couldn't. Since the zip would be combined with city and state, the computer couldn't isolate it. Thus, you should assign each single meaningful piece of information to a unique field. Therefore,

   NAME, ADDRESS, CITY, STATE, ZIP, PHONE

is a better structure because each piece of data is placed in a separate field. Learning to define meaningful items of information is an important aspect of database management, as you will see throughout this book. With the proper database structure, you can sort individuals by zip code, or search for individuals within a given zip code range. Because the zip code field is isolated from the city and state, it becomes a meaningful, individual piece of data for the computer to sort.

So then, how does the computer know what a given piece of information means? It doesn't. In the example above, you've told the computer that in each record there are six fields. The first field is NAME, the second is ADDRESS, the third field is CITY, etc. If you store "John Q. Smith" in the ZIP field, the computer is not going to think about this and say to you, "That looks more like a name to me!" It will just store John Q. Smith as the zip code. Therefore, it is up to you to put the correct data in the appropriate field. You're the brains of the operation, not the computer.

WHAT IS DATABASE MANAGEMENT?

Once you've structured your database, you need to manage it by giving the computer precise instructions. Managing a database primarily involves the following tasks:

1. ADD new data to the database.
2. SORT the database into some meaningful order.
3. SEARCH the database for types of information.
4. PRINT data from our database onto formatted reports.
5. EDIT data on the database.
6. DELETE data from the database.

You need to do similar tasks with a shoe-box file. Occasionally you may need to add some new index cards. You may also want to sort the index cards into some meaningful order (say, alphabetically or by zip code). You might want to search through them and find all the people who live in Los Angeles, or all the people in the 92123 zip code area, or perhaps just find out where a person named Clark Kenney lives. If Clark Kenney moves, you may want to edit the database and change his address. Then again, if Clark Kenney stops paying his dues, you may want to delete him from the mailing list altogether. This is database management. With the shoe box, you do all the work. With the computer, you think and the computer works.

Let's move on to Chapter 2 now and start talking about dBASE III PLUS more specifically.

REVIEWING DATABASE TERMINOLOGY

In this chapter you've learned some new vocabulary about databases:

A *database* is an organized collection of information.

▬

A *database management system* is a tool for managing information stored on a computer.

▬

On a database, information is stored in *records* (rows) and *fields* (columns) of information.

▬

The general tasks you perform in *managing a database* include adding new information, sorting, searching, printing reports, editing, and deleting data.

Building a Database

I n this chapter you'll learn the basic steps of getting dBASE III PLUS "up-and-running" on your computer. Notice that the instructions vary somewhat depending on the type of computer you have. You'll also learn techniques for managing the menu that appears once dBASE is running on your computer.

This chapter will also teach you how to create a database and add information to it. Techniques for getting immediate help on the screen are discussed too. Finally, you'll learn how to save your new data, retrieve it, and how to properly exit dBASE.

STARTING DBASE III PLUS

To try the examples in this section, you'll need to get dBASE III PLUS up-and-running on your computer. Before you can start dBASE you must install it according to the instructions in the *Getting Started* manual that came with your dBASE III PLUS package. Then follow these starting instructions for the type of computer you have:

Computers with Two Floppy-Disk Drives

If you are using a computer with two floppy-disk drives, place the dBASE III PLUS System Disk #1 in Drive A and a blank, formatted disk in Drive B. Next to the DOS A> prompt, type the command

DBASE ◄─┘

(*Note:* The symbol ◄─┘ means "Press the Return, or Enter key.") You'll see a copyright notice and these instructions:

Insert System Disk 2 and press ENTER, or press Ctrl-C to abort.

Remove the disk from Drive A. Place your dBASE III PLUS System Disk #2 in Drive A, and press the Return key. You'll see the dBASE menu screen appear.

Computers with Hard Disks

If you are using a hard disk system and have already installed dBASE III PLUS, simply log on to the appropriate directory on your hard disk (using the DOS CHDIR or CD command). At the

    C>

prompt, enter the command

    DBASE ⤶

When the copyright notice appears, press Return to move into the dBASE III PLUS menu screen.

Networked Computer Systems

For techniques in starting dBASE III PLUS on a networked system of computers, see the *Getting Started* manual that came with your dBASE III PLUS package. Procedures will vary depending upon your particular network configuration.

NAVIGATING THE MENU SCREEN

Figure 2.1 shows the on-screen dBASE III PLUS menu screen. This menu is also called the *Assistant,* because its job is to assist you in building commands that dBASE can interpret and execute. As you'll see later in the book, you can build your own commands without the Assistant menu.

This screen consists of eight main menu options listed in a bar across the top of the screen, eight submenus that pull down from the main menu bar as you highlight one of its options, a status bar and three message lines at the bottom of the screen.

If you press the ← or → keys on the numeric keypad, you'll notice that the highlighting moves across the main menu bar, and *pull-down menus* representing sub-options appear beneath the

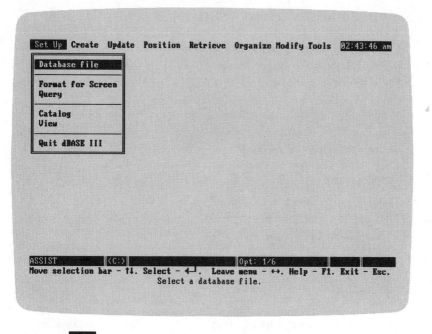

Figure 2.1: The dBASE III PLUS Assistant Menu Screen

highlighted option. (*Note:* If your arrow keys don't work and the "NUM" message appears at the bottom of your screen, press the Num Lock key and try again.) You can also highlight items from the main menu bar by typing the first letter of the option. For example, typing the letter **T** brings the pull-down menu for the *Tools* option.

Notice that some items on the pull-down menus are brighter than others. The brighter options are those that are available for selection. The dimmer options can only be selected after certain pre-conditions are met. Don't worry, though. Most of the options will be available to you the moment that you select a database.

Now type **S** to move the highlighting to the *Set Up* option. You'll notice that the first selection, *Database file,* is highlighted in reverse video. You can use the ↑ and ↓ keys to move this highlighting up and down within the pull-down menu. Pressing the Return key selects the currently highlighted option.

The Dot Prompt

Pressing the Escape (Esc) key "unselects" a pull-down menu option. If you press Esc before selecting a sub-option, the menu screen will disappear and the dBASE III PLUS dot prompt will appear (which we'll discuss in a later chapter). While the dot prompt is familiar to those with previous dBASE II or dBASE III experience, it may not mean a lot to the novice. If you should find that the menu disappears and only a period appears near the bottom of the screen, type the command

ASSIST ←⏎

to bring back the Assistant menu.

If you prefer entering commands at the dot prompt, there is a way to completely bypass the dBASE III PLUS menu screen (which we'll discuss in a later chapter). However, most of these same commands are available as Assistant menu options. For more details, see *Entering Commands at the Dot Prompt* later in this chapter.

The Status Bar

At the bottom of your screen (and at the bottom of Figure 2.1), you'll see the *Status Bar* in reverse video. The Status Bar keeps you informed of the current status of various optional settings. Just above the Status Bar, the *Action Line* will display the dBASE commands that you build from menu options. The action line is empty right now, but when you select menu options later, it will display dBASE III PLUS commands.

Beneath the status bar are the *Navigation Line* and *Message Line*. These two lines provide instructions and explain the currently highlighted option. When you're first learning, remember to read these lines beneath the Status Bar to see what your options are and to get instructions for your next selection.

GETTING HELP

Before we go any further, let's take a moment to discuss a way to get help *on-line* (on the screen) while working with dBASE. Any time a menu option is highlighted, you can press the Help (F1) key to get some additional information about the option. For example, if you press F1 while the *Create* option is highlighted, you'll see the brief description of the option shown in Figure 2.2.

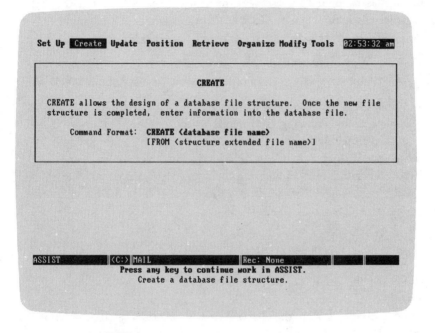

Figure 2.2: Help Screen for the *Create* Option

Some Help screens may seem a bit advanced at first because they explain techniques for working with dBASE III PLUS from the dot prompt (which we'll discuss later). Nonetheless, the F1 key is a quick way to get information without looking through the manuals.

When you finish viewing a help screen, press any key to resume your work. Now, let's build a database for managing a basic mailing list to put dBASE to work and start learning about the many capabilities dBASE III PLUS offers.

CREATING A DATABASE

To create a database, highlight the *Create* option from the main menu either by moving the highlighting to the word or by typing the letter **C**. The pull-down menu will present these options:

Database file
Format
View
Query
Report
Label

To create a database, select the *Database file* option by pressing the Return key. The screen will then display these options:

A:
B:
C:

If you are using a computer with two floppy-disk drives, select the **B:** option to create the database on the disk in Drive B. If you are using a hard disk system, select the **C:** option.

Next, dBASE will ask you to

Enter the name of the file:

The name you enter can be up to eight characters long, but it may not contain spaces or punctuation marks. For this example, type the file name

MAIL ⏎

If you make a mistake typing the name, you can use the Back-space key to back up and make corrections. dBASE will automatically add the extension .DBF (for **D**ata**B**ase **F**ile) to the file name you assign. Therefore, when you enter MAIL as the file name, dBASE will actually store the database under MAIL.DBF.

After you name your database, dBASE provides some help at the top of a new screen. *Note:* Some keys have a ^ symbol in front of them, which means that you must press the Ctrl key as you type the letter.

At the center of the screen, dBASE displays the blank form shown in Figure 2.3. You must fill in this form to create a database structure.

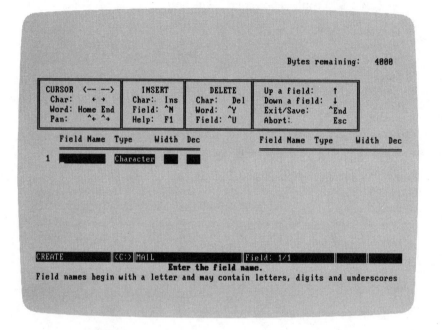

Figure 2.3: Form for Creating a Database Structure

Let's discuss what all of this means. Notice that dBASE is asking for information about the fields in each record. For each field, it needs to know the name, type, width, and number of decimal places. The name of the field can be up to ten characters long, but no spaces are allowed, and the only punctuation allowed is the underscore character (_). dBASE also needs to know the type of data being stored in the field. Data can be one of five types: 1) **C**haracter, for non-numeric data such as name, address, etc.; 2) **N**umeric, for numbers that we want to do some math with, like dollar amounts or inventory quantity; 3) **D**ate, for dates in MM/DD/YY format; 4) **M**emo, for long passages of text; 5) **L**ogical, where the field is either true or false. Then, dBASE needs to know the width of each field, the maximum number of characters that the field will contain. Finally, it needs to know how many decimal places are to be stored for numbers. For instance, in a dollar amount, we typically store two decimal places ($999.99).

To fill in information on the screen, simply type in the field name, followed by a press on the Return key. The cursor will move to the *type* prompt. Type the first letter of the type of data: **C**haracter data, **N**umeric data, **D**ates, **M**emos, or **L**ogical data. In your first example, just use all character types to keep things simple. The cursor will move to the "width" column. Type the maximum width for the field followed by a press on the Return key. If you make errors while typing data, you can use the arrow keys on the numeric keypad (on the right side of the keyboard) to position the cursor for making changes.

Structure the MAIL.DBF database like this:

Field	Field Name	Type	Width	Dec
1	LNAME	Character	15	
2	FNAME	Character	10	
3	ADDRESS	Character	25	
4	CITY	Character	15	
5	STATE	Character	5	
6	ZIP	Character	10	

Rather than typing in a seventh field, just press the Return key. dBASE will display the message

Press ENTER to confirm. Any other key to resume

Press the Return key.

Notice that we've broken the first and last names into separate fields. The last-name field (LNAME) can take a last name fifteen letters long. The first-name field (FNAME) can hold up to ten letters.

Why are there two separate fields? Because in the future, you might want to sort the data alphabetically by last name. If you just had one field for both first and last names, such as Joe Smith, when you did your sort, dBASE would sort by first name. You and I can look at Joe Smith and immediately see that Smith is the last name. Since the computer doesn't understand this, you've established the difference between first and last name by providing a separate field for each. You've also put address, city, state, and zip into separate fields. Note that **C** indicates that each of these is a Character data field.

Now you'll probably ask, "Why is zip code a Character string? Isn't 92122 a number?" Yes, it is, but hyphenated zip codes like 92038-2802 could cause problems. In dBASE, the hyphen means "subtract" when dealing with numbers. So at some point, 92038-2802 might become 89236 if stored as a number (92038 minus 2802 = 89236). This could wreak havoc on a mailing system.

Another problem is that some foreign zip codes have letters in them, like A132-09. In dBASE III PLUS, letters are not allowed in Numeric data fields. You will avoid a lot of trouble by making ZIP a Character field. The only time you must make a field Numeric is when you need to do math. Certainly, you'll never need to total up zip codes!

So we now have a structured database. All meaningful pieces of information are broken out into separate fields. Again, avoid the temptation to combine several pieces of information into one field (CITY:STATE:ZIP). dBASE III PLUS allows a maximum of 128 fields in each record, with their combined widths totalling up to a maximum of 4000 characters. There is plenty of room.

On your screen, you will now see that the computer is asking if you want to

Input data records now? (Y/N)

Type **N** to answer No and return to the main menu. There you have it—a database called MAIL.DBF. Now, let's discuss how to open the database and how to add some data to it.

OPENING A DATABASE

Imagine that you have a number of databases, like shoe boxes filled with index cards. Before you can add cards (*records*) to one of these databases, you must *open* its box. So let's discuss the easy technique for opening your MAIL.DBF database now.

First, move the highlighting to the *Set Up* option on the main menu bar. dBASE displays these options on the pull-down menu:

Database file

Format for Screen
Query

Catalog
View

Quit dBASE III

Press Return to select the *Database file* option. The screen displays

A:
B:
C:

for specifying a disk drive. As before, select **B:** if you are using a computer with two floppy-disk drives, or **C:** if you are using a hard disk. dBASE will display the names of all existing database files on the drive. Move the highlighting to MAIL.DBF and press Return. dBASE will ask

Is the file indexed? [Y/N]

We won't be creating index files until a later chapter, so just type **N** to answer No. At the bottom of the screen, on the highlighted status bar, you'll see

<B:> MAIL

or

<C:> MAIL

indicating that the MAIL.DBF database is open and ready for work on either Drive B or C. Now let's add some data.

ENTERING DATA

To add data to the file, highlight the *Update* option on the main menu, and select the *Append* option from the pull-down menu. A blank form for entering new data will appear, as in Figure 2.4.

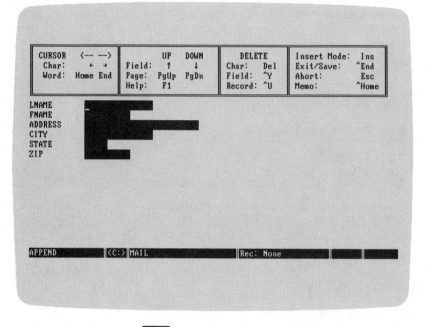

Figure 2.4: Blank Data Form

Notice the keys that appear at the top of the screen. You used some of the same keys creating the MAIL database structure. Now you'll have a chance to try some of them out as you add new records to the database.

A Sample Database Record

The following information will become the first record for your database:

John Q. Smith
123 A St.
San Diego, CA 92123

Because the order of the fields is slightly different than this Rolodex-card style, follow these steps to enter the first record.

Smith ↵
John Q. ↵
123 A St. ↵
San Diego ↵
CA ↵
92123

When you finish, your screen should look like Figure 2.5.

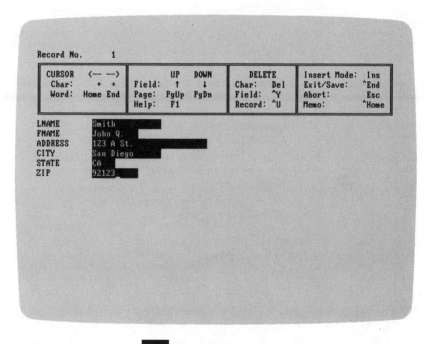

Figure 2.5: First MAIL Record

Press Return after entering the zip code, and a blank form for filling in the second record will appear.

The Numeric Keypad and Cursor-Movement Keys

When you are entering a number of new records, it's easy to

make mistakes. With dBASE it's also easy to correct mistakes as you enter data.

Before adding the second record to the database, take a moment to review the basic data-entry commands shown in Table 2.1. (Remember that the ^ symbol means, "Hold down the Ctrl key while typing the letter that follows.")

Key		Alternate Key	Effect
↑	*or*	^E	Move cursor up one field
↓	*or*	^X	Move cursor down one field
←	*or*	^S	Move cursor left one space
→	*or*	^D	Move cursor right one space
Del	*or*	^G	Delete character over cursor
Ins	*or*	^V	Turn the insert mode on/off
PgUp	*or*	^R	Move back to previous record
PgDn	*or*	^C	Move forward to next record
^End	*or*	^W	Save all newly added data and return to the menu
Home			Move to first letter of word
End			Move to end of word
^Y			Delete contents to the right of the cursor
^U			Delete/Undelete entire record

Table 2.1 Basic Data-Entry Control Keys

All of the control-key commands are in the left-hand portion of the keyboard, near the Ctrl key. This is so that you can hold down the Ctrl key with your little finger while pressing the appropriate key. The position of the keys suggests the direction that the cursor moves, as shown in Figure 2.6. The arrow keys and Ins and Del keys on the numeric keypad are shown in Figure 2.7.

The arrow and control-key commands hold true for most dBASE forms that appear on the screen, as you'll see throughout the following chapters.

Some enhanced keyboards offer a separate set of arrow keys that you can use instead of the cursor-control keys on the numeric keypad.

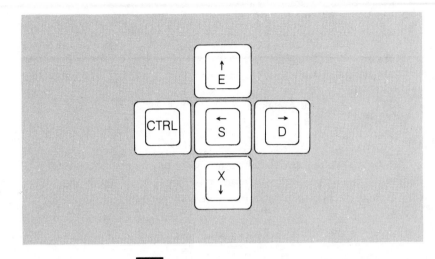

Figure 2.6: Cursor-Movement Keys

Figure 2.7: Numeric Keypad

Let's add a second record. Suppose that while adding the second record, you type the following data:

```
LNAME      :Appleby          :
FNAME      :Andy             :
ADDRESS    :35 Oak St.       :
CITY       :Los Angeless     :
STATE      :CA   :
ZIP        :_       :
```

Before typing the zip code, notice a couple of errors in the field above. To fix these, first, you can move the cursor up to the CITY field by pressing the ↑ key twice, or by holding down the Ctrl key and tapping the **E** key twice. The cursor moves to the beginning of the CITY field like so:

CITY:Los Angeless :

Now to move the cursor to the right, press the End key twice, and then ← twice. The cursor will move to the first s in Angeless, like this:

CITY:Los Angeless :

Delete the character above the cursor using a ^G or by pressing the Del key. Now the city field looks like this:

CITY:Los Angeles :

You've eliminated the extra s.

Next notice that the address is supposed to be 345 Oak St., instead of 35 Oak St. Press the ↑ key to move the cursor up to the ADDRESS field like so:

ADDRESS:35 Oak St._ :

Then press the ← key nine times to move the cursor to the 5 in the ADDRESS field:

ADDRESS:35 Oak St. :

Now you want to squeeze a **4** in between the 3 and the 5. To do so, you first have to go into an INSert mode by pressing the Ins key. This puts the message "INS" at the bottom of the screen.

Now if you just type the number **4**, the 4 is inserted between the 3 and the 5 like this:

ADDRESS:345̲ Oak St.   :

Now move back down to the ZIP field by pressing the ↓ key three times, then pressing the ← key twice to move the cursor to the left of the entry box. Then type a zip code (92123). Pressing Return after the zip code will then move the cursor onto record 3 for appending.

More Sample Records

So far so good. You've created a database and added two records to it. At this point, we suggest that you put in more data. If the *Append* form is still showing on the screen, just start keying in the following names and addresses. (Otherwise, use the *Set Up*, *Update*, and *Append* options to return to APPEND mode.) Here are some data (records 3-6) for you to type. You will use them for future examples:

LNAME	FNAME	ADDRESS	CITY	STATE	ZIP
Smith	Dave	619 Elm St.	San Diego	CA	92122
SMITH	Betsy	222 Lemon Dr.	New York	NY	01234
Smithsonian	Lucy	461 Adams St.	San Diego	CA	92122-1234
Doe	Ruth	1142 J. St.	Los Angeles	CA	91234

After you type the data for the last person on the list, dBASE will still ask for more data. To stop adding names, just press the Return key rather than typing a last name. Once you get all the data entered, you need to learn ways to retrieve the information.

RETRIEVING DATABASE RECORDS

Data stored in a database doesn't do you much good until you can get it back out. We'll discuss many ways to organize and retrieve data throughout the next couple of chapters, but let's take a moment now to try a simple retrieval to verify that the data you've typed are stored on the disk.

First, highlight the **Retrieve** option on the main menu bar. Then, select the *List* option by pressing Return. The screen will display new options, as shown in Figure 2.8.

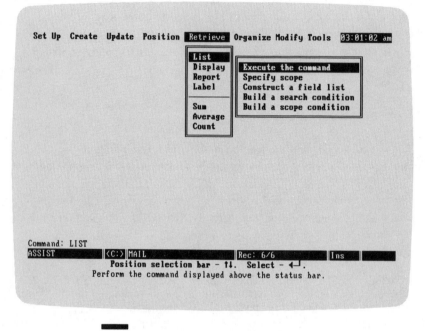

Figure 2.8: Menu Options for Data Display

Next, select the *Execute the command* option from the submenu by pressing Return once again. dBASE will ask

Direct the output to the printer? [Y/N]

If you answer **Y** to this question and if your printer is ready, the data will be printed. For now, simply type **N** to display the data on the screen. You'll see the six stored database records appear, as in Figure 2.9.

Notice that the records were too wide for the screen, so they *wrapped around,* placing the zip code over on the left side of the screen. You can clean up this display by asking that only certain

If you have a laser printer, and do choose to print your results, you may not see results right away. You'll need to eject the page *after* sending text to the printer. To do so, press Esc to access the dot prompt and type **EJECT** and press ◄┘. Then type **ASSIST** and press ◄┘ to return to the Assistant menu.

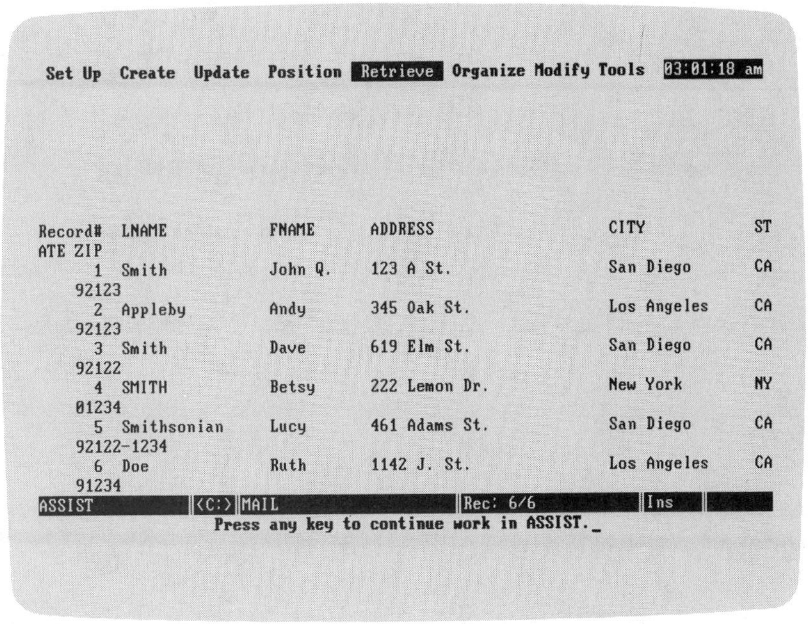

Figure 2.9: On-Screen Display of MAIL Records

fields be displayed. First, as the instructions at the bottom of the screen indicate, press any key to continue working in the Assist mode (working from the menu options rather than dot-prompt commands).

Specifying Fields for Display

Let's try another exercise, this time displaying only the LNAME, FNAME and CITY fields. Again, highlight the *Retrieve* option from the main menu bar, and select the *List* option from the submenu. From the next submenu, select the *Construct a field list* option. The screen displays a list of field names in the MAIL database, as shown in Figure 2.10.

You can move the highlighting from one option to the next by pressing the ↑ and ↓ keys. To select a field for display, simply press the Return key as the option is highlighted. In this example, press

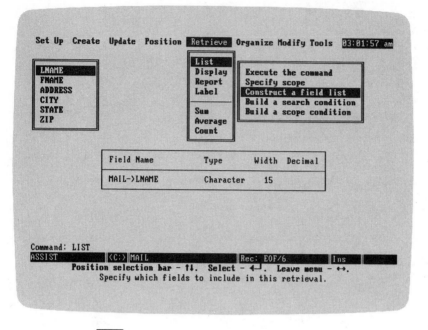

Figure 2.10: On-Screen Display of Field Names

Return to select the LNAME field. Then press Return again to select the FNAME field. Press ↓ to skip over the ADDRESS field, and then press Return to select the CITY field. When you finish, the LNAME, FNAME, and CITY fields will be dimmer than the others. (Because they have already been selected, they are no longer available for selection, and are shown in dimmer type). On the Action Line near the bottom of the screen, you'll see this command message:

Command: LIST LNAME, FNAME, CITY

Your menu selections have created a command that could have been entered at the dot prompt:

LIST LNAME, FNAME, CITY ↵

dBASE can understand this command in its own language. Now, press → to remove the submenu of field names. Then press ↑

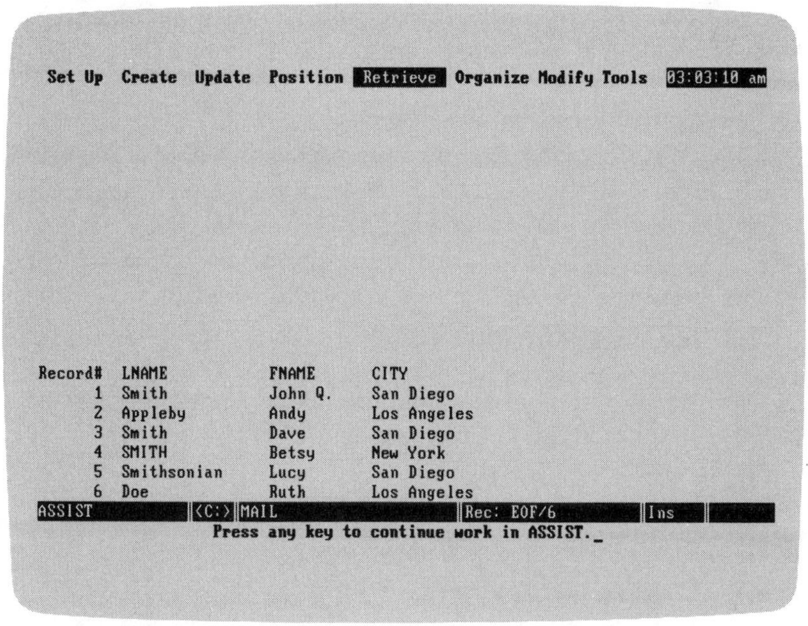

```
    Set Up  Create  Update  Position  Retrieve  Organize Modify Tools  03:03:10 am




      Record#  LNAME            FNAME        CITY
          1  Smith            John Q.      San Diego
          2  Appleby          Andy         Los Angeles
          3  Smith            Dave         San Diego
          4  SMITH            Betsy        New York
          5  Smithsonian      Lucy         San Diego
          6  Doe              Ruth         Los Angeles
   ASSIST              <C:> MAIL                    Rec: EOF/6         Ins
                          Press any key to continue work in ASSIST._
```

Figure 2.11: On-Screen Display of Selected MAIL Fields

twice to highlight the *Execute the command* option, and press Return.
When dBASE asks if you want to display the data on the printer,
answer **N.** dBASE will display the LNAME, FNAME, and CITY
fields from the MAIL database, as shown in Figure 2.11.

In the next chapter, we'll look at more advanced techniques
for displaying data on the screen and printer. Let's first take a
moment to discuss the dBASE dot prompt, which is an alternative
method for accessing your data.

ENTERING COMMANDS
AT THE DOT PROMPT

If you press the Esc key from the main menu, the menu will
disappear and a period will appear at the lower-left corner of the

screen. From here, you can enter commands using the dBASE language. Entering commands from the dot prompt is somewhat faster and less tedious for more advanced users, although it does require familiarity with the language.

Recall that when you selected menu options to display only the LNAME, FNAME, and CITY fields from the MAIL database, the screen displayed the command LIST LNAME, FNAME, CITY. You can type this command (or any command) at the dot prompt to achieve the same result. Type this command:

LIST LNAME, FNAME, CITY ←

As before, dBASE will display the three fields. When the dot prompt reappears, type this command:

LIST FNAME, LNAME, STATE

Notice that dBASE displays the fields you requested:

. LIST FNAME, LNAME, STATE

Record#	FNAME	LNAME	STATE
1	John Q.	Smith	CA
2	Andy	Appleby	CA
3	Dave	Smith	CA
4	Betsy	SMITH	NY
5	Lucy	Smithsonian	CA
6	Ruth	Doe	CA

To open a database when working at the dot prompt, you use the USE command. For example, to open the MAIL.DBF database on a hard-disk system, you could enter this command:

USE MAIL ←

For a floppy-disk system, you would need to specify Drive B. In this case, you would first enter the command

SET DEFAULT TO B ←

to tell dBASE that the data are stored on the disk in Drive B. Then you can enter the command

USE MAIL ←

to open the MAIL.DBF database.

For the novice or occasional user, the Assistant menu will probably be the preferred method for accessing your data for a while. Later, you may want to learn about the dBASE language for more speed or for more flexibility in entering your commands. If you plan on learning to program in dBASE III PLUS, you'll need to learn all the commands.

SAVING YOUR WORK

Before we proceed any further, there is one very important item of information that you need to learn: Always exit dBASE before turning off your computer. Failure to do so might cause you to lose some data that you've entered in a database.

To exit dBASE from the menu screen, highlight the *Set Up* option from the main menu bar, and select the *Quit dBASE III PLUS* option from the pull-down menu. (If the dot prompt is displayed, type the command ASSIST to bring the menu back onto the screen.) You can also exit dBASE by directly typing the command

   QUIT ⏎

at the dot prompt.

Quitting dBASE will ensure that all your data are safely stored on disk and return you to the DOS

   A>

or

   C>

prompt. To run dBASE again in the future, follow the steps we discussed at the beginning of this chapter.

For now, you might want to take a break and review the basic techniques we've discussed in this chapter for creating a database and adding data to it.

REVIEWING DATABASE BASICS

In this chapter we've discussed the following basic techniques for creating a database, storing records, and retrieving the data:

▬

To start dBASE on a single-user computer, enter the command DBASE at the DOS A> or C> prompt, and press Return.

▬

To select items from the main menu bar, use the ← and → keys to move the highlighting. (Optionally, you can select items from the main menu bar by typing the first letter of the option.)

▬

To select items from a pull-down menu, use the ↑ and ↓ arrows to move the highlight bar, and press Return to select the highlighted option.

▬

To create a new database, select the *Create* and *Database file* options from the menus.

▬

To get help on the screen at any time, just press the F1 key. After reading the help message, press any key to resume your work.

▬

To work with a particular database, select the *Set Up* and *Database file* options from the menus.

▬

To add new data to a database, select the *Update* and *Append* options.

▬

To see data stored in a database, select the *Retrieve* and *List* options from the menus. Then, select the *Execute the command* option from the submenu.

■

To work with dBASE from the dot prompt, press Esc to leave the Assistant menu. To return to the Assistant menu, enter the command ASSIST at the dot prompt.

■

To exit and save your work, select the *Set Up* and *Quit dBASE III PLUS* options from the menus.

Searching the Database

I n this chapter, we'll discuss basic techniques for searching, or *querying* a database. In other words, we'll be looking at techniques which allow you to view records that meet some search criteria, such as California residents, or people in the 92123 zip code area, or all the Smiths in the state of New York. As you'll see in this chapter and throughout the book, there is really no limit to the ways in which you can access data stored in a database.

If you've exited dBASE since the last chapter, be sure to run dBASE again and use the *Set Up* and *Database file* options from the menu to open the MAIL.DBF database. The examples in this chapter assume that the MAIL.DBF database is open.

BUILDING SEARCH COMMANDS WITH *LIST*

The easiest and most common technique for searching a database for records that meet some search criteria is with the *List* option. A simple example will demonstrate. Suppose that you want to retrieve records of all individuals who live in the 92123 zip code area. To do so, follow these steps from the Assistant menu screen

√ Highlight the **Retrieve** option on the menu.
√ Select *List*.
√ Select *Build a search condition*.

Notice that this menu of field names appears on the screen:

LNAME
FNAME
ADDRESS
CITY
STATE
ZIP

Because you want to view records from the 92123 zip code area, you need to search on the ZIP field. So the next step is to select the ZIP field. Next, a menu of *operators* will appear on the screen:

=	**Equal to**
< =	**Less than or equal to**
<	**Less than**
>	**Greater than**
> =	**Greater than or equal to**
< >	**Not equal to**

In this example, you're looking for zip codes that are equal to 92123, so select the *Equal to* option.

Finally, you have to specify what ZIP should be equal to. dBASE displays the prompt

Enter a character string (without quotes)

which translates into English as "Enter the thing that you're looking for, and don't use quotation marks." In this example, since you're looking for records with zip codes of 92123, type

92123 ↵

At this point, you've built the command that appears on the Action Line at the bottom of your screen:

Command: LIST FOR ZIP = '92123'

You've built this command from your menu selections. When dBASE executes this command, it will display all records that contain the 92123 zip code. Before you execute the command, you'll need to select the *No more conditions* option, which tells dBASE that you've completed your request and are now ready to execute the command on the Action Line. The last step now is to select the *Execute the command* option.

When dBASE asks if the display should be printed, answer **No**. dBASE will then display records in which the zip code is 92123:

1	**Smith**	**John Q.**	**123 A St.**	**San Diego**	**CA**	**92123**
2	**Appleby**	**Andy**	**345 Oak St.**	**Los Angeles**	**CA**	**92123**

(*Note:* Although the records may wrap around on your screen, this text shows each record on a single line.) Press any key to return to the Assistant menu screen.

BUILDING SEARCH CONDITIONS

As you'll see in future chapters, the *Build a search condition* option can be used in many situations, including those for printing reports and mailing labels, for deleting records, and changing information in groups of records. In fact, probably the biggest advantage to using a computer to store information is the ability to define search conditions which pull out information that meets some criterion.

Now, on a different note, recall that in the last chapter we displayed only specified fields. You can specify display fields while performing a search, too. For example, suppose that you want to view only Los Angeles residents, and furthermore, you only want to see the name of each individual. You need to use the *Construct a field list* and the *Build a search condition* options from the *List* submenus, as in these steps from the Assistant menu screen:

- √ Highlight the *Retrieve* option.
- √ Select *List*.
- √ Select *Construct a field list*.
- √ Select the CITY, LNAME, and FNAME fields.
- √ Press → to leave the field-names menu.
- √ Select *Build a search condition*.
- √ Select CITY.
- √ Select = .
- √ Type **Los Angeles.**
- √ Press the ⏎ key.

At this point, you've built the command that appears on the Action Line at the bottom of your screen:

Command: LIST CITY, LNAME, FNAME FOR CITY = 'Los Angeles'

To execute this command, follow these steps:

- √ Select *No more conditions*.
- √ Select *Execute the command*.
- √ Enter **N**o in response to printer question.

The result will be a listing of the city, last name, and first name of Los Angeles residents:

2	Los Angeles	Appleby	Andy
6	Los Angeles	Doe	Ruth

Let's try a couple of other searches using operators other than the equal sign. First, press any key to return to the menu.

Suppose that you want to view all residents whose zip codes are greater than, or equal to, 90000. You'd need to use the > = operator, rather than the = operator. (*Note:* You're displaying only the ZIP, LNAME, and FNAME fields.) Here are the steps:

√ Highlight the *Retrieve* option.
√ Select *List.*
√ Select *Construct a field list.*
√ Select the ZIP, LNAME, and FNAME fields.
√ Press → to leave the field-name menu.
√ Select *Build a search condition.*
√ Select ZIP.
√ Select > = .
√ Type **90000.**
√ Press ←.
√ Select *No more conditions.*

At this point, your on-screen command looks like this:

Command: LIST ZIP, LNAME, FNAME FOR ZIP > = '90000'

When you select the *Execute the command* option, and respond to the printer question, you'll see records with zip codes greater than or equal to 90000:

1	92123	Smith	John Q.
2	92123	Appleby	Andy
3	92122	Smith	Dave
5	92122-1234	Smithsonian	Lucy
6	91234	Doe	Ruth

The less-than (<) and less-than/equal-to (< =) operators can be used in a fashion similar to the > and > = operators. For example, to list records that have zip codes that are less than 90000, you would follow these steps:

✓ Highlight the *Retrieve* option.
✓ Select *List.*
✓ Select *Construct a field list.*
✓ Select the ZIP, LNAME, and FNAME fields.
✓ Press → to leave the field-name menu.
✓ Select *Build a search condition.*
✓ Select ZIP.
✓ Select <.
✓ Type **90000.**
✓ Press ←┘.
✓ Select *No more conditions.*

This results in the command:

Command: LIST ZIP, LNAME, FNAME FOR ZIP < '90000'

When you select the *Execute the command* option and a printing option, you'll see the only record on this database that has a zip code less than 90000:

4   01234   SMITH   Betsy

To view every record in the database *except* California residents, you could use the < > (does not equal) operator, as in these steps:

✓ Highlight the *Retrieve* option.
✓ Select *List.*
✓ Select *Build a search condition.*
✓ Select STATE.
✓ Select < >.
✓ Type **CA.**
✓ Press ←┘.
✓ Select *No more conditions.*

The command on the Action Line looks like this:

Command: LIST FOR STATE < > "CA"

When the command is executed, the only non-California resident will be displayed:

4   SMITH   Betsy   222 Lemon Dr.   New York   NY   01234

Combining Search Conditions

You can combine search conditions with *AND* and *OR* options to be more specific about the information you wish to pull out of the database. For example, suppose that you want to view all the Smiths in the state of California. In computer argot, you want to view records that have the name Smith in the LNAME field, AND the word CA in the STATE field. To perform such a query, displaying the STATE, LNAME, and FNAME fields in the results, follow these steps:

- √ Highlight *Retrieve.*
- √ Select *List.*
- √ Select *Construct a field list.*
- √ Select STATE.
- √ Select LNAME.
- √ Select FNAME.
- √ Press →.
- √ Select *Build a search condition.*
- √ Select LNAME.
- √ Select =.
- √ Type **Smith.**
- √ Press ⏎.

At this point, this command appears at the bottom of your screen:

Command: LIST STATE, LNAME, FNAME FOR LNAME = 'Smith'

The screen also displays these options:

No more conditions
Combine with .AND.
Combine with .OR.

You need to add an AND condition, so continue by following these steps:

    √ Select *Combine with .AND.*

    √ Select STATE.

    √ Select = .

    √ Type **CA.**

    √ Press ◄┘.

    √ Select *No more conditions.*

Now this command is displayed at the bottom of your screen:

Command: LIST STATE, LNAME, FNAME FOR LNAME = 'Smith'
.AND. STATE = 'CA'

In English, this command that you've constructed through menu selections means, "Show me records that have *Smith* in the LNAME field, AND *CA* in the STATE field." When you select the *Execute the command* option, you'll see these results:

Record #	STATE	LNAME	FNAME
1	CA	Smith	John Q.
3	CA	Smith	Dave
5	CA	Smithsonian	Lucy

You're probably wondering why Smithsonian was included in the list. Well, unless you specify otherwise, *Smith* is the same as *Smithsonian* because the first five letters match. Later in the chapter, you'll learn a technique that forces all letters in a specified field to match exactly.

SEARCHING
FROM THE DOT PROMPT

By now you have probably noticed that as you select menu items, dBASE builds a command with a very specific syntax:

```
<command> <field list> <search condition>
```

For example, the command

```
LIST LNAME, FNAME, CITY FOR CITY = "San Diego"
```

can be built first by selecting *List* from the **Retrieve** menu. Then select LNAME, FNAME, and CITY from the *Select a field list* menu option, and select CITY and = from the *Build a search condition* submenus. Eventually, you may find it easier just to key in commands for searches at the dot prompt. Also, you'll find that the dot prompt offers more flexibility.

Searching with the LIST Command

Let's try searching with dot-prompt commands rather than from menu options. Press the Esc key from the main menu, and you'll see the dot prompt. Then type the command

```
LIST LNAME, FNAME, CITY FOR CITY = "San Diego" ⏎
```

You'll see the San Diego residents displayed on the screen:

Record #	LNAME	FNAME	CITY
1	Smith	John Q.	San Diego
3	Smith	Dave	San Diego
5	Smithsonian	Lucy	San Diego

Now, let's take a look at some other searches typed at the dot prompt, and some of the unexpected results a search in dBASE might produce. Suppose that you type a simple command to view everyone with the last name Smith in the database:

```
LIST LNAME, FNAME FOR LNAME = 'Smith' ⏎
```

The somewhat surprising result is

Record #	LNAME	FNAME
1	Smith	John Q.
3	Smith	Dave
5	Smithsonian	Lucy

There are a couple of problems here. First, Betsy SMITH is missing. Why? Because somebody typed her last name as SMITH, and *Smith* is not the same as *SMITH* from the computer's point of view. Second, what is Smithsonian doing in there? You wanted Smiths, not everyone with Smith as the first five letters in their last name. Let's start solving these problems.

You can get rid of Smithsonian easily. Recall that when you created the MAIL.DBF structure, you allowed fifteen spaces for the last name field. So all the Smiths are actually "Smith_____" as far as dBASE is concerned. You can omit Smithsonian in your display by specifying that only Smith, followed by a blank space, be displayed:

LIST LNAME, FNAME FOR LNAME = 'Smith ' ↵

Now only the name Smith is listed:

Record #	LNAME	FNAME
1	Smith	John Q.
3	Smith	Dave

Smithsonian didn't make it this time, because the first six letters of her last name are Smiths, not Smith . But you still have to deal with the absence of SMITH.

The uppercase function UPPER() displays all lowercase letters in a character field in uppercase. You can test this out by typing the command

LIST UPPER(LNAME) ↵

to get this list:

Record #	UPPER(LNAME)
1	SMITH
2	APPLEBY
3	SMITH

4   SMITH
5   SMITHSONIAN
6   DOE

Here every last name on the list is displayed in uppercase.
(They're still in upper and lowercase in the database, though.)
Now you can get dBASE to list all Smiths, ignoring upper and
lowercase by asking it to list all the people whose *uppercase equivalent*
last name is SMITH. In dBASE, that looks like this:

LIST FOR UPPER(LNAME) = 'SMITH ' ⏎

In English, this statement reads, "List all the people whose last
name, when translated to uppercase, is SMITH."

Now dBASE displays the list you want:

Record #	LNAME	FNAME	ADDRESS	CITY	STATE	ZIP
1	Smith	John Q.	123 A St.	San Diego	CA	92123
3	Smith	Dave	619 Elm St.	San Diego	CA	92122
4	SMITH	Betsy	222 Lemon Dr.	New York	CA	01234

You really have to spell it out for these machines. They're so
literal. They hardly ever do what you *mean;* they always do what
you *say.* No imagination! You got rid of Smithsonian by listing for
Smith followed by a blank space, and you got SMITH in by
checking to see if the uppercase equivalent (UPPER) of the last
name was SMITH.

Searching with the LOCATE Command

The LOCATE command is used for locating the position of a
record based upon a desired characteristic. Since LOCATE does
not display its data like LIST, you have to use the DISPLAY command along with it to see what dBASE has located. Like the LIST
command, you use the FOR statement to indicate the characteristic you wish to find.

Let's assume that you want dBASE to locate information on
Dave Smith. You could ask dBASE to search for Dave Smith by
last name:

LOCATE FOR LNAME = 'Smith' ⏎

This would give you the dBASE display

Record = 1

This number doesn't do much good, but you can see the contents of the record by typing

DISPLAY ↵

This record is displayed on the screen:

Record #	LNAME	FNAME	ADDRESS	CITY	STATE	ZIP
1	Smith	John Q.	123 A St.	San Diego	CA	92123

Whoops, this isn't Dave Smith. You can continue the search for Dave with the CONTINUE command. So type

CONTINUE ↵

which gives you

Record = 3

If you display this record by typing

DISPLAY ↵

you have found Dave:

Record #	LNAME	FNAME	ADDRESS	CITY	STATE	ZIP
3	Smith	Dave	619 Elm St.	San Diego	CA	92122

Not too bad. However, if you had 10,000 names on your mailing list, this process could take a long time. A quicker approach would be to ask for the desired record more specifically. To do this, use the .AND. operator:

LOCATE FOR LNAME = 'Smith' .AND. FNAME = 'Dave' ↵

Now, *two* statements must be true for LOCATE to find the correct record. That is, the last name must be Smith, *and* the first name must be Dave. The result of this command is

Record = 3

on the first shot. If you type

   DISPLAY ↵

you see the following record:

Record #	LNAME	FNAME	ADDRESS	CITY	STATE	ZIP
3	Smith	Dave	619 Elm St.	San Diego	CA	92122

Got it in one try. If you type CONTINUE, you get

   End of LOCATE scope

because dBASE has checked all other records and there is not
another Dave Smith to be found.

   Now, last but certainly not least, we will discuss the type of
search where you need to know if a field roughly matches something you are looking for. For example, suppose you want to
search for people living on a street named Lemon, no matter what
the address number is or whether or not they live on Lemon St.,
Lemon Ave., or Lemon Blvd. If you LIST or LOCATE FOR
ADDRESS = 'Lemon', no match will be found, because the
word Lemon is embedded in the middle of the address field (222
Lemon Dr.). You need some way to say, "Display all records that
have the word Lemon embedded in the address field." That's
quite a mouthful, but not in dBASE, because the $ function will
find the embedded word. So, to locate an individual living on
Lemon, use the command

   LOCATE FOR 'Lemon' $ADDRESS ↵

Notice that the grammar is reversed from what you've used
before. This is because the $ means *embedded in*. The syntax makes
sense because the above command says, "Find a record with the
word Lemon embedded in the address field." When you type the
above command, you see on your screen

   Record = 4

If you then type

   DISPLAY ↵

you see

Record #	LNAME	FNAME	ADDRESS	CITY	STATE	ZIP
4	SMITH	Betsy	222 Lemon Dr.	New York	CA	01234

Pretty good! It found a person living on Lemon. Keep in mind that any of the search examples we've shown with the LOCATE command work as well with the LIST command, and vice versa. That is, you could also LIST FOR 'Lemon' $ADDRESS. With this command, all individuals who live on Lemon would be displayed on the screen.

You can also combine search conditions to your heart's content. For example, if you want a listing of everyone who lives on either Elm or Oak streets, you could

    LIST FOR 'Elm' $ADDRESS .OR. 'Oak' $ADDRESS ↵

which would give you

Record #	LNAME	FNAME	ADDRESS	CITY	STATE	ZIP
2	Appleby	Andy	345 Oak St.	Los Angeles	CA	92123
3	Smith	Dave	619 Elm St.	San Diego	CA	92122

The result is a listing of the individuals who live on either Oak or Elm streets. Be careful to distinguish *and* and *or*. If you had asked for a LIST FOR 'Elm' $ADDRESS .AND. 'Oak' $ADDRESS, you would end up with nothing, because a given individual in your database can't possibly live on both Elm and Oak streets at the same time (unless he did happen to live at 3421 OakElm St.).

In summary, the .OR. operator requires that only one of the conditions has to be true to get a listing. The .AND. command requires that both search conditions be true. For instance, the command

    LIST FOR 'Elm' $ADDRESS .AND. 'San Diego' $CITY ↵

would tell dBASE to display all of the individuals who live on Elm St. *and* in San Diego (San Diego residents who live on Elm). The command

    LIST FOR 'Elm' $ADDRESS .OR. 'San Diego' $CITY ↵

would display all individuals living on Elm St., regardless of what city, and all people living in San Diego, regardless of what street. The .OR. command generally broadens a search, since only one condition out of two must be met for dBASE to bring the data to the screen. On the other hand, the .AND. function narrows the search, since both search conditions must be met to find the correct data.

We can combine .AND. and .OR. search conditions. Try the following command:

```
LIST FOR STATE = 'CA' .AND. ('Oak' $ADDRESS .OR.;
'Elm' $ADDRESS) ←
```

Note: Command lines that are too wide to fit on the page in this book are broken with a semicolon (;). You must type the command as one long line without the semicolon.

This command would first require that the individual live in California. Furthermore, the individual must live on either Oak or Elm to make it to the list. In other words, this command lists all California residents who live on either Oak or Elm.

Incidentally, a LOCATE command can be built from the menu just as a LIST command can. For example, to view data for Ruth Doe, you would first follow these steps from the Assistant menu screen to create the LOCATE command line:

√ Highlight the *Position* option.
√ Select *Locate.*
√ Select *Build a search condition.*
√ Select LNAME.
√ Select = .
√ Type **Doe** ←.
√ Select *Combine with .AND.*
√ Select FNAME.
√ Select = .
√ Type **Ruth** ←.

At this point, your menu selections have built this command displayed on the Action Line:

Command: LOCATE FOR LNAME = 'Doe' .AND. FNAME = 'Ruth'

To continue, you need to execute the command by following these steps:

√ Select *No more conditions.*
√ Select *Execute the command.*

The screen displays the message

Record = 6

indicating that dBASE is now *pointing* at Record 6. To verify this, select the *Display* option from the menu (which displays only a single record) by following these steps:

√ Highlight the **Retrieve** option.
√ Select *Display.*
√ Select *Execute the command.*

You'll see Ruth Doe's record appear on the screen, along with the instructions to press any key to return to the menu.

EXACT SEARCHIING

Recall that earlier in the chapter, a search for people with the last name Smith displayed Smithsonian as well as the Smiths. You were able to leave Smithsonian out by performing a search for Smith   (with a blank space after the h). Another way to accomplish the same goal is to change the way in which dBASE makes search comparisons. To do so, press Esc until the menu disappears and the dot prompt appears. Then type this command:

SET EXACT ON ↵

If you now enter the command

LIST FOR LNAME = "Smith" ↵

or the command

> LIST FOR UPPER(LNAME) = "SMITH" ↵

you'll see the Smiths, but not Smithsonian, because *Smithsonian* is not an exact match to *Smith*.

To return to the original EXACT setting, enter the command

> SET EXACT OFF ↵

at the dot prompt.

To check the status of the EXACT parameter at anytime, just enter the command

> SET ↵

at the dot prompt. You'll see a whole menu of SET parameters, as in Figure 3.1.

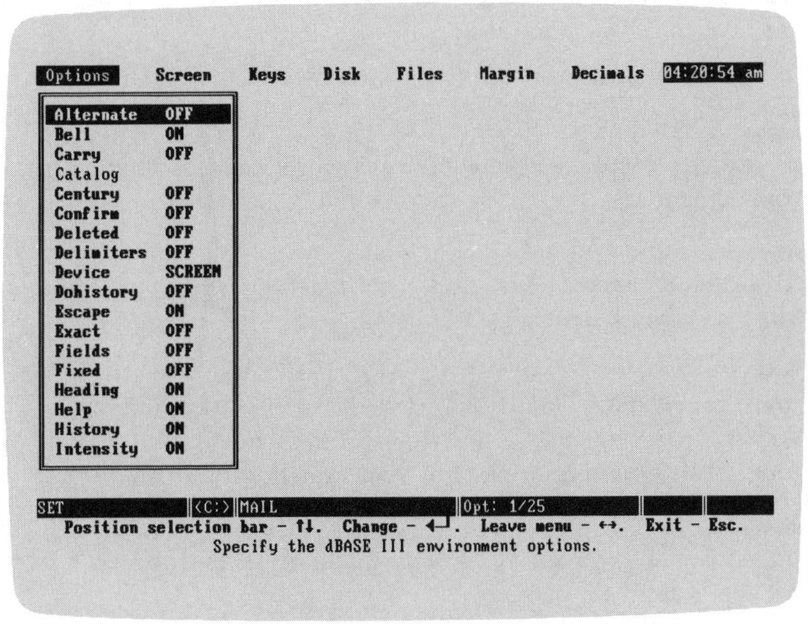

Figure 3.1: Menu of SET Parameters

You'll see the *Exact* option in its alphabetical position and either ON or OFF next to it. You can change the EXACT parameter while this menu is displayed by using ↑ and ↓ to move the highlighting to the *Exact* option and pressing the Return key to change settings on the highlighted parameter. Press Esc to return to the dot prompt. Type

ASSIST ⏎

to return to the Assistant menu screen.

If you have a color monitor, you can use the *Screen* option on this menu to change the colors displayed on your screen. See Chapter 17 for details.

REVIEWING SEARCH TECHNIQUES

In this chapter we've discussed numerous techniques and commands for searching through records in a database. Take a moment to review these topics:

▬

To search, or *query*, a database means to view records that match some criterion.

▬

To search for records that meet some criterion, select the *Build a search condition* option from the *List* submenu.

▬

You can use the = (equal), < (less than), < = (less than or equal), > (greater than), > = (greater than equal), and < > (not equal) operators to perform your searches from the menu.

▬

To display only certain fields in a search, select the *Construct a field list* option from the submenu.

▬

When performing searches from the dot prompt with the LIST

and LOCATE command, you can also use the $ (embedded in) operator, and the UPPER function to manage upper and lowercase.

The SET EXACT command allows you to change the way in which searches are performed.

Sorting the Database

I n most situations you add new records to a database as they become available. Then, at some point, you need to rearrange the records into some meaningful order, such as by zip code for bulk mailing, or by last name for a directory. dBASE provides two options for sorting databases, *Sort* and *Index*. We'll discuss each option in this chapter.

SORTING WITH THE *SORT* OPTION

When you use the *Sort* option to sort a database file, dBASE requires that you create a new database to store the sorted records. Once the sorting is done, you can *Copy* the contents of the sorted database back into the original file. Let's try an alphabetical sort with the MAIL file. When you *Sort*, store the newly arranged data to a file called TEMP (for temporary). After dBASE sorts the data, you will copy the contents of TEMP back over to MAIL, so that the records in MAIL will be properly sorted.

First, make sure that the MAIL.DBF database is in use. (The database name appears on the Status Bar). If not, use the *Set Up* and *Database file* options from the Assistant menu screen to open your database. Next, take a quick look at the current contents of the database by highlighting the *Retrieve* option and selecting the *List* and *Execute the command* options. You'll see the contents of the MAIL.DBF database:

1	Smith	John Q.	123 A St.	San Diego	CA	92123
2	Appleby	Andy	345 Oak St.	Los Angeles	CA	92123
3	Smith	Dave	619 Elm St.	San Diego	CA	92122
4	SMITH	Betsy	222 Lemon Dr.	New York	NY	01234
5	Smithsonian	Lucy	461 Adams St.	San Diego	CA	92122-1234
6	Doe	Ruth	1142 J. St.	Los Angeles	CA	91234

Now let's say that your database is not indexed, and you want to put these records into alphabetical order by last name. To do so, follow these steps from the Assistant menu screen:

√ Highlight the *Organize* option.
√ Select *Sort*.

√ Select LNAME.
√ Leave the submenu by pressing →.
√ Select a drive for the sorted file.
√ Type TEMP for the sorted file name.

After a few seconds, the screen displays this message:

100% Sorted   6 records sorted

Next, highlight the *Retrieve* option, and select the *List* and *Execute the command* options to view the database again. You'll see these records on the screen, along with a message to press any key to continue:

1	Smith	John Q.	123 A St.	San Diego	CA	92123
2	Appleby	Andy	345 Oak St.	Los Angeles	CA	92123
3	Smith	Dave	619 Elm St.	San Diego	CA	92122
4	SMITH	Betsy	222 Lemon Dr.	New York	NY	01234
5	Smithsonian	Lucy	461 Adams St.	San Diego	CA	92122-1234
6	Doe	Ruth	1142 J. St.	Los Angeles	CA	91234

Whoops! It doesn't look like anything happened here. That's because you're looking at the MAIL.DBF database, but it is TEMP.DBF that actually contains the sorted records. To verify this, use the *Set Up* and *Database file* options from the menu to open TEMP.DBF. Then, use the *Retrieve, List,* and *Execute the command* options to view the contents of the database. You'll see that the records are indeed in alphabetical order:

1	Appleby	Andy	345 Oak St.	Los Angeles	LA	92123
2	Doe	Ruth	1142 J. St.	Los Angeles	CA	91234
3	SMITH	Betsy	222 Lemon Dr.	New York	NY	01234
4	Smith	John Q.	123 A St.	San Diego	CA	92123
5	Smith	Dave	619 Elm St.	San Diego	CA	92122
6	Smithsonian	Lucy	461 Adams St.	San Diego	CA	92122-1234

So TEMP.DBF has the sorted records on it, but the MAIL database is still in random order. How do you put the sorted contents of TEMP into MAIL? Simple. Since the TEMP.DBF database is open, you can just copy it to the MAIL.DBF database, overwriting the existing contents of MAIL.DBF. To do so, follow these steps:

✓ Highlight the *Organize* option.
✓ Select *Copy.*
✓ Select a drive.
✓ Type MAIL as the name of the database to copy to.
✓ Select *Execute the command.*

To make sure that you don't accidentally overwrite an important file, dBASE III PLUS will double check before copying the file. You'll see this message:

MAIL.DBF already exists, overwrite it? (Y/N)

If you answer yes, the existing contents of the mail database will be replaced by the data in TEMP.DBF. Answer yes by typing **Y**.

Now, you need to open the MAIL.DBF database and see what's in it. As usual, select the *Set Up* and *Database file* options to open MAIL.DBF. Then use the *Retrieve, List,* and *Execute the command* options to view the contents of the database. You'll see the records displayed like this:

1	Appleby	Andy	345 Oak St.	Los Angeles	CA	92123
2	Doe	Ruth	1142 J. St.	Los Angeles	CA	91234
3	SMITH	Betsy	222 Lemon Dr.	New York	NY	01234
4	Smith	John Q.	123 A St.	San Diego	CA	92123
5	Smith	Dave	619 Elm St.	San Diego	CA	92122
6	Smithsonian	Lucy	461 Adams St.	San Diego	CA	92122-1234

Everything is in alphabetical order now.

Let's illustrate what took place on the disk with some pictures. To start with, the disk had a database called MAIL.DBF on it, with the records in random order (the order in which they were entered). Figure 4.1 shows the contents of the disk.

dBASE requires that when you *Sort* the database, you must sort to another file. In this example, you sorted to a database called TEMP.DBF. After the sort was complete, you had two databases on the disk: MAIL.DBF, still in random order, and TEMP.DBF,

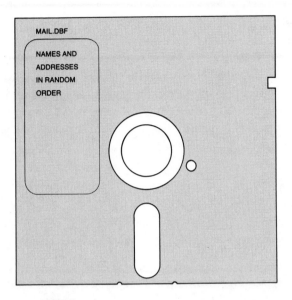

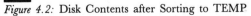

Figure 4.1: Disk Contents before Sorting

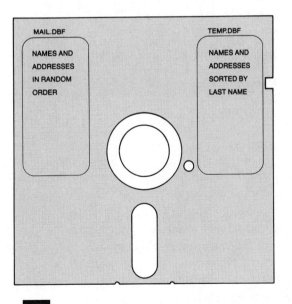

Figure 4.2: Disk Contents after Sorting to TEMP

which had the same contents as MAIL.DBF, but in sorted order, as in Figure 4.2.

To see the names and addresses in sorted order, you needed to open TEMP, then LIST the records. However, you wanted the data on MAIL to be sorted too, so you used the COPY command to copy the sorted contents of TEMP over to MAIL. After the copy was complete, you had two identical databases, as shown in Figure 4.3.

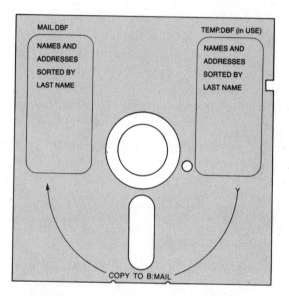

MAIL.DBF

NAMES AND
ADDRESSES
SORTED BY
LAST NAME

TEMP.DBF (in USE)

NAMES AND
ADDRESSES
SORTED BY
LAST NAME

COPY TO B:MAIL

Figure 4.3: Copying a Sorted TEMP File

You just needed TEMP to temporarily hold the sorted records. We'll discuss techniques for deleting unnecessary data files in the next chapter.

Now suppose that you want to do a bulk mailing, and you need these records in zip code order. What do you do? I bet you can guess.

Select the *Organize* and *Sort* options from the menus. When the submenu of field names appears on the screen, use ↓ or ↑ to highlight the field name ZIP, and press Return to select it. Press → to leave the submenu, select a drive from the next menu, and then type **TEMP** for a file name. Before overwriting the TEMP file with the new sorted file, dBASE will once again double check and ask for permission before proceeding with the copy. Answer **Y** to this prompt.

Now you can just quickly copy the contents of the TEMP.DBF file over to the MAIL.DBF file. To do so, open the TEMP.DBF database by selecting the *Set Up* and *Database file* options from the menus.

Next, select *Organize* and *Copy* from the menus to begin copying. Select a drive, enter MAIL as the database to copy to, and select *Execute the command.* Once again dBASE will double check before overwriting the MAIL.DBF database. Just type **Y** in response.

Finally, use the *Set Up* and *Database file* options to open the MAIL.DBF database. Select the *Retrieve, List,* and *Execute the command* options to view the records. You'll see that they are now in order by zip code:

1	SMITH	Betsy	222 Lemon Dr.	New York	NY	01234
2	Doe	Ruth	1142 J. St.	Los Angeles	CA	91234
3	Smith	Dave	619 Elm St.	San Diego	CA	92122
4	Smithsonian	Lucy	461 Adams St.	San Diego	CA	92122-1234
5	Appleby	Andy	345 Oak St.	Los Angeles	CA	92123
6	Smith	John Q.	123 A St.	San Diego	CA	92123

Sorting in this fashion is useful, but there are disadvantages. First, sorting wastes disk space. Since dBASE does the sorting to another database file, you need at least as much empty space on a disk as the database itself fills. That means you can only use half a disk for your entire database since you may need the other half for the TEMP file. Second, sorting is quite slow. You may not think so with this little database, but you would if you had 5000 records. This can be especially painful when you want them sorted by name for a directory, sorted by zip code for mailings, and so forth. Also, since everyone's record number changes as the records become rearranged, you can never be sure of an individual's record number using the SORT command. This last disadvantage may seem trivial now, but with large databases, it's nice to have record numbers remain constant. The *Index* option is the solution to these problems.

SORTING WITH THE *INDEX* OPTION

The *Index* option provides you with a much quicker and more efficient method of sorting records than does the *Sort* option.

Creating an Index File

Let's give it a whirl by putting the MAIL.DBF back into alphabetical order by name.

Highlight the *Organize* option from the main menu bar, and select the *Index* option from the submenu. dBASE will display these somewhat cryptic instructions:

The index key can be any character, numeric, or date expression involving one or more fields in the database file. It is usually a single field. Enter an index key expression:

For now, simply type the name of the field you want to sort. In this example, type

   LNAME ⏎

(We'll deal with more complex *index expressions* later in the chapter, as well as in Chapter 8.)

Next, you need to select a drive for storing the index file. dBASE then displays the message:

Enter a file name (consisting of up to 8 letters or digits) followed by a period and a file name extension (consisting of up to 3 letters or digits.) Enter the name of the file:

Names for index files follow the same rules as database files; they can be up to eight characters long but may not contain spaces or punctuation. dBASE will automatically assign the extension .NDX to the file name you provide. For this example, type the file name

   NAMES ⏎

Now, to verify that the records are indeed back in alphabetical order, select the *Retrieve, List,* and *Execute the command* options once again. You'll see these results:

5	Appleby	Andy	345 Oak St.	Los Angeles	CA	92123
2	Doe	Ruth	1142 J. St.	Los Angeles	CA	91234
1	SMITH	Betsy	222 Lemon Dr.	New York	NY	01234
3	Smith	Dave	619 Elm St.	San Diego	CA	92122
6	Smith	John Q.	123 A St.	San Diego	CA	92123
4	Smithsonian	Lucy	461 Adams St.	San Diego	CA	92122-1234

The records have changed to proper order, but the record numbers have remained the same. This is helpful, because that means Andy Appleby is still Record 5, Ruth Doe is still Record 2, etc. Also, you didn't have to go through the *Copy* rigamarole to see the records listed in proper order.

In the command you created, you asked dBASE to INDEX to NAMES. Isn't NAMES a data file? Yes, but it is not a database. It is a special file, an *index file* named NAMES.NDX. Its contents look very much like an index in a book. A book's index has a list of keywords in alphabetical order, and page numbers where the keywords appear in text. Your database index has a list of last names in alphabetical order, and the record numbers where they appear in the database, like so:

Appleby	5
Doe	2
SMITH	1
Smith	3
Smith	6
Smithsonian	4

After the index is complete, when you view the records, dBASE automatically uses information from the index file to determine the proper order to display the records in MAIL.DBF. The records in the MAIL.DBF database are still in their original order; the index file, however, tells dBASE the correct order in which to display the records.

After you do an index, the MAIL.DBF and NAME.NDX files exist on the disk, as in Figure 4.4.

Let's try another example. This time you'll index on the ZIP field. First, highlight the *Organize* option and select *Index*. Then, enter *Zip* as the field to index, and select a drive for the index file.

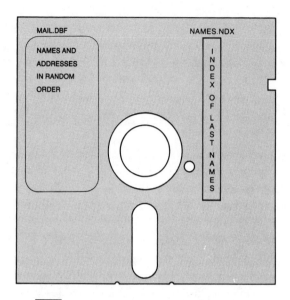

Figure 4.4: Disk Contents with an Index File

Type ZIP as the file name. When the indexing is done, select the *Retrieve* and *List* options. Then use the *Construct a field list* option to place the zip codes in the leftmost column to better show the new order. Select the *Execute* option to view the records in the new sorted order:

Record#	ZIP	LNAME	FNAME	ADDRESS
1	01234	SMITH	Betsy	222 Lemon Dr.
2	91234	Doe	Ruth	1142 J. St.
3	92122	Smith	Dave	619 Elm St.
4	92122-1234	Smithsonian	Lucy	461 Adams St.
5	92123	Appleby	Andy	345 Oak St.
6	92123	Smith	John Q.	123 A St.

The records are now displayed in zip code order. Furthermore, you have a file called ZIP.NDX which tells dBASE the order in which to display the records, as in Figure 4.5.

If you want a quick view of your mailing list sorted alphabetically by name, you don't have to sort it again. Just use the *Set Up*

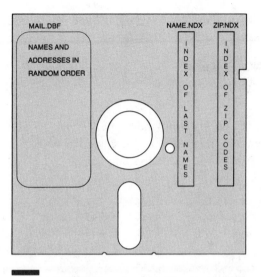

Figure 4.5: Disk Contents with Two Index Files

option from the Assistant menu screen to open the database with the appropriate index file. Here's how:

- √ Highlight *Set Up* from the main menu bar.
- √ Select *Database file.*
- √ Specify a drive.
- √ Select MAIL.DBF.
- √ Answer **Y** to the "Is file indexed?" prompt.

At this point, a menu of all existing index file names will appear on the screen. As with most menu options, you can simply use ↑ and ↓ to move the highlighting through the options, and press Return to select items. The *order* in which you select items is important, though.

Because you want to see names in alphabetical order in this example, you need to select the NAMES.NDX index first. Then, you can select other index files that were created for this database, in any order you wish. (dBASE allows a maximum of seven index files per database.) We'll discuss reasons for selecting multiple index files in a moment.

When you select the NAMES.NDX and ZIP.NDX index files, you'll notice that the NAMES.NDX is called the *Master* index file:

```
NAMES.NDX    Master
TEMP.NDX
ZIP.NDX      02
```

When you finish selecting index files, press → to leave the sub-menu. If you then select *Retrieve, List,* and *Execute* from the menus, you'll see the names in alphabetical order:

Record#	LNAME	FNAME	ADDRESS	CITY
5	Appleby	Andy	345 Oak St.	Los Angeles
2	Doe	Ruth	1142 J. St.	Los Angeles
1	SMITH	Betsy	222 Lemon Dr.	New York
3	Smith	Dave	619 Elm St.	San Diego
6	Smith	John Q.	123 A St.	San Diego
4	Smithsonian	Lucy	461 Adams St.	San Diego

When you want a quick look at your mailing list in zip code order, you don't have to re-sort anything because you've already indexed on ZIP, and ZIP.NDX still exists. Just use the *Set Up* and *Database file* options again to open the MAIL.DBF database. Answer Yes to the "Is the file indexed?" prompt. This time, when you select index files, be sure to select ZIP.NDX first, and NAMES.NDX second, so the screen looks like this:

```
NAMES.NDX    02
TEMP.NDX
ZIP.NDX      Master
```

When you select the *Retrieve* and *List* options to view the database, you'll see that the records are back in zip code order:

Record#	ZIP	LNAME	FNAME	ADDRESS
1	01234	SMITH	Betsy	222 Lemon Dr.
2	91234	Doe	Ruth	1142 J. St.
3	92122	Smith	Dave	619 Elm St.
4	92122-1234	Smithsonian	Lucy	461 Adams St.
5	92123	Appleby	Andy	345 Oak St.
6	92123	Smith	John Q.	123 A St.

Don't Resort to Re-sorting

Now, you are probably wondering why I keep selecting more than one index file, when only the Master (first selected) index file affects the sorted order of the database. The reason for doing so is to make the index files *active*.

Once an index file is active, it is automatically updated anytime the database is altered. That means that as you add, change, or delete records in the MAIL.DBF database, both the NAMES.NDX and ZIP.NDX index files are also updated accordingly and instantly re-sorted! Therefore, once you have created index files, you need never use the *Sort* or *Index* options from the *Organize* menu again. With a large database, this will save you a great deal of time because you won't need to use the *Index* or *Sort* options to reorganize the database each time you add or change information.

You must remember to make the index files active before you add or change data on the database. If you don't, the index files will become *corrupted*. That is, they'll need to be recreated. If you only make one index file active before adding, changing, or deleting data, then the active index file will still be correct, but the unlisted index files will be corrupted.

You know when an index file has been corrupted because either

1. dBASE does not display newly added records when you enter the *List* option or command.

2. dBASE will display the error message "Record out of range" when you attempt to list the records.

In either case, the index files will have to be recreated from scratch. You'll have to select the *Organize* and *Index* options from the menus again, and create the index file just as though you were doing so for the first time.

dBASE III PLUS allows you to have up to seven index files active at a time. You may want to wait until you have more experience before you try managing that many index files, but you should practice working with index files and experiment a bit.

Don't worry about damaging the database; it's impossible to do so by experimenting with index files.

SORTS WITHIN SORTS

Although your MAIL.DBF database is too small to demonstrate the point, sometimes a single field is not sufficient for organizing a database. For example, suppose that there were 10,000 names on the MAIL.DBF database, and 100 people had the last name Smith. If you indexed on the LNAME field only, the Smiths might end up in a somewhat haphazard order:

    Smith Rudolph
    Smith Abigail
    Smith Terri
    Smith Barbara
    Smith Prudence
    Smith Zeke
    Smith Oscar

This order won't do you much good when you're attempting to find a particular Smith.

To remedy this situation, you need to sort on more than one field (or in other words, do a sort-within-a-sort). If you indexed this hypothetical database on both the LNAME and FNAME fields, your Smiths would come out in alphabetical order:

    Smith Abigail
    Smith Barbara
    Smith Oscar
    Smith Prudence
    Smith Rudolph
    Smith Terri
    Smith Zeke

To index on multiple fields like this, you merely need to *concatenate* (stick together) the fields in the index expression with a plus (+) sign. Let's give it a whirl. Select the *Organize* and *Index* options.

When dBASE displays the instructions

The index key can be any character, numeric, or date expression involving one or more fields in the database file. It is usually a single field. Enter an index key expression:

type this expression:

LNAME + FNAME ↵

Select a drive. Then enter a file name (**BOTH**).

When the indexing is complete, use the *Retrieve, List* and *Execute the command* options to view the records. You'll see the records in alphabetical order by last name and by first name within identical last names:

5	Appleby	Andy	345 Oak St.	Los Angeles	CA	92123
2	Doe	Ruth	1142 J. St.	Los Angeles	CA	91234
1	SMITH	Betsy	222 Lemon Dr.	New York	NY	01234
3	Smith	Dave	619 Elm St.	San Diego	CA	92122
6	Smith	John Q.	123 A St.	San Diego	CA	92123
4	Smithsonian	Lucy	461 Adams St.	San Diego	CA	92122-1234

More advanced examples of sorts-within-sorts, and descending sorts with Numeric and Date fields, will be presented in Chapters 8 and 17.

Suppose now that you want all the records sorted by zip code, but within each zip code area, you want them sorted by last name. Furthermore, just in case there are several Smiths in the 92123 zip code area, you want the names sorted by first name within common last names. This would be simple enough to accomplish. You would just select the *Organize* and *Index* options once again, and enter this *Index expression:*

ZIP + LNAME + FNAME

Notice the order of the entries. Since ZIP is listed first, the records will be sorted into zip code mailing. However, within common zip codes, records will be sorted by last and first name, as in this small sample:

92111	Zeepers	Zach
92122	Adams	Archie
92122	Baker	Anne
92122	Miller	Arnie
92122	Miller	Millie

```
92122    Miller      Pia
92122    Miller      Wanda
92122    Peterson    Wayne
92122    Wilson      Arthur
92123    Ascii       Antoine
```

INDEXING FROM THE DOT PROMPT

You can sort or index a database file using commands from the dot prompt. As we discussed earlier, the USE command opens a database file from the dot prompt. If you are using a computer with two floppy-disk drives, you can store the database and index files on Drive B simply by making B the *default* drive. To do so, enter the command:

SET DEFAULT TO B ↵

Now to open MAIL.DBF enter this command:

USE MAIL ↵

To create an index file from the dot prompt, you use the INDEX ON command, along with the field(s) to be used in the index file, and the name of the index file. For example, to create the BOTH.NDX index file of the last and first name fields, you would enter this command:

INDEX ON LNAME + FNAME TO BOTH ↵

To view the results of the index, enter this command:

LIST ↵

Type the field names next to the LIST command to view specific fields using the LIST command. For example, to view the LNAME and FNAME fields only, enter this command:

LIST LNAME, FNAME ↵

To use existing index files from the dot prompt, you can use the INDEX command directly with the USE command. For example, to open the MAIL.DBF database, with the NAMES.NDX index files as the Master, and ZIP.NDX index files as secondary (02), you would enter the command:

    USE MAIL INDEX NAMES,ZIP ←┘

You can use the SET INDEX command as well. For example, to switch to zip code order, but still keep the NAMES.NDX index file active, you could simply enter this command:

    SET INDEX TO ZIP,NAMES ←┘

From this point on, records are displayed in order by zip code, but both ZIP.NDX and NAMES.NDX are updated automatically should any data be added to, deleted from, or changed in the MAIL.DBF database.

SEARCHING FOR RECORDS WITH AN INDEX FILE

Index files are certainly useful for creating and maintaining sort orders, as we've seen in this chapter. Index files can also speed up searches for information on very large databases. For example, if you used LIST or LOCATE to look up information in a very large database, you might have to wait a couple of minutes to get the results. With an index file and the FIND option, the same search would probably take only a second or two.

Even though your MAIL.DBF database is too small to demonstrate the full speed of searching with an index file, you can use it to get some practice with general techniques. Suppose that you want to find Doe in the MAIL.DBF database using an index file. First of all, you'll have to make sure that NAMES.NDX is the Master index, because searches only work with the Master index. Hence, from the dot prompt, enter this command:

    USE MAIL INDEX NAMES,ZIP ←┘

Next, to quickly locate Doe, just enter this command:

    FIND Doe ←┘

Enter this command to verify that the correct record was located:

DISPLAY ⏎

To locate a particular zip code, first enter the command

USE MAIL INDEX ZIP,NAMES

and then the command

FIND 92122

Again, entering the command DISPLAY will show the record found, if any.

From the menus, you can assign indexes in the usual fashion through the *Set Up* and *Database file* options. Then, to look up data in the Master index, highlight the *Position* option on the menu and select *Seek*. dBASE will ask that you enter an expression. You need to type the item that you are looking for, enclosed in quotation marks (if it is the Character data type). For this example, type

"Doe" ⏎

dBASE will give you the message to press any key to return to the menu. After doing so, highlight the **Retrieve** option, and select the *Display* and *Execute the command* options. This will display the single record located by the *Seek* option.

REVIEWING DATABASE ORGANIZATION

In this chapter we've discussed numerous techniques and commands for organizing a database:

▬

dBASE provides two options for organizing a database into some meaningful order, *Sort* and *Index*.

▬

To Sort a database, highlight the **Organize** option and select *Sort*. You'll need to assign a file name for the sorted records, and then use the *Copy* option to copy the sorted records back to the original file.

▬

To Index a database, highlight the *Organize* option and select the *Index* option. Enter names for the index file and fields to index.

▬

The *Index* option is much faster and more efficient than the *Sort* option, and it allows you to define and maintain sort orders automatically.

▬

For sorts-within-sorts, you can simply string together several fields in an Index expression, using a plus sign

    ZIP + LNAME + FNAME

▬

When several index files are open, the first-selected (*Master*) index file determines the sort order for displays of data, but any other *active* index files are also updated instantly and automatically.

▬

Another advantage of index files is quick lookups with the *Find* or *Seek* options. Only the Master index file can be used in a search, though.

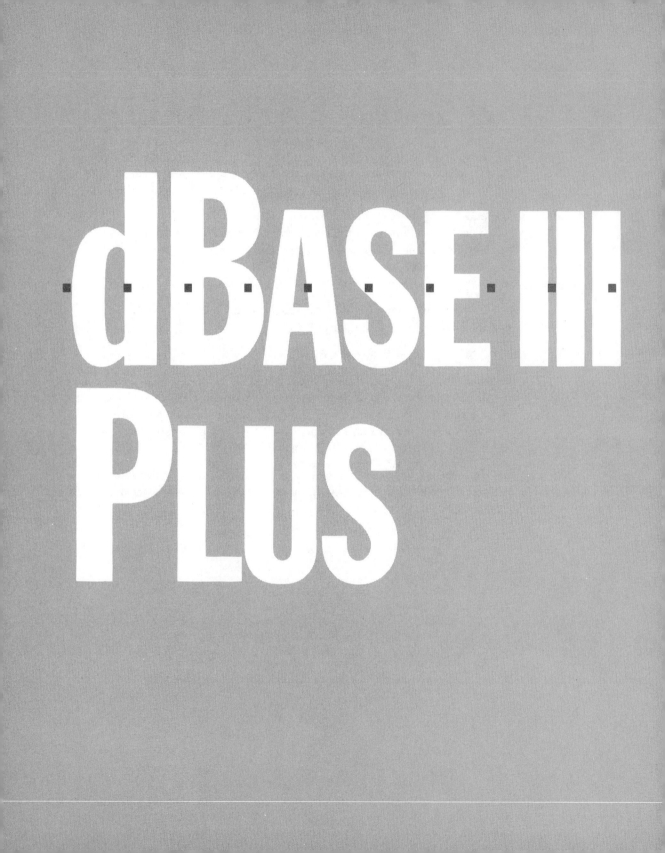

Editing and Modifying Databases

W hen working with computers, the term *edit* means to change existing data on the database. For instance, if a certain individual who is already on our database moves to a new house, you would want to change his street address. That would be a database edit. Suppose you decide that you want to include phone numbers for each individual on our database, even though you did not originally designate a field for storing phone numbers. You would have to modify the structure of the database. The options you can use to perform such feats are discussed in this chapter.

EDITING WITH *EDIT*

Computer databases need editing for a variety or reasons. People move and change their addresses, we make mistakes while entering data and have to fix them, and so forth. Editing with dBASE is a rather simple task if you know the number of the particular record you are looking for. You can't possibly remember all those numbers, but you can use the knowledge you've gained thus far to look up a record number quickly.

Getting Ready

Before you actually begin editing a database, make sure that the database is open, and that any index files that are used regularly with the database are also open. The index files must be open to be automatically updated as information is changed in the database.

In this example, select the *Set Up* and *Database file* options, and open the MAIL.DBF database. When dBASE asks if the file is indexed, answer **Yes**. Select the NAMES.NDX and ZIP.NDX index files, so these will remain active throughout the exercises in this chapter. Press → to remove the index file menu.

Changing a Record

Now, let's suppose that Dave Smith moves, and you want to update his record with his new address. If this were a large data-

base, your first task would be to find his record in the database
file. There are a number of ways that you can do so, but the easiest in this example would be to use the *Locate* option, as in these
steps from the Assistant menu screen:

√ Highlight the *Position* option on the main menu bar.
√ Select *Locate*.
√ Select *Build a search condition*.
√ Select LNAME.
√ Select = .
√ Type **Smith** ↵.
√ Select *Combine with .AND*.
√ Select FNAME.
√ Select = .
√ Type **Dave** ↵.
√ Select *No more conditions*.

Notice that your menu selections have created a command on
the Action Line:

Command: LOCATE FOR LNAME = 'Smith' .AND. FNAME = 'Dave'

which tells dBASE, "Find the first record that has 'Smith' in the
LNAME field, AND 'Dave' in the FNAME field." Select *Execute
the command*.

Now, to edit this record, move the highlight to the *Update*
option and select *Edit*. You'll see Dave Smith's data on the screen
ready for editing, as in Figure 5.1.

Notice that the cursor is under the S in Smith. Now we can use
the arrow keys and cursor-control keys to position the cursor to
make changes. (Remember that the ^ symbol means, "Hold
down the Ctrl key while pressing the next key.") Cursor commands for the EDIT mode are explained in Table 5.1.

To change Dave's address, press the ↓ key twice to move down
two lines. This positions the cursor to the beginning of the
ADDRESS field. Press ^Y to empty out the current address field,
and type the new address, **123 B St**. Press the ↓ key, then the ←

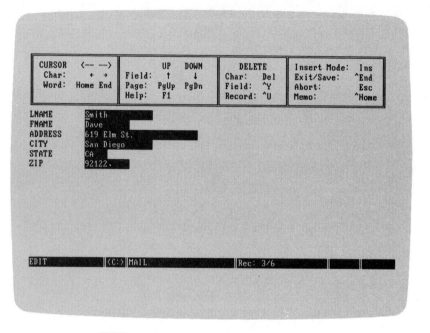

Figure 5.1: Record Displayed in EDIT Mode

key a few times to move the cursor to the beginning of the CITY field. Press ^Y to erase the current city and type **Los Angeles** as the new city. Press the ↓ key twice, then the ← key a few times to move to the beginning of the ZIP field. Press ^Y to delete the current zip code and type the new zip code, **90123.** Now Dave Smith's data looks like this:

```
LNAME     :Smith       :
FNAME     :Dave        :
ADDRESS   :213 B St.   :
CITY      :Los Angeles :
STATE     :CA     :
ZIP       :90123_      :
```

At this point, check to see if the data looks ok. If it does, save the new data by pressing a ^W or ^End. This will bring back the Assistant menu.

Key	Alternate Key		Effect
↑	*or*	^E	Moves cursor up one line.
↓	*or*	^X	Moves cursor down one line.
←	*or*	^S	Moves cursor left one space.
→	*or*	^D	Moves cursor right one space.
Backspace			Moves cursor left and erases.
Del	*or*	^G	Deletes character over cursor.
^T			Erases one word to the right.
^Y			Erases all field contents to the right of the cursor
^U			Deletes entire record.
Ins	*or*	^V	Turns INSert mode on/off.
PgUp	*or*	^R	Moves back one record.
PgDn	*or*	^C	Moves forward one record.
^End	*or*	^W	Saves changes and returns to Assistant or dot prompt.
Esc	*or*	^Q	Abandons changes and returns to Assistant or dot prompt.

Table 5.1: EDIT-Mode Control Keys

If you practice using the EDIT mode, you will find it easy to use. It is a straightforward procedure; there is nothing particularly tricky about it. At this point, you can try editing a few records of your own.

EDITING WITH *BROWSE*

The *Browse* option allows you to scroll through the database, horizontally and vertically, to edit or add records. As you pan, dBASE shows as much data as will fit on the screen. You can move the cursor to change whatever information you please. This is a very useful technique for locating easily-corrected errors, like misspellings.

You can use the *Locate* option to pinpoint a particular record to edit, as you did in the last example. But in this case, since the MAIL.DBF database is so small, you can just start editing from the top of the database.

To start at the top of the database with the first record, highlight the *Position* option on the main menu bar, and select the *Goto Record* and *Top* options. To enter the BROWSE mode now, highlight the *Update* option and select the *Browse* option. You'll see as much information as will fit on the screen, as shown in Figure 5.2.

```
┌─────────────────┬───────────────────┬──────────────────┬────────────────────┐
│ CURSOR  <-- -->  │          UP   DOWN │    DELETE         │ Insert Mode:  Ins  │
│   Char:    ← →   │ Record:  ↑    ↓    │   Char:    Del    │ Exit:        ^End  │
│   Field: Home End│ Page:   PgUp  PgDn │   Field:   ^Y     │ Abort:        Esc  │
│   Pan:    ^← ^→  │ Help:    F1        │   Record:  ^U     │ Set Options: ^Home │
└─────────────────┴───────────────────┴──────────────────┴────────────────────┘
LNAME---------- FNAME------ ADDRESS-------------------- CITY----------- STATE
Appleby         Andy        345 Oak St.                 Los Angeles     CA
Doe             Ruth        1142 J. St.                 Los Angeles     CA
SMITH           Betsy       222 Lemon Dr.               New York        NY
Smith           Dave        123 B St.                   Los Angeles     CA
Smith           John Q.     123 A St.                   San Diego       CA
Smithsonian     Lucy        461 Adams St.               San Diego       CA




BROWSE          |<C:>|MAIL                     |Rec: 5/6   |    |    |
                    View and edit fields.
```

Figure 5.2: Records on a BROWSE Screen

You can use the arrow keys to move the large highlighting bar and the cursor within this bar. Then make whatever changes you want. The menu at the top of the screen summarizes the command keys. The control-key commands for the BROWSE mode are explained in more detail in Table 5.2.

Key		Alternate Key	Effect
↑	*or*	^E	Moves cursor up one line.
↓	*or*	^X	Moves cursor down one line.
←	*or*	^S	Moves cursor one space to the left.
→	*or*	^D	Moves cursor one space to the right.
Home	*or*	^A	Moves cursor one field to the left.
End	*or*	^F	Moves cursor one field to the right.
^→	*or*	^B	Pans one field to the right.
^←	*or*	^Z	Pans one field to the left.
Del	*or*	^G	Deletes character over cursor.
^Y			Deletes information to the right of the cursor in the field.
Ins	*or*	^V	Enters INSert mode, so that newly entered data is inserted into the field without overwriting existing data.
^Home			Displays/erases help menu on the top of the BROWSE screen.
^End	*or*	^W	Saves all newly edited data and returns to dot prompt.
Esc	*or*	^Q	Returns to dot prompt without saving changes made in the BROWSE mode.

Table 5.2: BROWSE-Mode Control Keys

To change the information of a field or record, just position the cursor where you want to make the change, and type the new data on top of the old data.

In the above example, the ZIP field is not displayed because it can't fit on the screen with all the other information. To look at that field, you need to pan to the right. Press ^→ to pan to the right one field, so the zip code will be displayed and the last name will be invisible. Press ^← to pan the screen back to the left.

For more options that you can use in BROWSE mode, press ^Home. A menu of options will appear:

Bottom   Top   Lock   Record No.   Freeze   Find

These options are described in more detail in Table 5.3.

Option	Purpose
Bottom:	Positions the highlighting to the last record in the database.
Top:	Places the highlighting on the first record in the database.
Lock:	Maintains the on-screen display of one or more fields to the left of the screen even as you pan to the right using the ^→ or ^B keys.
Record No:	Asks you to enter the number of a record to highlight.
Freeze:	Locks the highlighting into a single field (like ZIP) for easier editing of the same field in a number of records.
Find:	Looks up data in an indexed field. For example, with NAMES.NDX assigned as the Master index file, you could select *Find* and type **Doe** to quickly move the highlighting to Doe's record.

Table 5.3: BROWSE Menu Options

When you finish browsing, you can use a ^W or ^End to save all data and return to the Assistant menu.

DOT-PROMPT COMMANDS FOR EDITING

Like all Assistant menu options, you can edit a database directly from the dot prompt. For example, to browse through the database, just use the database (and any index files) and enter the BROWSE command at the dot prompt, as in these commands:

```
USE MAIL INDEX NAMES,ZIP   ←┘
BROWSE                     ←┘
```

To edit an open database (and index files), use the EDIT command with the number of the record to edit:

```
USE MAIL INDEX NAMES,ZIP   ←┘
EDIT 2                     ←┘
```

GLOBAL EDITING

The term *global edit* refers to a change to a database that affects more than one record. Global edits are used quite often in database management to perform a large task quickly. For example, if you had an inventory system with several thousand parts on it, and one of your manufacturers raised the price of all his products by 10%, you could perform a global edit to increase the price of all items made by that manufacturer in a single step.

Let's give it a try using the MAIL.DBF database and a hypothetical example. Suppose that you have two different secretaries entering information into your MAIL.DBF database. One always spells out Los Angeles, while the other uses the abbreviation L.A. You decide to standardize the entry so that searches for Los Angeles residents do not require two separate searches for *Los Angeles* and *L.A.*

The least efficient way to make this change would be to work through the database, finding each occurrence of Los Angeles and retyping it as **L.A.** If there were 500 such cases, you'd be spending a lot of time.

The faster way is to follow these steps from the Assistant menu screen:

√ Highlight the *Update* option.
√ Select the *Replace* option.

✓ Select CITY.
✓ Type **L.A.** ←┘
✓ Press →.

Notice the command you've created on the Action Line:

Command: REPLACE CITY WITH 'L.A.'

This will replace the CITY field with the abbreviation L.A. in the current record, but you want dBASE to do so for those records which currently contain Los Angeles. Therefore, you need to build a search condition for these records following these steps:

✓ Select *Build a search condition.*
✓ Select CITY.
✓ Select = .
✓ Type **Los Angeles.** ←┘

Now the command is more specific:

Command: REPLACE CITY WITH 'L.A.' FOR CITY = 'Los Angeles'

In English, this translates to "Everywhere you see the words *Los Angeles* in the CITY field, put in the abbreviation *L.A.* instead." Select *No more conditions* to leave the submenu, and then select *Execute the command*. The screen will display this message:

3 records replaced

If you now use the *Retrieve* and *List* options, you'll see that the records which once contained Los Angeles now contain the abbreviation L.A.:

Record#	LNAME	FNAME	ADDRESS	CITY
5	Appleby	Andy	345 Oak St.	L.A.
2	Doe	Ruth	1142 J. St.	L.A.
1	Smith	Betsy	222 Lemon Dr.	New York
3	Smith	Dave	123 B St.	L.A.
6	Smith	John Q.	123 A St.	San Diego
4	Smithsonian	Lucy	461 Adams St.	San Diego

You can use the REPLACE command quite easily from the dot prompt as well, as long as you remember to use the *FOR* condition to clearly define which records get changed. For example, exit the menu by pressing Esc. Then enter this command at the dot prompt:

REPLACE CITY WITH 'Los Angeles' FOR CITY = 'L.A.'

All the L.A. records will change back to Los Angeles.

The REPLACE command can be helpful with standardizing case in some situations. For example, in MAIL.DBF, you have a record with SMITH in uppercase. From the dot prompt, you can enter the command

REPLACE LNAME WITH "Smith" FOR LNAME = "SMITH"

to globally change all SMITHs to Smith. After trying these two REPLACE commands from the dot prompt, you can enter the command

LIST LNAME, CITY ↵

to quickly view the results.

Whether you make your global changes from the menu or from the dot prompt, you must be certain to enter the correct FOR condition to ensure that the command only acts upon the appropriate records. REPLACE has a high *whoops factor,* which means that by the time you realize that you've entered the wrong FOR condition, dBASE has already changed all the wrong records. So do be careful.

Now type

ASSIST ↵

to return to the Assistant menu screen.

DELETING RECORDS

Deleting records from a dBASE database actually involves two steps. First, you mark the record for deletion. You can review these marked records prior to permanently deleting them, or you can temporarily delete them to perform a certain task. Second, whenever it's convenient, you can *pack* the database, which permanently deletes the records that have been marked for deletion.

Marking Records

The easiest way to mark a record for deletion is to press ^U while the record is being edited via the *Edit* or *Browse* options. For example, suppose that you want to delete Dave Smith from the MAIL.DBF database. First, enter BROWSE mode from the Assistant menu screen:

✓ Select *Update.*
✓ Select *Browse.*

Next, move the highlighting to Dave Smith's record, as shown in Figure 5.3. Then press ^U so that "Del" appears in the lower right corner of the screen (also shown in the figure). The ^U key acts as a *toggle,* which means that pressing it repeatedly marks and unmarks records for deletion.

After marking the record for deletion, save your work in BROWSE by typing ^W or ^End. If you now select the *Retrieve* and *List* options from the Assistant menu, you'll see that this record is marked for deletion with a leading asterisk, but it has not been deleted yet:

2	Doe	Ruth	1142 J. St.	Los Angeles	CA
3	*Smith	Dave	123 B St.	Los Angeles	CA
6	Smith	John Q.	123 A St.	San Diego	CA
1	Smith	Betsy	222 Lemon Dr.	New York	NY
4	Smithsonian	Lucy	461 Adams St.	San Diego	CA

Packing the Database

Now, to permanently remove this record from the database, you

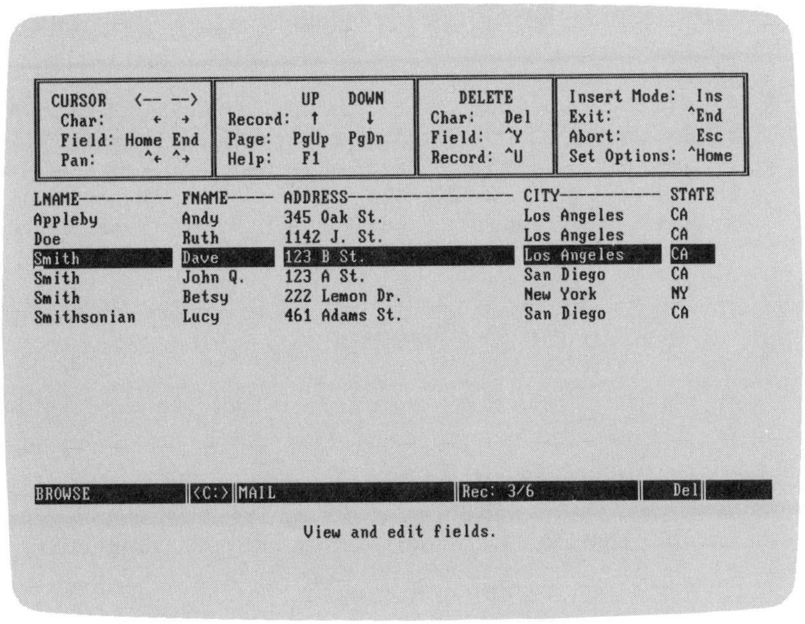

Figure 5.3: Record Highlighted on a BROWSE Screen

must select the *Pack* option from the Assistant menu screen:

√ Highlight the *Update* option.
√ Select *Pack.*

dBASE will display the message

5 records copied

which means that there are now only five records on the database. You'll also see messages that the NAMES.NDX and ZIP.NDX index files are being updated. (When records are deleted from the MAIL.DBF database, they are automatically removed from NAMES.NDX and ZIP.NDX if you remembered to open your index files when you opened your database.)

If you select the *Retrieve* and *List* options now, you'll see that Dave Smith's record has indeed been deleted from the database:

4	Appleby	Andy	345 Oak St.	Los Angeles	CA
2	Doe	Ruth	1142 J. St.	Los Angeles	CA
1	Smith	Betsy	222 Lemon Dr.	New York	NY
5	Smith	John Q.	123 A St.	San Diego	CA
3	Smithsonian	Lucy	461 Adams St.	San Diego	CA

Deleting from the Dot Prompt

You can easily perform deletions from the dot prompt using the DELETE command. As usual, begin by pressing the Esc key to leave the Assistant menu and bring up the dot prompt. Now, suppose that you want to delete all California residents from the MAIL.DBF database. At the dot prompt, type this command:

```
DELETE ALL FOR STATE = 'CA' ↵
```

dBASE would respond with

4 records deleted

The effect of this command would be to mark all records with CA in the STATE field for deletion. If you were to list the contents of the database now, you'd see

1	*Appleby	Andy	345 Oak St.	Los Angeles	CA	92123
2	*Smith	John Q.	123 A St.	San Diego	CA	92123
3	*Smithsonian	Lucy	461 Adams St.	San Diego	CA	92122-1234
4	*Doe	Ruth	1142 J. St.	Los Angeles	CA	91234
5	Smith	Betsy	222 Lemon Dr.	New York	NY	01234

All individuals who live in California are marked for deletion. Don't PACK them now, or you'll end up with only one record in your database, Betsy Smith, since she lives in New York. Rather than packing, let's

```
RECALL ALL ↵
```

so that you don't lose all your California residents permanently. (The earthquake hasn't hit yet, but the practice might be useful.)

If you LIST after recalling all the records you'll see

1	**Appleby**	**Andy**	**345 Oak St.**	**Los Angeles**	**CA**	**92123**
2	**Smith**	**John Q.**	**123 A St.**	**San Diego**	**CA**	**92123**
3	**Smithsonian**	**Lucy**	**461 Adams St.**	**San Diego**	**CA**	**92122-1234**
4	**Doe**	**Ruth**	**1142 J. St.**	**Los Angeles**	**CA**	**91234**
5	**Smith**	**Betsy**	**222 Lemon Dr.**	**New York**	**NY**	**01234**

Everyone is back in shape.

Global deletes are useful for getting the job done quickly, but there is an element of danger: you might accidentally delete records you wanted to keep. It's a good idea always to LIST the records that are marked for deletion prior to packing the database. For example, suppose that you decided to take a shortcut method for deleting John Smith from the database using the command

DELETE ALL FOR LNAME = 'Smith ' ⏎

You would end up with the response

2 records deleted

Whoops. You had actually only planned to delete one Smith, but ended up with two deletions. So to see who else you've accidentally deleted, you would ask dBASE to

LIST FOR DELETED() ⏎

That is, list all the records that are marked for deletion. The result would be

2	**∗Smith**	**John Q.**	**123 A St.**	**San Diego**	**CA**	**92123**
5	**∗Smith**	**Betsy**	**222 Lemon Dr.**	**New York**	**NY**	**02134**

Apparently we've gotten a little carried away with our global delete here. We only meant to delete John Q. Smith, but unfortunately our global delete marked Betsy Smith for deletion also. You can bring back Betsy with the command to

RECALL RECORD 5 ⏎

dBASE would release Record 5 from deletion. Global deletes are useful in cases where you want to delete records of a certain type, but be sure to LIST FOR DELETED() prior to PACKing to make sure you won't be deleting any innocents. Now type this command:

    RECALL ALL ↵

so that you don't lose John Q. Smith permanently.

MODIFYING THE DATABASE STRUCTURE

It is not at all unusual to change your mind about what to store in a database after you have entered some records. For example, phone numbers might come in handy on your MAIL database, but you didn't make a field for them. dBASE III PLUS offers a very easy technique to change the structure of a database, no matter how much data you've already stored.

For example, to add a new phone number field to the MAIL.DBF database, follow these simple steps from the Assistant menu screen:

*Remember: to leave the dot prompt and return to the Assistant menu, type **ASSIST** and press ↵.*

    √ Highlight the *Modify* option.
    √ Select the *Database file* option.

The current structure of the database appears on the screen, ready for modification, as in Figure 5.4.

Now, pop quiz. What type of data will the phone number be? At first you might think it should be Numeric data, but this is incorrect. Phone numbers contain non-numeric characters, like parentheses and hyphens. Remember, the numeric data type is for real numbers only. Therefore, the phone number will be character data.

Most phone numbers look something like (123)456-7890, therefore we'll assign a width of 13 characters to this new field.

You can insert fields using the ^N key, but in this case, field 7 seems as good a place as any for a phone number. Using the ↓ arrow key to move the cursor to the first empty field slot on the screen, type the field name PHONE, use the Character data type,

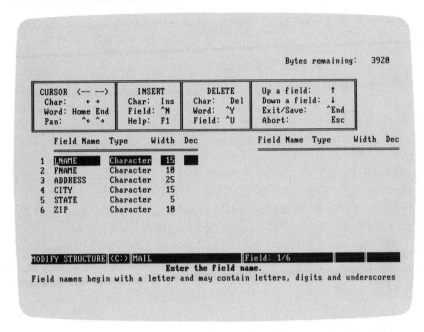

Figure 5.4: MODIFY STRUCTURE Screen for MAIL.DBF

and enter the length, 13. Your screen display should look something like this:

MAIL.DBF

	Field Name	Type	Width	Dec
1	LNAME	Character	15	
2	FNAME	Character	10	
3	ADDRESS	Character	25	
4	CITY	Character	15	
5	STATE	Character	5	
6	ZIP	Character	10	
7	PHONE	Character	13	
8		Character		

After adding the new field to the database, save the new struc-ture by typing a ^W or ^End. dBASE displays this message:

Press ENTER to confirm—any other key to resume
Database records will be APPENDED from backup fields of the same name only!!

This somewhat cryptic message is a little easier to understand if you know how the MODIFY STRUCTURE command works. When you ask dBASE to MODIFY STRUCTURE, it first copies all of the records from the database to a separate database. Then, it deletes all records in the current database and allows the user to make changes. When you are done changing the structure, it reads all the records from the backup database back into the current database. However, if you changed the name of any field, it does not read in data for the new field name. For example, if you had changed the LNAME file to LAST_NAME, you would have lost all of the last names in the database. This is a useful reminder, because if you have changed a field name, you can press any key and then change the field name back to its original name.

For this example, you didn't change any field names; you just added a new field, so it's safe to proceed. Press the Return key

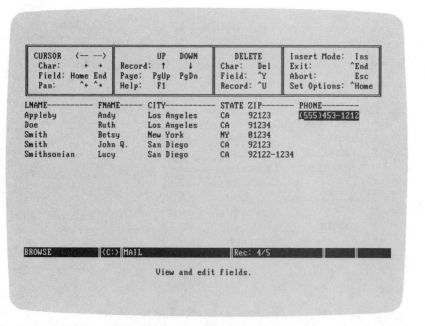

Figure 5.5: Modified BROWSE Screen

now to complete the modification of the database. You'll be returned to the assistant menus.

Unfortunately, there is no command to fill in the phone numbers automatically in the MAIL database. To add new phone numbers, you'll need to do so one record at a time.

The easiest way to do this would be to highlight the *Update* option and select *Browse*. Then press ^Home to bring up the menu, and select the *Lock* option. Type **2** and press Return to lock the two leftmost fields. Next, type ^Home again to bring up the menu, and select Freeze. Type the field name PHONE to keep the highlighting in the PHONE field.

Next, press ^→ a few times to bring the new phone number field onto the screen. Now you can easily move from record to record and add new phone numbers. Figure 5.5 shows the MAIL.DBF BROWSE screen with the new PHONE field.

Type ^End or ^W when done filling in phone numbers to save your work and return to the menu.

REVIEWING EDITING

In this chapter we've discussed many techniques for changing an existing database:

▬

When editing (making changes to) a database, make sure to first open your database and the index files you use regularly.

▬

To bring a single record to the screen for editing, select the *Update* and *Edit* options from the menu.

▬

To bring the entire database to the screen for editing, select the *Update* and *Browse* options from the menu.

▬

To mark records for deletion, use the *Update* and *Delete* options from the menu.

■

To permanently delete records from the database, select *Pack* from the *Update* menu.

■

To globally edit a database, use the *Update* and *Replace* options from the menu.

■

To change the structure of an existing database, select the *Modify* and *Database file* options from the menu.

Creating and Printing Formatted Reports

S o far you've been displaying data on the screen without any particular format. I've even cheated a little in displaying LISTs in this book so that they would fit the page. If you don't provide dBASE with an exact format for displaying data, dBASE will list records and fields in its own fashion. To print formatted reports with dBASE III PLUS, you use its built-in report generator.

CREATING A REPORT

You can create as many report formats for a database as you wish. Like database and index files, you assign a name (maximum of eight characters long, no spaces or punctuation) to the report, and dBASE stores it on disk with the file name extension .FRM. Let's give it a try by creating a simple directory for the MAIL.DBF database.

The first step is to make sure that the MAIL.DBF database is in use. If the MAIL file name does not appear in the Status Bar at the bottom of the screen, use the *Set Up* and *Database file* options to open the MAIL.DBF database and the NAMES.NDX and ZIP.NDX index files. For this example, be sure to open NAMES .NDX before ZIP.NDX to create an alphabetized report.

Next, highlight the *Create* option on the main menu bar. Select *Report* from the submenu. dBASE will ask for the drive and a file name for the report format. As usual, select a drive and then type the file name

BYNAME ⤶

dBASE first displays a menu of the format options for printing reports, as shown in Figure 6.1. The meaning of each of these options is summarized in Table 6.1.

For your first sample report, follow these steps to set up the page format:

✓ Select *Page Title*.
✓ Type **Mailing List by Name**.

✓ Press ←⊥.

✓ Press ^End to finish the title.

```
  Options           Groups         Columns          Locate        Exit  02:44:37 am

  ┌─────────────────────────────────────────┐
  │ Page title                              │
  │ Page width (positions)        88        │
  │ Left margin                    4        │
  │ Right margin                   8        │
  │ Lines per page                58        │
  │ Double space report           No        │
  │ Page eject before printing    Yes       │
  │ Page eject after printing     No        │
  │ Plain page                    No        │
  └─────────────────────────────────────────┘


  ┌──────────────────────────────────────────────────────────────────────────────┐
  │ CURSOR   <-- -->  │ Delete char:   Del │ Insert column:  ^N │ Insert:     Ins │
  │ Char:      ←  →   │ Delete word:    ^T │ Report format:  F1 │ Zoom in:  ^PgDn │
  │ Word:   Home End  │ Delete column:  ^U │ Abandon:       Esc │ Zoom out: ^PgUp │
  └──────────────────────────────────────────────────────────────────────────────┘

  CREATE REPORT  |<C:>|C:BYNAME.FRM           |Opt: 1/9
         Position selection bar - ↑↓.  Select - ←⊥.  Leave menu - ↔.
  Enter up to four lines of text to be displayed at the top of each report page.
```

Figure 6.1: Format Options Menu

Next, adjust the left margin to zero spaces. Here are the steps:

✓ Press ↓ twice.

✓ Select *Left Margin*.

✓ Type **0**.

✓ Press ←⊥.

The rest of the settings on the menu are sufficient for this report. Now let's define the contents of the report itself. You can skip the *Group* option on the main menu, because that is used primarily for subtotals—a topic we'll discuss in a later chapter. Here

On-Screen Prompt	Effect of Your Response
Page title:	Defines a title to be printed at the top of the report.
Page width:	Defines the maximum page width for the report (usually 80 columns, although can be extended to 500 columns for very wide printer paper).
Left margin:	Defines a left margin measured in number of spaces.
Right margin:	Defines a right margin in number of spaces.
Lines per page:	Defines the number of lines to be printed on each page (usually 58 for 8 1/2 by 11 inch paper).
Double space report:	Prints the report without blank lines between rows unless you change this option to **Yes**.
Page eject before printing:	**Yes** ensures that the printed report starts on a new page. **No** prints the report starting at the current printer position of the paper.
Page eject after printing:	**Yes** makes the printer move to the top of the next page after printing the last page of the report.
Plain page:	**No** prints the report title, page numbers, and current date.

Table 6.1: Summary of Format Options

are the steps to put the last name in the first column of the report:

√ Highlight *Columns* on the Report menu.
√ Select *Contents*.
√ Press F10 to display a menu of field names.
√ Select LNAME.
√ Press ⏎ to finish the entry.
√ Select *Heading*.
√ Type **Last Name**.
√ Press ⏎.
√ Press ^End to finish the entry.

Now let's narrow the column just a bit to try to conserve space. Here are the steps:

√ Select the *Width* option.
√ Press ↓ until the width is 12.
√ Press ↵.

That defines the contents of the first column of the report. Notice that a template of the report appears in the bottom half of the screen with the Last Name heading displayed, and 12 X's to show the width of this column on the report, as in Figure 6.2.

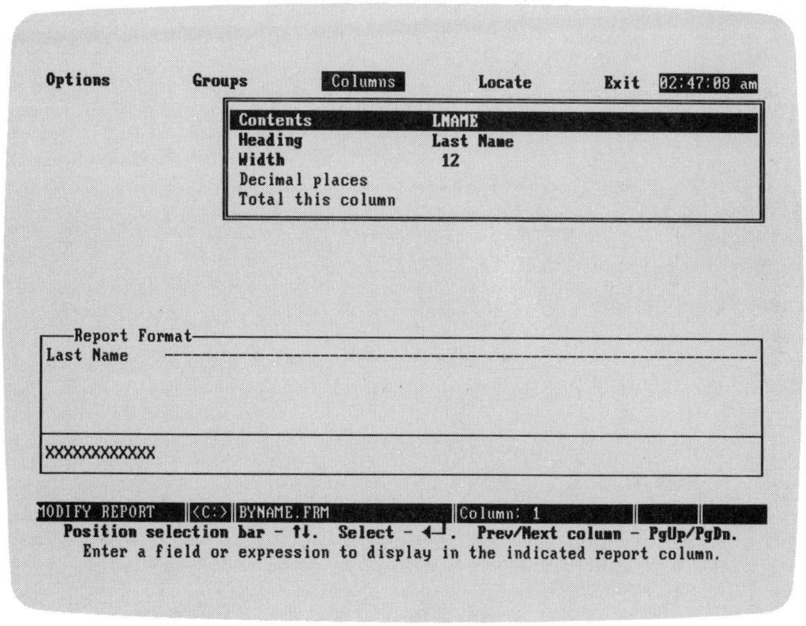

Figure 6.2: Template of BYNAME Report

Next, put the First Name in the next column of the report. The steps are outlined below.

√ Press PgDn to move to the next column.
√ Select *Contents*.
√ Type FNAME.
√ Press ◄┘ to enter the field name.
√ Select *Heading*.
√ Type **First Name**.
√ Press ◄┘.
√ Press ^End to finish the entry.

The column should be defined like this:

Contents	**FNAME**
Heading	**First Name**
Width	**10**
Decimal places	
Total this column	

Now press PgDn to define the next column. Place the ADDRESS field in this column by filling in these options:

Contents	**ADDRESS**
Heading	**Address**
Width	**20**
Decimal places	
Total this column	

Press PgDn to define the next column, and place the CITY field in this column by filling in these options:

Contents	**CITY**
Heading	**City**
Width	**15**
Decimal places	
Total this column	

Press PgDn to move to the next column, and fill in the STATE column:

Contents	**STATE**
Heading	**St**
Width	**2**
Decimal places	
Total this column	

Finally, press PgDn to describe a column for the zip code. Your screen should look like Figure 6.3 when you have selected the last format option for BYNAME. Now you must save your report format.

| Options | Groups | Columns | Locate | Exit | 02:52:25 am |

Contents	Zip
Heading	Zip Code
Width	10
Decimal places	
Total this column	

```
┌─Report Format─
 irst Name Address              City        St Zip Code    ───────────

 ┌─────────────────────────────────────────────────────────────┐
 │ XXXXXXXX XXXXXXXXXXXXXXXXXXX XXXXXXXXX XX XXXXXXXXX          │
```

`MODIFY REPORT  <C:> BYNAME.FRM                Column: 6`
Position selection bar - ↑↓. Select - ◄┘. Prev/Next column - PgUp/PgDn.
Enter a field or expression to display in the indicated report column.

Figure 6.3: Report Format Selections

Saving a Report Format

When you've defined the basic format for your report, save your work by highlighting the *Exit* option on the menu at the top of your screen and selecting *Save.* dBASE will return to the main menu where you can now print your report.

Printing the Report

To print your report, highlight the ***Retrieve*** option, and select *Report.* Specify a drive and select BYNAME.FRM. For this first run, simply select the *Execute the command* option, and answer **Y**es to the question about printing the report. Your finished report will look like Figure 6.4.

Mailing List by Name

Last Name	First Name	Address	City	St	Zip Code
Appleby	Andy	345 Oak St.	Los Angeles	CA	92123
Doe	Ruth	1142 J. St.	Los Angeles	CA	91234
Smith	Betsy	222 Lemon Dr.	New York	NY	01234
Smith	John Q.	123 A St.	San Diego	CA	92123
Smithsonian	Lucy	461 Adams St.	San Diego	CA	92122-1234

Figure 6.4: Sample Directory Report from MAIL.DBF

Like the *List* and *Locate* options, you can specify that only certain records be printed on the report. For example, to list only California residents, follow these steps:

✓ Highlight the **Retrieve** option.
✓ Select *Report.*
✓ Select the BYNAME.FRM report format.
✓ Select *Build a search condition.*
✓ Select STATE.
✓ Select the = option.
✓ Type **CA** as the state to search for.
✓ Select *No more conditions.*
✓ Select *Execute the command.*

Your report will display only California residents. Betsy Smith's data will not be printed in this report.

Of course, index files will determine the order of information printed in the report. If you select the NAMES.NDX file first

Whenever you wish to print a report in the future, you must remember to first open the database that was used to create that report format. You'll also need to open an index if you want a specific sort order.

when you open the database, the names will be displayed in alphabetical order. However, if you select ZIP.NDX first, the data will be displayed in order by zip code. Of course, if you do not open your index files, then the records in the report will be printed in the same order in which they were entered into the database.

MODIFYING REPORT FORMATS

Defining a report format is often a trial-and-error process. What you see on the screen or page may not be exactly what you had in mind. You can easily change the format of any report by highlighting the *Modify* option from the main menu bar and selecting the *Report* option. As usual, specify the drive, and select the BYNAME.FRM report for this example. Then you can use the arrow keys to scroll through the report format and make changes. The *Locate* option on the top menu allows you to select a specific report column to alter.

To insert a column in a report format, press ^N while the column to the right of the new column is displayed on the contents box. A blank form for filling in the new column definition will appear.

To remove a column, use PgUp or PgDn to bring the appropriate column definition to the screen. Then type ^U to delete the column. For help while modifying field definitions in a report format, just press the F1 key.

When you finish changing your report format, highlight the *Exit* option from the top menu, and select *Save*. You'll be returned to the menu where you can print a copy of the modified report using the usual *Retrieve* and *Report* options from the menu.

CREATING MAILING LABELS

If you've ever had to type a number of mailing labels, you're sure to love dBASE's mailing label printer. You create formats for mailing labels in much the same way that you create formats for reports. Let's give it a try.

First, highlight the *Create* option from the main menu bar, and select the *Label* option. dBASE will ask for a name for the label format (to which it will add the extension .LBL). For this example, select a drive, and type the file name TWOCOL (for two-column labels).

dBASE will display the most commonly used setting for a label format: 3-1/2 by 15/16 inches, one column across. Suppose that you want this size, but you want two columns of labels. Simply select the last option, *Labels across page*. Then press ↑ once to change the 1 to a **2**. Your selections are shown in Figure 6.5.

```
┌─────────┐                                      ┌──────────────┐
│ Options │          Contents           Exit     │ 02:59:04 am  │
└─────────┘                                      └──────────────┘
  ┌──────────────────────────────────────────────────┐
  │ Predefined size:       3 1/2 x 15/16 by 1         │
  │                                                    │
  │ Label width:           35                          │
  │ Label height: -        5                           │
  │ Left margin:           0                           │
  │ Lines between labels:  1                           │
  │ Spaces between labels: 0                           │
  │ Labels across page:    2                           │
  └──────────────────────────────────────────────────┘



  ┌─────────────────────────────────────────────────────────────────────┐
  │ CURSOR:   <-- -->  │ Delete char: Del │ Insert row:    ^N │ Insert:    Ins  │
  │  Char:     ←  →    │ Delete word: ^T  │ Toggle menu:   F1 │ Zoom in:  ^PgDn  │
  │  Word:  Home End   │ Delete row:  ^U  │ Abandon:      Esc │ Zoom out: ^PgUp  │
  └─────────────────────────────────────────────────────────────────────┘

 CREATE LABEL    <C:> C:TWOCOL.LBL            Opt: 7/7
         Position selection bar - ↑↓.  Select - ↵.  Leave menu - ↔.
                 Enter the number of labels across the page.
```

Figure 6.5: Menu Selections for Two-Column Labels

Next, highlight the *Contents* option from the menu, which lets you define the contents of each line of the label. Type the field names and punctuation exactly as shown in Figure 6.6.

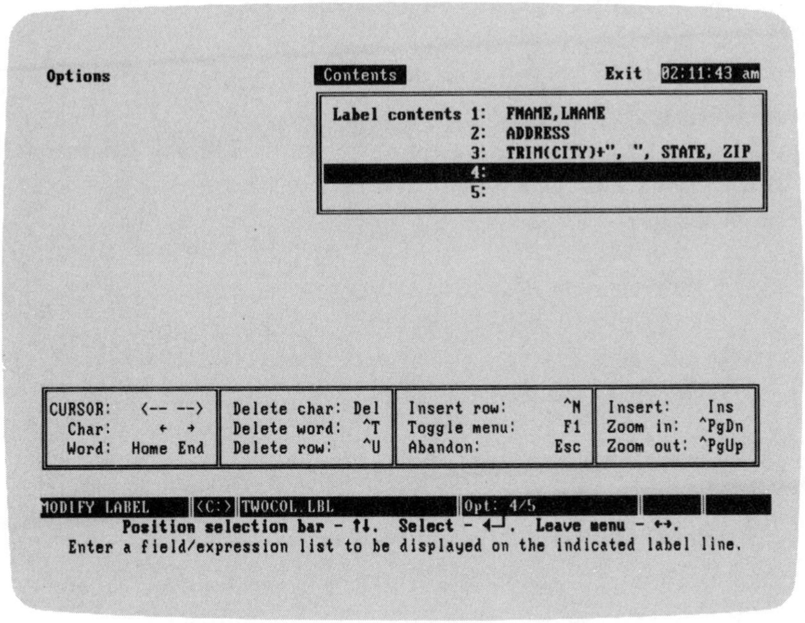

Figure 6.6: Contents for MAIL.DBF Labels

Notice that the first line contains

FNAME, LNAME

To put two spaces between the State and Zip fields, you would use the expression **TRIM(CITY) + ", " + TRIM(STATE) + " " + ZIP** where there is one blank space after the comma, and two blank spaces between the second pair of quotation marks.

This command tells dBASE to print the FNAME and LNAME fields from each database record on the first line of the label, with a single space between fields. The next line contains only the ADDRESS field. The third line of the label contains

TRIM(CITY) + ", ",STATE,ZIP

This line tells dBASE to place the CITY, STATE, and ZIP fields on the third row of the label. You've had to go to some lengths to get it just right, though. First, the TRIM function tells dBASE that if a city's name is shorter than the 15 spaces you defined for your database CITY field, leftover blank spaces should be trimmed, not printed. (These extra blank spaces are called *trailing blanks*.) The plus sign tells dBASE to *concatenate* (link) the following text or symbols (in this case, a comma) directly to the CITY field without inserting a blank space. The comma in quotation marks (", ") tells dBASE to print a comma and a blank space. (*Note:* The quotation marks distinguish this comma from the others. Usually commas tell dBASE to leave a blank space between two fields.) The final portion of this line

    ,STATE,ZIP

simply places the state and the zip code on the same line, with a blank space in front of each.

After defining the label format, highlight the *Exit* option and select *Save*.

Printing Labels

No doubt you'll want to print mailing labels in zip code order rather than alphabetical order, so you'll want to make the ZIP.NDX index file primary. To do so, select the *Set Up* and *Database file* options from the Assistant menu, and select MAIL.DBF. When you select index files, be sure to select ZIP.NDX first.

Then, to print labels, highlight the *Retrieve* option, and select *Label*. Specify a drive, and select the TWOCOL.LBL file. Select the *Execute the command* option, and answer **Y**es to the printer question. Your labels will look like Figure 6.7.

Betsy Smith   Ruth Doe
222 Lemon Dr.   1142 J. St.
New York, NY 01234   Los Angeles CA 91234

Lucy Smithsonian   Andy Appleby
461 Adams St.   345 Oak St.
San Diego, CA 92122-1234   Los Angeles CA 92123

John Q. Smith
123 A St.
San Diego, CA 92123

Figure 6.7: Two-Column MAIL.DBF Labels

Of course, as with most options, you can also specify search conditions for your mailing labels (such as ZIP > = 90000) to print only labels that meet some criterion.

Modifying Label Formats

To modify a label format file, highlight the *Modify* option from the main menu, and select *Label*. Specify the drive and file name. Then you can change the label format. (Use the arrow keys to move the cursor and the F1 key to get help.)

USING LABEL AND REPORT COMMANDS

Like everything else in dBASE III PLUS, reports and mailing labels can be accessed directly from the dot prompt. To create a report format for a database, set the default drive, open the appropriate database, then enter the command MODIFY REPORT with the name of the report format file. For example, to modify the BYNAME.FRM report format from the dot prompt, you would enter the commands:(On a hard-disk system, omit the SET DEFAULT TO B).

```
SET DEFAULT TO B ←
USE MAIL ←
MODIFY REPORT BYNAME ←
```

To print a report, make sure the appropriate database is open, and any index files that you want to use are active. Then, enter the command REPORT FORM with the name of the report format file. In this example, the commands open the MAIL.DBF database with the NAMES.NDX index file primary (so the records are listed in alphabetical order) and print the data in the BYNAME .FRM report format:

```
SET DEFAULT TO B ←
USE MAIL INDEX NAMES, ZIP ←
REPORT FORM BYNAME TO PRINT ←
```

Adding the command TO PRINT to the end of the REPORT FORM command prints the report rather than displaying it on-screen.

You can use the FOR option to specify a search condition for printing reports. For example, this command prints data for people whose last names begin with the letters A through M:

```
REPORT FORM BYNAME FOR LNAME > = "A";
  .AND. LNAME < = "M" TO PRINT
```

To create or change a mailing label format for a database, use the command MODIFY LABEL along with the name of the for-mat file. The appropriate database must be open:

```
SET DEFAULT TO B ←
USE MAIL ←
MODIFY LABEL TWOCOL ←
```

To display labels, use the LABEL FORM command with the name of the label format file. If you want them in zip code order, use the appropriate index file, too:

```
USE MAIL INDEX ZIP, NAMES ←
LABEL FORM TWOCOL ←
```

To print labels, add the TO PRINT command to the end of the LABEL FORM command:

```
LABEL FORM TWOCOL TO PRINT ←
```

When printing labels, you can use the SAMPLE option to dis-play a facsimile of the labels to be printed, which will help you to line up the labels properly in the printer. For example, this com-mand allows you to check the alignment of the labels in the printer before printing labels from the TWOCOL.LBL format file:

```
LABEL FORM TWOCOL SAMPLE TO PRINT ←
```

You can, of course, build a search condition with the FOR option when printing labels. This command prints mailing labels for individuals in the 90000 to 95000 zip code areas, using the

TWOCOL.LBL format file:

```
LABEL FORM TWOCOL FOR ZIP > = '90000';
.AND. ZIP < = '95000' TO PRINT
```

REVIEWING REPORTS AND LABELS

In this chapter, you have learned how to use formats to create reports and mailing labels.

▬

To create a report format for a database, select the *Create* and *Report* options from the menus.

▬

To print a report, select the *Retrieve* and *Report* options from the menus.

▬

To modify an existing report format, select the *Modify* and *Report* options from the menu.

▬

To create a mailing label format for a database, select the *Create* and *Label* options from the menu.

▬

To print mailing labels, select the *Retrieve* and *Label* options from the menu.

▬

To print a report or mailing labels in sorted order, use an existing index file, or optionally, create a new one.

▬

Commands for creating report and label formats, as well as for printing reports and labels, can be entered at the dot prompt.

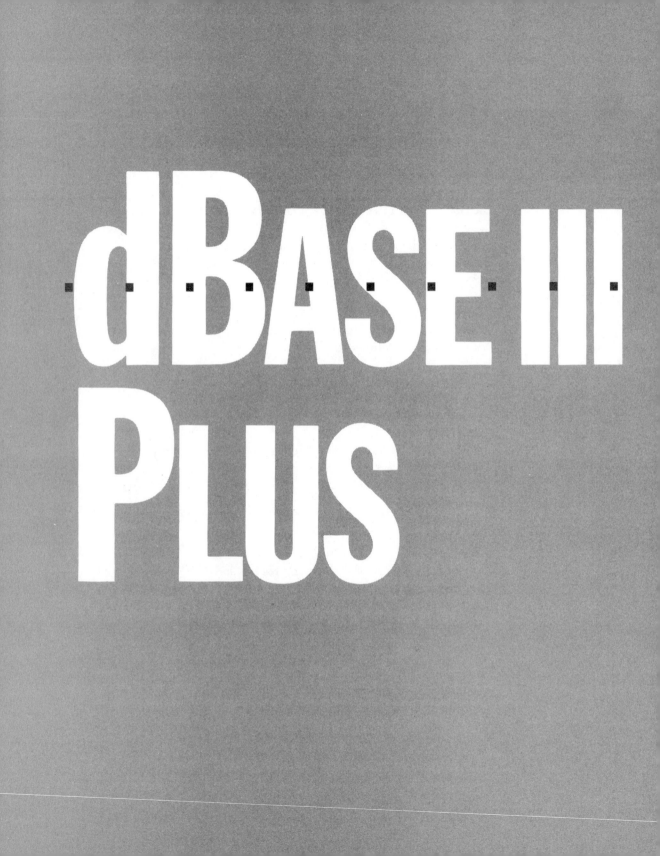

Designing Custom Screen Displays

A s you've seen in previous chapters, the *Append* and *Edit* options allow you to enter and edit data through a simple screen which displays the fields in a vertical row.

Through the use of the dBASE III PLUS Screen Painter, you can create your own custom screens for adding and editing data. Figure 7.1 shows such a custom screen for MAIL.DBF, which you'll develop in this chapter. However, you'll see that being creative is easy, so you might prefer to try your own screen as you go through the chapter.

CREATING A CUSTOM SCREEN

To get started creating a form, follow these steps:

√ Highlight the *Create* option.
√ Select *Format.*
√ Select a drive.
√ Type **ADDNAMES,** or create your own form name.

A screen for developing a form will appear, as well as a menu of options. First, you need to tell dBASE which database this form will be used for. So, follow these steps:

√ Select *Select Database file.*
√ Specify MAIL.DBF.

Now, as a shortcut to developing a form, we can have the screen painter put together a general purpose form, which we in turn will modify. (This is easier than trying to create the form completely from scratch.) Follow these steps:

√ Select *Load fields.*
√ Highlight each field, and press ⏎.

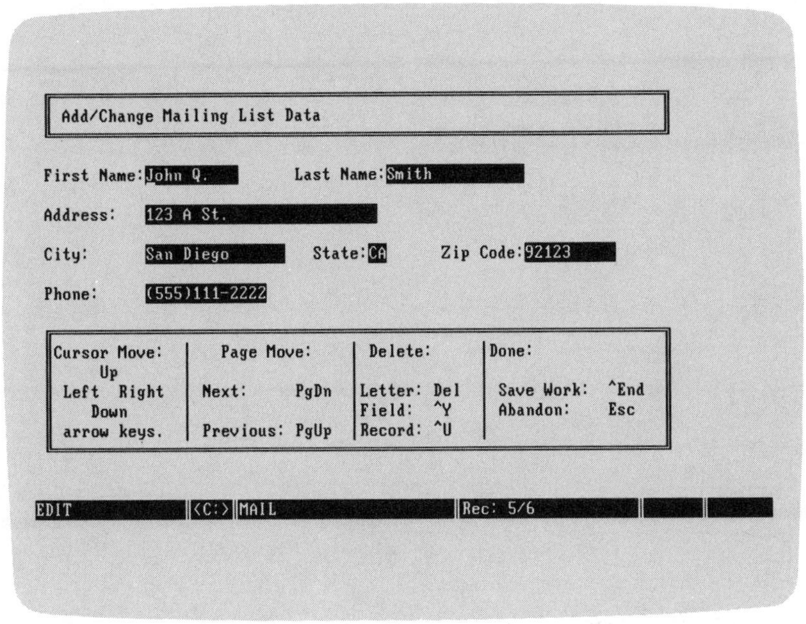

```
┌─────────────────────────────────────────────────────────────────┐
│ Add/Change Mailing List Data                                     │
└─────────────────────────────────────────────────────────────────┘

First Name: John Q.          Last Name: Smith

Address:    123 A St.

City:       San Diego     State: CA      Zip Code: 92123

Phone:      (555)111-2222

┌──────────────┬───────────────┬──────────────┬──────────────────┐
│ Cursor Move: │ Page Move:    │ Delete:      │ Done:            │
│     Up       │               │              │                  │
│ Left  Right  │ Next:   PgDn  │ Letter: Del  │ Save Work:  ^End │
│     Down     │               │ Field:  ^Y   │ Abandon:    Esc  │
│ arrow keys.  │ Previous: PgUp│ Record: ^U   │                  │
└──────────────┴───────────────┴──────────────┴──────────────────┘

EDIT              <C:> MAIL                 Rec: 5/6
```

Figure 7.1: Custom Data-Entry Screen

You'll notice that as you press ↓, the highlighting moves through each field name on the menu. If you press Return while a field name is highlighted, a triangle appears next to it, indicating that the field has been selected for inclusion on the custom form. For this exercise, use this method to select all the field names for your screen:

LNAME
FNAME
ADDRESS
STATE
ZIP
PHONE

Press → after all field names have been selected. You'll see a simplified form appear on the screen, as in Figure 7.2. This screen is called the *blackboard* because, as you'll see, it is easy to move, add, and change information on the screen.

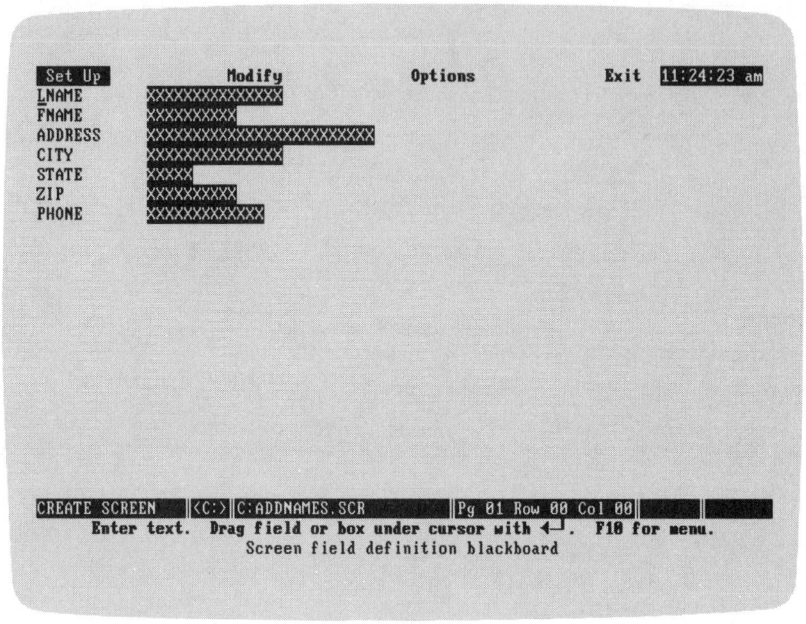

Figure 7.2: Loaded Fields on the Screen Painter Blackboard

Notice that there are field labels (such as LNAME, FNAME, etc). There are also field highlights which show where the reverse video portion of the screen will appear when the form is used for entering and editing data. The Xs show the number of characters in each field.

MOVING INFORMATION ON THE BLACKBOARD

It's pretty easy to move information around on the blackboard after you've practiced a bit. Take a moment to review the basic editing keys listed in Table 7.1.

Now let's start shifting some things around. First, press ^N four times to put some blank lines at the top of the screen for a title (which you'll add later). Make sure that the cursor is in the

Key	Alternate Key	Effect
F10		Switches between menu and blackboard.
←		Moves cursor left one character.
→		Moves cursor right one character.
↑		Moves cursor up one line.
↓		Moves cursor down one line.
Ins	*or* ^V	Turns the INSert mode ON and OFF when cursor is not in a field, or extends the length of the highlighted field where the cursor rests.
^N		Adds a blank line between two lines.
End	*or* ^F	Moves cursor to beginning of next word.
Home	*or* ^A	Moves cursor to beginning of current or previous word.
↵	*or* ^M	Inserts a new line if INSert is ON. Otherwise, moves cursor down one line. Also moves field highlighting and boxes.
Del	*or* ^G	Deletes character at the cursor or decreases the size of a highlighted field where the cursor rests.
Backspace		Deletes character to left of cursor.
^T		Deletes word to right of cursor.
^Y		Deletes an entire line from form.
^U		Deletes a field or box.
PgDn	*or* ^C	Scrolls down 18 lines on screen.
PgUp	*or* ^R	Scrolls up 18 lines on screen.

Table 7.1: Blackboard Editing Keys

upper-left corner of the screen and that the blackboard is still displayed on the screen. (*Note:* Press F10 if you want to switch from Blackboard to menu.) Next, let's move the LNAME field highlighting next to the FNAME field. Follow these steps to move a single field:

✓ Press ↓ four times to move the cursor to LNAME.

✓ Press the End key to put the cursor inside the field highlighting.

✓ Press ⟵ to enter DRAG mode.

✓ Press → 12 times to move the cursor 12 spaces to the right.

✓ Press ↓.

✓ Complete the move by pressing ⟵.

The LNAME field highlighting will now be next to the FNAME field highlighting, as shown in Figure 7.3.

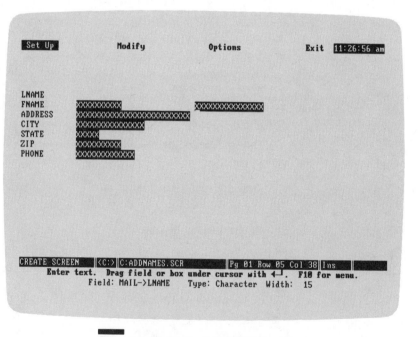

Figure 7.3: Customized LNAME Location

Notice the general steps that you used to move the field highlighting. First, you put the cursor inside the field highlighting that you wanted to move. When the cursor was inside the highlighting, you pressed the Return key to begin the *Dragging* option. The bottom of the screen then read:

Move field with ↑ ↓ ← →. Complete with ↵

You used the → and ↓ keys to move the cursor to the new location, and pressed Return to complete the move. (You'll have a chance to practice this again in a moment.)

Now, let's add a few blank lines to this form. To move the ADDRESS field down a line, follow these steps:

✓ Press ↓.
✓ Press ^←.
✓ Press ↵.

To move the CITY field down a line, follow these steps:

✓ Press ↓.
✓ Press ↵.

Now, to move the STATE field next to the CITY field, follow these steps:

✓ Press ↓ and End to move the cursor into the STATE field.
✓ Press ↵ to start the move.
✓ Using → and ↑, move the cursor to row 09, column 36. (The Status Bar lists the cursor's row and column position.)
✓ Complete the move by pressing ↵.

Now move the ZIP field over by the STATE field. Here are the steps:

✓ Press ↓ twice, and then press Home to move cursor inside the ZIP field.

✓ Press ◄— to start the move.
✓ Move the cursor to row 09, column 53.
✓ Complete the move by pressing ◄—.

Now you can delete the STATE and ZIP field labels by following these steps:

✓ Press ↓.
✓ Press ^←.
✓ Press ^Y.
✓ Press ^T.

The form is taking shape now, as shown in Figure 7.4. Next let's create some more appropriate field labels to be displayed on a custom data-entry screen.

ADDING FIELD LABELS

Field labels like LNAME and FNAME may be easy for you to remember, but they are not the best labels for other people who will enter data through your custom screen. You can create field labels simply by typing them on the screen. Here are some simple steps to put a whole new set of field labels on the ADDNAMES form. *Note:* If pressing the Space bar moves text to the right, press the Ins key while the cursor is not inside a field.

✓ Press Ins if the "INS" message appears at the bottom of your screen.
✓ Move the cursor to the L in LNAME, and press ^T.
✓ Press ↓.
✓ Press the Space bar, and type **First Name:**.
✓ Move the cursor to row 05, column 28.
✓ Type **Last Name:**.
✓ Move the cursor to row 07, column 00.

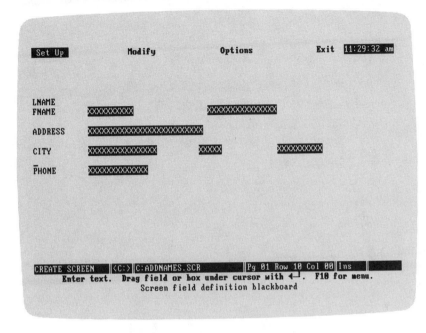

Figure 7.4: Customized Field Locations

✓ Press the Space bar, and type **Address:**.
✓ Move the cursor to row 09, column 00.
✓ Press the Space bar, and type **City:**.
✓ Move the cursor to row 09, column 30.
✓ Type **State:**.
✓ Move the cursor to row 09, column 44.
✓ Type **Zip Code:**.
✓ Move the cursor to row 11, column 00.
✓ Press the Space bar, and type **Phone:**.

Notice that you pressed Space bar for cosmetic reasons—to move field names away from the left edge of the screen. When you've finished, your custom form will look like Figure 7.5.

Let's customize this form a little more, by adding some boxes and titles.

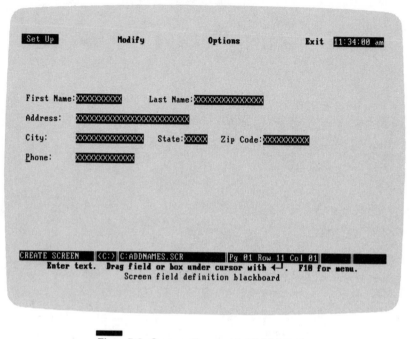

Figure 7.5: Custom Form with Field Labels

DRAWING BOXES

Let's continue creating a custom data-entry screen by drawing a box for the title. First, call up the menu by pressing F10. Then, highlight *Options*. This will display these choices:

Generate text file image
Draw a Window or a Line
  Single Bar
  Double Bar

Select the *Double Bar* option. These instructions appear at the bottom of the screen:

Position cursor to box corner with ↑ ↓ ← →. Complete with ↵

In this exercise, use the arrow keys to move the cursor to row 01, column 01, and press Return to mark the starting position.

The screen instructions then display:

Position cursor to other corner with ↑ ↓ ← →. Complete with ↵

Now follow these steps:

- √ Press ↓ twice.
- √ Press → until the cursor gets to row 03, column 68.
- √ Press ↵ to finish marking the corner.
- √ Move the cursor inside the box that appears on the screen.
- √ Type **Add/Change Mailing List Data,** or create your own title.

Now your screen has a boxed title.

If you are feeling particularly ambitious or if the people who will use your screen are novices, you may want to try adding your own Help Menu to your custom data-entry screen. Figure 7.6 shows some help information added to the bottom of the ADD-NAMES form. Create the box with Double Bar and Single Bar lines. Type the rest of the text just as you see it in Figure 7.6.

SAVING THE FORM

By this time you've put quite a bit of work into your form. So, you might want to save the form now, just to play it safe. To do so, move the highlighting to the *Exit* option. (If the menu is not showing, press F10 first.) Then, select the *Save* option. You'll be returned to the main menu.

To resume working on a form, (or to make changes in the future), highlight the *Modify* option from the main menu, and select *Format.* Select a drive and the form name (ADDNAMES.SCR in this example). Then press F10 to view the blackboard.

TEMPLATES

Templates are used to reduce the likelihood of errors being typed into forms, as well as to simplify data entry. For example, you can add a template like this to the PHONE field:

:( ) -   :

Because the parentheses and hyphen are already in the field, the template encourages a standardized format for entering telephone numbers and simplifies their entry.

To add this template to the ADDNAMES form, first move the cursor to the first character in the PHONE field highlighting. Then call up the menu (F10) and highlight the *Modify* option. At the bottom of the pull-down menu, you'll see these options:

Picture Function
Picture Template
Range

Select the *Picture Template* option. You'll see a menu of special

```
 Set Up            Modify              Options          Exit  11:42:18 am

  ┌─────────────────────────────────────────────────────────────┐
  │ Add/Change Mailing List Data                                 │
  └─────────────────────────────────────────────────────────────┘

   First Name: XXXXXXXXX      Last Name: XXXXXXXXXXXXXX

   Address:      XXXXXXXXXXXXXXXXXXXXXXXXX

   City:        XXXXXXXXXXXXX    State: XXXX    Zip Code: XXXXXXXXX

   Phone:       XXXXXXXXXXXXX

  ┌──────────────┬────────────────┬─────────────┬──────────────┐
  │ Cursor Move: │  Page Move:    │  Delete:    │ Done:        │
  │     Up       │                │             │              │
  │ Left  Right  │  Next:    PgDn │ Letter: Del │ Save Work: ^End │
  │    Down      │                │ Field:  ^Y  │ Abandon:   Esc  │
  │ arrow keys.  │  Previous: PgUp│ Record: ^U  │  _           │
  └──────────────┴────────────────┴─────────────┴──────────────┘

 CREATE SCREEN  <C:> C:ADDNAMES.SCR        Pg 01 Row 18 Col 50  Ins
      Enter text.  Drag field or box under cursor with ←┘.  F10 for menu.
                   Screen field definition blackboard
```

Figure 7.6: ADDNAMES Form with Custom Help Menu

characters that you can use in your picture template. These characters are explained in Table 7.2.

Special Character	Effect
A	Allows letters only to be entered.
L	Allows logical data only (T, F, Y, or N).
X	Allows entry of any character.
#	Allows numbers and + or − signs.
9	Allows numeric digits only.
!	Converts entry to uppercase.
other	Adds any other character to the entry.

Table 7.2: Special Template Characters

dBASE will also ask you for the template. Type this template:

(999)999-9999

Notice that you've specified that only numbers can be entered into the field (by placing the special character **9** into the template). Therefore, the template also helps to prevent mistakes in entering data.

Let's discuss a few other tricks that you could do with picture templates. For example, if you put the template

!AAAAAAAAAAAA

in the LNAME field highlighting, and the template

!AAAAAAAA

in the FNAME field highlighting, both of these fields would automatically switch the first letter of the entry to uppercase. The special **A** characters will allow the other characters to remain as they were entered.

Placing the template

!!

into the STATE field automatically converts any state abbreviation to all uppercase. Placing the template

##########

into the ZIP field allows numbers, spaces, periods, plus (+) and minus (−) signs to be entered for the zip code. (If your mailing list includes foreign zip codes, however, you'll want to stay with the XXXXXXXXXX template which allows any characters.) Figure 7.7 shows how the ADDNAMES screen form looks with all these new picture templates entered.

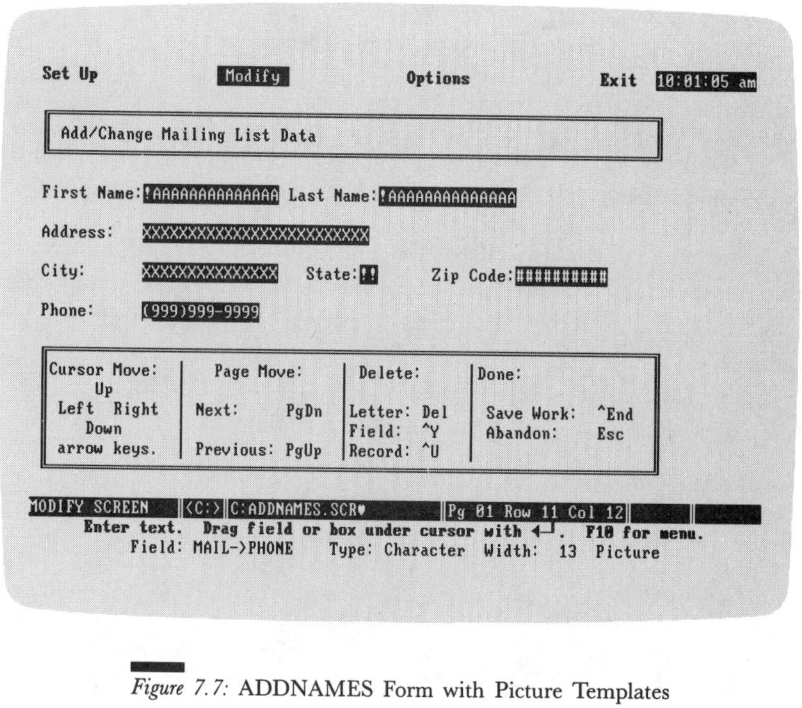

Figure 7.7: ADDNAMES Form with Picture Templates

When you're done adding the picture templates to the ADD-NAMES form, highlight the *Exit* option and select *Save*. Now let's look at ways to put the custom form to work.

USING A CUSTOM FORM

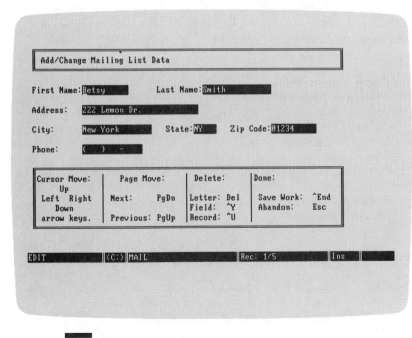

To use a custom form, you simply highlight the *Set Up* option from the main menu, and select the *Format for screen* option. dBASE will ask for the drive and file name. In this example, select the appropriate drive, and select ADDNAMES.FMT from the menu of form names.

To use a custom form to add or edit database records, you must first remember to open the appropriate database (that is, the one you used to design the form in the first place).

The custom form will now be displayed whenever you add new records, or edit through the EDIT mode. For example, if you highlight the *Update* option and select *Edit,* you'll see the first record from your database displayed on your custom screen, as in Figure 7.8.

Figure 7.8: MAIL.DBF Record Displayed on Custom Screen

All keys work with the new form as they did in the normal APPEND and EDIT modes. That is, the arrow keys move the cursor, Del and ^Y delete characters and fields, PgUp and PgDn scroll up and down through records, and ^End saves your work and returns to the Assistant menu.

USING OTHER SCREEN PAINTER OPTIONS

There are several other options available in the screen painter which we'll discuss briefly now. Some of these features are quite advanced and are discussed in more detail in Chapter 17.

The *Modify* Menu Options

While working on the blackboard, you can place the cursor in any field, and press F10 to call up the Screen Painter menu. If you highlight the *Modify* option from the Screen Painter menu, you'll see a pull-down menu that looks something like this:

Screen Field Definition
Action: **Edit/GET**
Source: **MAIL**
Content: **FNAME**
Type: **Character**
Width: **10**
Decimal:

Picture Function:
Picture Template:
Range:

Let's briefly discuss what each of these options provides:

Action: Toggles between Edit/GET and Display/SAY. In the Edit/GET mode, the field can be modified in the EDIT and APPEND modes. In the Display/SAY mode, data are only displayed and cannot be changed in either APPEND or EDIT mode. The latter is most commonly used in advanced applications where a field value, such as an account number, is fixed and cannot be changed.

Source: *Source* is the name of the file that the field is from, and this option cannot be changed.

Content: *Content* is the name of the field associated with the field highlighting that contains the cursor.

Type: This is the data type, as defined in the database structure (Character, Numeric, Date, Logical, or Memo).

Width: The field width as defined in the database structure. The number that you enter will change the width of the field definition in the database structure, so use this option with caution.

Decimals: The number of decimal places used with Numeric data.

Picture
Function: Like picture templates, but only requires that you enter a single character. Options are: ! (convert all letters to uppercase), A (allow only alphabetic characters to be entered into field), D (display dates in American mm/dd/yy format—for Date data type only), E (display dates in European dd/mm/yy format—for Date data type only). The S option limits the size of a field display on a form, but allows data to scroll horizontally within it. Hence, if you use the picture function S5 in the LNAME field, then the highlighting on the screen will only be five characters wide when entering or editing data. However, longer names will scroll through the five-character "window." The R option, rarely used, displays literals in a date, even if a non-Date data type is used. For example, picture function RE will request data in DATE mode, even if a field is numeric.

Picture
Template: Allows standardized entry formats and data-entry

checking. See Table 7.2 for options.

Range: Used with Numeric and Date data only, this option allows you to define a highest and lowest acceptable range of entries.

Adding, Changing, Deleting Fields

The *Width* option from the *Modify* pull-down menu allows you to change the width of a field. However, this option makes the same change to the database structure. More often than not, you'll simply want to change the size of a field on a form for aesthetic reasons.

To increase the size of a field highlighting on the data-entry screen without affecting the database structure, follow these steps:

√ Call up ADDNAMES.SCR.
√ Move the cursor to the field that you want to lengthen.
√ Press the Ins key until the field looks wide enough.
√ Press ^End to save the form.

Similarly, to decrease the field width on the data-entry screen and not in the database structure, follow these steps but press the Del key instead of the Ins key.

To add a new field from your database to this form, follow these steps:

√ Call up ADDNAMES.SCR.
√ Move the cursor to the additional field location.
√ Press F10.
√ Highlight *Modify* on the Screen Painter menu.
√ Select the *Content* option.
√ Select the field name from the submenu that appears.
√ Highlight the *Width* option, and enter a width.
√ Finally, press F10 to return to the blackboard.

To delete a field from a form, move the cursor to the appropriate field highlighting and type ^U. dBASE will ask if you want to delete the field from the database structure as well. If you answer **Y**es, all data in that field will be lost. Therefore, answer **N**o unless you are absolutely certain that you will never need this information in your database.

CREATING SCREENS FROM THE DOT PROMPT

If you begin working from the dot prompt, there are several simple techniques you can use to handle forms. First, the command MODIFY SCREEN <file name> will enter the Screen Painter. For example, entering the command

    MODIFY SCREEN ADDNAMES ↵

will allow you to create a screen format named ADDNAMES.SCR (screens always have the extension .SCR).

The Screen Painter automatically creates a separate file with the same name but the extension .FMT (ADDNAMES.FMT). This is the file dBASE actually uses to display forms on the computer's screen. The .SCR file is used only while you are designing a screen through the Screen Painter.

From the dot prompt, you can activate a .FMT file with the SET FORMAT command. For example, the commands below open the MAIL.DBF database with the NAMES.NDX and ZIP.NDX index files. Then, the SET FORMAT command opens the ADDNAMES.FMT format file:

    SET DEFAULT TO B ↵
    USE MAIL INDEX NAMES,ZIP ↵
    SET FORMAT TO ADDNAMES ↵

To add new records to the MAIL.DBF database using the custom screen, you merely need to enter the command

    APPEND ↵

at the dot prompt.

To edit data on the MAIL.DBF database, simply enter this command at the dot prompt:

    EDIT ↵

Optionally, you can specify a record number:

    EDIT 4 ↵

You can use a FOR condition with EDIT as well. For example,

    EDIT FOR LNAME = "Doe" .AND. FNAME = "Ruth" ↵

will edit all records with Ruth Doe as the name.

To stop using the custom form and return to the normal APPEND and EDIT screens, simply enter this command at the dot prompt:

    CLOSE FORMAT ↵

REVIEWING CUSTOM DATA-ENTRY SCREENS

In this chapter, you have learned many techniques for creating custom data-entry screens:

▬

To create a custom form for a database, select the *Create* and *Format* options from the Assistant menu screen.

▬

To move fields on the Screen Painter blackboard, place the cursor inside the field highlighting that you want to move, and press Return. Use the arrow keys to move the cursor to the new location, and press Return to complete the move.

▬

To change field labels on a form, simply position the cursor and type over existing labels. Use the arrow, Ins, and Del keys to move the cursor and add/delete text.

■■■

To draw boxes on the form, select *Draw a window or line* from the Screen Painter options menu.

■■■

To save a custom form, highlight the *Exit* option from the Screen Painter menu and select *Save*.

■■■

To add templates to a field highlight, move the cursor to the first character in the field and call up the menu (F10). Select the *Picture Function* or *Picture Template* option.

■■■

To use a custom form, highlight the *Set Up* option from the main menu bar and select the *Format for screen* option. The custom form will be used in the APPEND and EDIT modes when selected from the menu.

■■■

To change the size of a field highlight on the screen, move the cursor to within the field and press Ins to increase its length, or Del to decrease it. Press ^U to delete the field altogether.

■■■

From the dot prompt, the commands MODIFY SCREEN, SET FORMAT TO, APPEND, EDIT, and CLOSE FORMAT access a custom screen.

Managing Numbers and Dates

U p to this point, our database has contained only Character data. Eventually, you'll probably want to include dates and numbers in a database. There are several techniques for managing dates and numbers, and for performing basic arithmetic on them. These are the topics of this chapter.

CREATING A SALES DATABASE

For the exercises in this chapter we'll create a database named SALES.DBF. From the Assistant menu, highlight the *Create* option and select *Database file*. Select the appropriate drive for your computer, and type the file name SALES. Define the database fields structure as shown in Figure 8.1.

You have defined five fields for your SALES.DBF database. Notice that CODE and TITLE are Character data fields. Only

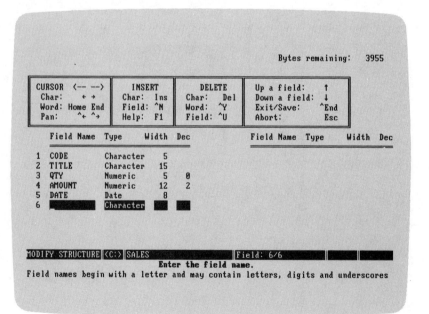

Figure 8.1: SALES.DBF Database Structure

Numeric data with a maximum of five digits (99999) and no decimal places can be entered in your QTY (quantity) field. AMOUNT is also a Numeric data field, but its maximum width is twelve with two decimal places (for pennies). dBASE automatically assigns a width of eight characters (mm/dd/yy) to the DATE field.

Once you've entered the database structure, press Return rather than defining a sixth field, or press ^End to save the structure. When dBASE asks you to confirm the new structure, press Return. When dBASE asks if you want to add new data now, answer **Y**es and fill in the following sample records. (*Note:* You need not enter the record numbers because dBASE keeps track of those automatically.)

Record#	CODE	TITLE	QTY	AMOUNT	DATE
1	AAA	Rakes	3	15.00	03/01/86
2	BBB	Hoes	2	12.50	03/01/86
3	CCC	Shovels	3	21.50	03/01/86
4	AAA	Rakes	2	10.00	03/01/86
5	CCC	Shovels	4	26.50	03/01/86
6	AAA	Rakes	2	11.00	03/02/86
7	CCC	Shovels	1	7.50	03/01/86
8	BBB	Hoes	2	12.50	03/02/86
9	AAA	Rakes	5	23.50	03/02/86

SUMMING NUMBERS

To sum a numeric field, highlight the **Retrieve** option from the Assistant menu, and select *Sum*. If you immediately select *Execute the command* after selecting *Sum*, dBASE will display the sum of all numeric fields for every record in the database:

9 records summed
QTY   AMOUNT
  24   140.00

You can use the *Construct a field list* option from the submenu to specify that only certain fields be summed. For example, suppose that you want to know the sum of sales to date. The steps that tell dBASE to add only the numbers in the AMOUNT field are outlined below.

✓ Highlight *Retrieve* from the main menu bar.
✓ Select *Sum.*
✓ Select *Construct a field list.*
✓ From the menu of field names, select AMOUNT.
✓ Press → to finish selecting fields.
✓ Select *Execute the command.*

Then dBASE will add all of the numbers you've entered in the AMOUNT field and display the results:

9 records summed
AMOUNT
140.00

By using the *Build a search condition* option from the Assistant menu you can also tell dBASE that only certain records be included in the sum. For example, suppose that you want to know how many rakes you have sold. To find out, ask dBASE to sum the QTY field for records with Part Number AAA. Here are the steps:

✓ Highlight the *Retrieve* option from the main menu bar.
✓ Select *Sum.*
✓ Select *Construct a field list.*
✓ Select QTY.
✓ Press → to finish selecting fields to sum.
✓ Select *Build a search condition.*
✓ Select CODE.
✓ Select = .
✓ Type **AAA**.
✓ Press ◄┘.
✓ Select *No more conditions.*
✓ Select *Execute the command.*

With these menu selections, you have built

Command: SUM QTY FOR CODE "AAA"

dBASE will display the result

4 records summed
QTY
  12

indicating that the sum of the QTY field for records with CODE AAA is twelve. In other words, you've sold twelve rakes.

If you are interested in sales on a certain date, follow these steps:

√ Highlight the *Retrieve* option from the main menu bar.
√ Select *Sum.*
√ Select *Build a search condition.*
√ Select DATE.
√ Select = .
√ Type **03/02/86.**
√ Select *No more conditions.*
√ Select *Execute the command.*

dBASE will show the sum of the QTY and AMOUNT fields for all records with dates of 03/02/86:

3 records summed
QTY   AMOUNT
  9   **47.00**

Of course, you can be even more specific in your sums by using .AND. and .OR. in your search condition. For example, if you want to know how many AAA rakes you sold on March 1, 1986, and how much these sales came to, follow these steps:

√ Highlight *Retrieve* from the main menu bar.
√ Select *Sum.*
√ Select *Build a search condition.*
√ Select CODE.
√ Select = .
√ Type **AAA.**
√ Press ⬅.
√ Select *Combine with .AND.*

✓ Select DATE.
✓ Select =.
✓ Type **03/01/86**.
✓ Select *No more conditions.*
✓ Select *Execute the command.*

dBASE displays the sum of the QTY and AMOUNT fields for sales of part number AAA on March 1, 1986:

2 records summed
QTY   AMOUNT
    5   25.00

AVERAGING NUMERIC AMOUNTS

The *Average* option from the **Retrieve** menu works in exactly the same way as the *Sum* option, but it calculates an average rather than a sum. For example, if you select *Average* and *Execute the command,* dBASE will display

9 records averaged
QTY   AMOUNT
    3   15.56

the average QTY and AMOUNT of all nine records.

You can use the *Construct a field list* option from the menu to specify numeric fields to average. Of course, you can use the *Build a search condition* option to average only records, such as Part Number AAA or Date = 03/01/86, just as you did with the *Sum* option.

COUNTING RECORDS

The *Count* option works on any data type because it simply counts the number of occurrences in records. For example, if you highlight the **Retrieve** option and select *Count,* and then select *Execute* *the command,* dBASE will display

9 records

indicating that there are nine records on the database.

Suppose that you want to know how many sales records about BBB hoes have been entered into your database. If you select *Count* and *Build a search condition* from the menus, and specify CODE = BBB, dBASE will display

2 records

because only two records in the database have the code BBB.

PRINTING TOTALS AND SUBTOTALS IN REPORTS

You can also total and subtotal columns of information in dBASE III PLUS reports. The most important point to keep in mind with subtotals, however, is that the database must either be sorted or indexed by the field which determines how the records are subtotaled. For example, if you want your sales report to present quantity and price totals and subtotals for each product (the CODE field), you need to first index the SALES.DBF database by the CODE field. Here are the steps to create a CODE.NDX index file from your SALES.DBF database:

- √ Highlight the *Organize* option.
- √ Select *Index*.
- √ Type **CODE**.
- √ Press ◄┘.
- √ Select a drive.
- √ Type **CODE** as the name for the index file.
- √ Press ◄┘.

When the indexing is complete, press any key to return to the Assistant menu screen.

Now you can develop a report using the report generator. Let's build one now, just for the practice. First, highlight the *Create* option, and select *Report*. Select a drive for storing the report format, and type the report file name SUBTOTS.

Fill in these options on the first report menu:

Page title	Sales by Product Code
Page width (positions)	80
Left margin	0
Right margin	0
Lines per page	58
Double space report	No
Page eject before printing	Yes
Page eject after printing	No
Plain page	No

Next, highlight the *Group* option, and specify CODE as the field to group. Also, you can assign the group title Product Code.

Group on expression	CODE
Group heading	Product Code
Summary report only	No
Page eject after group	No
Sub-group on expression	
Sub-group heading	

Next you'll want to fill in individual columns. Begin by highlighting the *Columns* option and defining the first report column:

Contents	CODE
Heading	Part No.
Width	8
Decimal places	
Total this column	

Press PgDn, and define the second report column:

Contents	TITLE
Heading	Part Name
Width	15
Decimal places	
Total this column	

Press PgDn again, and fill in the specifications for the third report column:

Contents	QTY
Heading	Qty
Width	5
Decimal places	0
Total this column	Yes

Notice that the *Total this column* option is marked **Y**es, which means that this numeric field will be automatically totaled and subtotaled in the printed report.

Press PgDn. The *Total this column* option is marked **Y**es in the fourth column definition so that the AMOUNT field will be totaled and subtotaled.

Contents	AMOUNT
Heading	Amount
Width	12
Decimal places	2
Total this column	Yes

Finally, press PgDn and place DATE in the last column of the report by filling in these options:

Contents	DATE
Heading	Date
Width	8
Decimal places	
Total this column	

After the report format is defined, your screen should look like Figure 8.2. Highlight the *Exit* option and select *Save* to store the report format and return to the Assistant menu.

Now, to print the report, highlight the **Retrieve** option on the main menu bar and select *Report*. Select the appropriate drive and the SUBTOTS.FRM report. Select *Execute the command*. Your report will look like Figure 8.3 with subtotals and totals of sales for each product.

Sub-subtotals in a Report

You can subtotal on two separate fields in a report, so that you get subtotals of subtotals. For example, suppose that you want

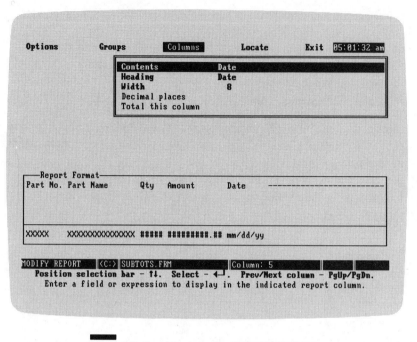

Figure 8.2: Specifications for SUBTOTS.FRM

your report to subtotal each day's sales, but you also want subtotals for each product within each date. As with other subtotals, the database needs to be presorted or indexed on the two subtotaling fields. For this example, you need to create an index file of dates and product codes, and here is where data types tend to get a little tricky.

If you attempt to index on DATE + CODE, you'll see the error message

Data Type Mismatch

because the DATE field is the Date data type and CODE is the Character data type. dBASE won't let you combine mismatched data types. However, if you go through the usual process of creating an index file, but enter the expression

DTOC(DATE) + CODE ↵

when dBASE asks for the index expression, everything will be fine. The DTOC function changes the Date data type to the Character data type, but only in the index file. In other words, there is no longer a data type mismatch error, but your database still accepts

Sales by Product Code

Part No.	Part Name	Qty	Amount	Date
** Product Code AAA				
AAA	Rakes	3	15.00	03/01/86
AAA	Rakes	2	10.00	03/01/86
AAA	Rakes	2	11.00	03/02/86
AAA	Rakes	5	23.50	03/02/86
** Subtotal **				
		12	59.50	
** Product Code BBB				
BBB	Hoes	2	12.50	03/01/86
BBB	Hoes	2	12.50	03/02/86
** Subtotal **				
		4	25.00	
** Product Code CCC				
CCC	Shovels	3	21.50	03/01/86
CCC	Shovels	4	26.50	03/01/86
CCC	Shovels	1	7.50	03/01/86
** Subtotal **				
		8	55.50	
*** Total ***				
		24	140.00	

Figure 8.3: Subtotaled Report Organized by Code

only dates entered in this field. (We'll discuss DTOC and other functions in more detail later in the chapter.)

Next, just create the report format in the usual fashion using *Create* and *Report* from the Assistant menu screen. Name the report DATECODE. You can fill out the first menu of report options as shown here, or use your own formatting:

Page title	**Sales by Date and Product Code**
Page width (positions)	**80**
Left margin	**0**
Right margin	**0**
Lines per page	**58**
Double space report	**No**
Page eject before printing	**Yes**
Page eject after printing	**No**
Plain page	**No**

Next, highlight the *Group* option, and specify DATE as the field to group, and CODE as the Sub-group:

Group on expression	**DATE**
Group heading	**Date**
Summary report only	**No**
Page eject after group	**No**
Sub-group on expression	**CODE**
Sub-group heading Product	**Code**

(*Note:* If you change the *Page eject after group* option to **Y**es, each day's sales will be printed on a separate page.)

Finally, use this summary to define the columns for your DATECODE report:

Contents	**Heading**	**Width**	**Decimal Places**	**Total?**
DATE	Date	12	0	No
CODE	Part No.	5	0	No
TITLE	Part Name	15	0	No
QTY	Qty	5	0	Yes
AMOUNT	Amount	12	2	Yes

These column specifications appear at the bottom of your screen:

Report Format

Date	**Part No.**	**Part Name**	**Qty**	**Amount**
mm/dd/yy	XXXXX	XXXXXXXXXXXXXXX	#####	#########.##

After you save your DATECODE report form, select the *Retrieve* and *Report* options, and specify DATECODE.FRM to display the report shown in Figure 8.4. The report presents each day's sales subtotals for each product.

Sales by Date and Product Code

Date	Part No.	Part Name	Qty	Amount

** Date 03/01/86

* Product Code AAA

| 03/01/86 | AAA | Rakes | 3 | 15.00 |
| 03/01/86 | AAA | Rakes | 2 | 10.00 |

* Subsubtotal *

| | | | 5 | 25.00 |

*Product Code BBB

| 03/01/86 | BBB | Hoes | 2 | 12.50 |

* Subsubtotal *

| | | | 2 | 12.50 |

* Product Code CCC

03/01/86	CCC	Shovels	3	21.50
03/01/86	CCC	Shovels	4	26.50
03/01/86	CCC	Shovels	1	7.50

* Subsubtotal *

| | | | 8 | 55.50 |

** Subtotal **

| | | | 15 | 93.00 |

Figure 8.4: Report Subtotaled by Date and Product Code

Sales by Date and Product Code (continued)

Date	Part No.	Part Name	Qty	Amount

** Date 03/02/86

* Product Code AAA

| 03/02/86 | AAA | Rakes | 2 | 11.00 |
| 03/02/86 | AAA | Rakes | 5 | 23.50 |

* Subsubtotal *

| | | | 7 | 34.50 |

* Product Code BBB

| 03/02/86 | BBB | Hoes | 2 | 12.50 |

* Subsubtotal *

| | | | 2 | 12.50 |

** Subtotal **

| | | | 9 | 47.00 |

*** Total ***

| | | | 24 | 140.00 |

Figure 8.4: Report Subtotaled by Date and Product Code (continued)

CREATING SUMMARY REPORTS

Under the *Group* option, you may have noticed the *Summary report only* suboption on the report generator menu. Changing this option to Yes displays only the subtotals without the data used in the calculations. To test this option, slightly change the SUB-TOTS.FRM report format.

Remember that the SUBTOTS.FRM report format required presorting the database by product CODE, and that you created an index file named CODE.NDX to perform the sort. Before you reprint the report, you'll need to reactivate that index file. Here are the steps:

✓ Highlight *Set Up* from the main menu bar.
✓ Select *Database file.*
✓ Select a drive.
✓ Select SALES.DBF.
✓ Answer **Yes** to the "Is the File Indexed?" prompt.
✓ Select CODE.NDX.
✓ Press → to finish selecting database and index files.

Now the SALES.DBF database is sorted by the CODE field. Here are the steps to change the SUBTOTS.FRM report to a summary report:

✓ Highlight the *Modify* option from the main menu bar.
✓ Select *Report.*
✓ Select a drive.
✓ Specify SUBTOTS.FRM.
✓ Highlight the *Groups* option from the report menu.
✓ Highlight the *Summary report only* option.
✓ Press ← to switch the option to **Yes.**

At this point, your menu selections look like this:

Group on expression	**CODE**
Group heading	**Product Code**
Summary report only	**Yes**
Page eject after group	**No**
Sub-group on expression	
Sub-group heading	

Now, save the report format with the *Exit* and *Save* options. From the Assistant menu screen, select the *Retrieve* and *Report* options, and specify SUBTOTS.FRM. Select *Execute the command.* Your summary report of product sales will look like Figure 8.5.

Sales by Product Code

Part No.	Part Name	Qty	Amount	Date
✶✶ Product Code AAA				
✶✶ Subtotal ✶✶				
		12	59.50	
✶✶ Product Code BBB				
✶✶ Subtotal ✶✶				
		4	25.00	
✶✶ Product Code CCC				
✶✶ Subtotal ✶✶				
		8	55.50	
✶✶✶ Total ✶✶✶				
		24	140.00	

Figure 8.5: Summary Product Sales Report

USING DOT-PROMPT COMMANDS

As we've discussed before, working from the dot prompt does require some fluency with the dBASE language and may go beyond your requirements. However, to fully explore techniques for managing numbers and dates, you'll need to use some commands from the dot prompt for options that the Assistant menu cannot provide.

To practice these dot-prompt commands, press Esc to get rid of the Assistant menu. Then, to make sure that the SALES.DBF database is in use, enter the command:

    USE SALES ⏎

if you're using a hard-disk system, or

    USE B:SALES ⏎

if you're using a computer with two floppy-disk drives.

To sum a numeric field from the dot prompt, you use the SUM command with the names of the fields to sum. For example, if you ask dBASE to add the data in the QTY field of your database records with the command

SUM QTY ←┘

this answer displays just as though data were summed from the menu options:

9 records summed
QTY
24

To specify certain records in the sum, use the FOR option in the command:

SUM QTY FOR CODE = "AAA" ←┘

This command sums the QTY field for records that have AAA as the product CODE. dBASE displays this answer:

4 records summed
QTY
12

The COUNT command is used in a similar fashion, and performs the same task as the *Count* option from the Assistant menu. For example, the command

COUNT FOR CODE &LT> "AAA" ←┘

displays the number of records in the database that do not have part number AAA:

5 records

Now let's look at a more advanced technique from the dot prompt, using the AVERAGE command.

If you want the average selling price of part AAA, you need to take into account the quantity sold for each transaction. That is, the average selling price is the average of the amounts divided by

> If you do not see the results of a SUM, COUNT, or AVERAGE command at the dot prompt, type the command **SET TALK ON** and press ←┘. Then press ↑ twice to re-access your command, and ←┘ to execute it.

the quantities. So, tell dBASE to average the amount divided by the quantity for part number AAA with the following command:

AVERAGE (AMOUNT/QTY) FOR CODE = 'AAA' ←┘

(The / symbol stands for divided by, as in the fraction 3/4.) dBASE displays

4 records averaged
(AMOUNT/QTY)
5.05

The average selling price for part number AAA is $5.05.

In some cases you might prefer to know how many records contain certain information, rather than knowing about sums of fields. For example, you might wish to know how many transactions involved part AAA. You use the COUNT command for this. To find out how many records on the database have AAA as the part number, ask dBASE to

COUNT FOR CODE = 'AAA' ←┘

dBASE will tell us

4 records

There are four records with part AAA.

USING COMMANDS
TO MANAGE DATES

In our SALES database, we've included a field named DATE, and assigned it the Date data type. dBASE III PLUS contains many *functions* for managing dates. The DATE( ) function displays today's date, as it was typed when you first booted up your system. For example, if you ask dBASE what the date is (using the ? command)

? DATE( ) ←┘

you'll see today's date on the screen. To change that date, type

The basic dBASE math operators are + (add), – (subtract), / (divide), and * (multiply). Chapter 11 provides additional information.

this command:

RUN DATE ←┘

The screen will display the current date and allow you to change it:

Current date is Tue 11-06-1986
Enter new date:_

To try out some new exercises, fill in the new date as 03/01/86, and press Return:

Current date is Tue 11-06-1986
Enter new date: 03/01/86 ←┘

Now, let's try out some new exercises. First, with the SALES database still in use, ask dBASE to display all records that match today's date, using the command

LIST FOR DATE = DATE() ←┘

dBASE displays

Record#	CODE	TITLE	QTY	AMOUNT	DATE
1	AAA	Rakes	3	15.00	03/01/86
2	BBB	Hoes	2	12.50	03/01/86
3	CCC	Shovels	3	21.50	03/01/86
4	AAA	Rakes	2	10.00	03/01/86
5	CCC	Shovels	4	26.50	03/01/86
7	CCC	Shovels	1	7.50	03/01/86

Next, ask dBASE to display all records that have dates that are later than today's date:

LIST FOR DATE > DATE() ←┘

These records appear on your screen:

Record#	CODE	TITLE	QTY	AMOUNT	DATE
6	AAA	Rakes	2	11.00	03/02/86
8	BBB	Hoes	2	12.50	03/02/86
9	AAA	Rakes	5	23.50	03/02/86

The dBASE *functions* for managing dates are explained in Table 8.1.

Function	Purpose
CDOW	Day of week as a Character type (Monday).
CMONTH	Month as a Character type (January).
CTOD	Character-to-date conversion.
DAY	Day of month (31).
DOW	Day of week as number (Sunday = 1, Monday = 2, etc.).
DTOC	Date-to-character conversion.
MONTH	Month as number (1-12).
TIME	Time expressed as HH:MM:SS.
YEAR	Year of date (1985).

Table 8.1: Date Functions

Test these out with the SALES database. This command asks dBASE to list the date, day of week (DOW), month (CMONTH), day (DAY) and year (YEAR) of each date in the SALES database:

```
LIST  DATE,CDOW(DATE),CMONTH(DATE),DAY(DATE),YEAR(DATE)
←
```

dBASE displays

Record#	DATE	CDOW(DATE)	CMONTH(DATE)	DAY(DATE)	YEAR(DATE)
1	03/01/86	Saturday	March	1	1986
2	03/01/86	Saturday	March	1	1986
3	03/01/86	Saturday	March	1	1986
4	03/01/86	Saturday	March	1	1986
5	03/01/86	Saturday	March	1	1986
6	03/02/86	Sunday	March	2	1986
7	03/01/86	Saturday	March	1	1986
8	03/02/86	Sunday	March	2	1986
9	03/02/86	Sunday	March	2	1986

To view records that fall upon a certain day (as is often useful when scheduling), you can use the CDOW (Character Day of Week) function:

```
LIST FOR CDOW(DATE) = "Saturday" ←
```

dBASE displays records with dates that fall on a Saturday (March 1, 1986, is a Saturday):

Record#	CODE	TITLE	QTY	AMOUNT	DATE
1	AAA	Rakes	3	15.00	03/01/86
2	BBB	Hoes	2	12.50	03/01/86
3	CCC	Shovels	3	21.50	03/01/86
4	AAA	Rakes	2	10.00	03/01/86
5	CCC	Shovels	4	26.50	03/01/86
7	CCC	Shovels	1	7.50	03/01/86

To see which records have dates in March, use the CMONTH function:

LIST FOR CMONTH(DATE) = "March" ↵

dBASE displays

Record#	CODE	TITLE	QTY	AMOUNT	DATE
1	AAA	Rakes	3	15.00	03/01/86
2	BBB	Hoes	2	12.50	03/01/86
3	CCC	Shovels	3	21.50	03/01/86
4	AAA	Rakes	2	10.00	03/01/86
5	CCC	Shovels	4	26.50	03/01/86
6	AAA	Rakes	2	21.00	03/02/86
7	CCC	Shovels	1	7.50	03/01/86
8	BBB	Hoes	2	12.50	03/02/86
9	AAA	Rakes	5	23.50	03/02/86

To display a specific date, you need to convert the date in the database to a Character type with the DTOC function. This command lists all records with the date March 2:

LIST FOR DTOC(DATE) = "03/02" ↵

dBASE displays

Record#	CODE	TITLE	QTY	AMOUNT	DATE
6	AAA	Rakes	2	11.00	03/02/86
8	BBB	Hoes	2	12.50	03/02/86
9	AAA	Rakes	5	23.50	03/02/86

Incidentally, in case you should need to know the time at any given moment, you can use this TIME function:

? TIME() ◄┘

dBASE will display the time in HH:MM:SS format:

14:26:18

(That's 2:26 pm, plus 18 seconds.) The time that dBASE displays is based upon the time you keyed in when you first booted up the system. To change the time, enter this command:

RUN TIME ◄┘

Date Arithmetic

You can perform *date arithmetic,* too. For example, if you want to know at what date the amounts in the SALES file became ninety days overdue, just add 90 to each of the dates:

LIST DATE + 90 ◄┘

dBASE displays

Record#	DATE + 90
1	05/30/86
2	05/30/86
3	05/30/86
4	05/30/86
5	05/30/86
6	05/31/86
7	05/30/86
8	05/31/86
9	05/31/86

Let's reverse the order of the operation a bit. Suppose that today is May 30, and you want to know which records on the SALES database are 90 or more days past due. You want to list for those dates in which the difference between the current date minus the database DATE was greater than or equal to (> =) 90:

LIST FOR CTOD("05/30/86") – DATE > = 90 ◄┘

dBASE displays the appropriate records:

Record#	CODE	TITLE	QTY	AMOUNT	DATE
1	AAA	Rakes	3	15.00	03/01/86
2	BBB	Hoes	2	12.50	03/01/86
3	CCC	Shovels	3	21.50	03/01/86
4	AAA	Rakes	2	10.00	03/01/86
5	CCC	Shovels	4	26.50	03/01/86
7	CCC	Shovels	1	7.50	03/01/86

When you want to determine how many days have passed between two dates, just subtract the smaller, earlier date from the larger, later date. Make sure the dates are Date data types. If not, use the CTOD function to convert them. For example, suppose you were born on March 31, 1956, and today is November 6, 1986. To find out how many days you've been alive, subtract your birth date from today's date. If you forget to convert the data first and type the equation

? "11/06/86" – "03/31/56" ⏎

you get a strange result:

11/06/8603/31/56

However, if you remember to use the CTOD conversion function

? CTOD("11/06/86") – CTOD("03/31/56") ⏎

dBASE will tell you exactly how many days have passed between the two dates:

11177

Similarly, if you forget to do the date conversion when working with a database

LIST DATE – "01/01/86" ⏎

dBASE will produce an error message because you are trying to subtract the character string "01/01/86" from a date (the DATE field). On the screen, you'll see

Data type mismatch
?

```
LIST DATE - "01/01/86"
Do you want some help? (Y/N)
```

Just remember to use the CTOD function to convert the character string surrounded by quotation marks ("01/01/86") to a date:

```
LIST DATE - CTOD("01/01/86") ◄┘
```

and everything will be fine.

Sorting by Date

If you want your records to be displayed in chronological order, you can index on the DATE field:

```
INDEX ON DATE TO DATES ◄┘
```

Chapter 17 provides examples of other complex index (sorting) expressions.

When you list the database or print a report, the records will be in order by date:

Record#	CODE	TITLE	QTY	AMOUNT	DATE
1	AAA	Rakes	3	15.00	03/01/86
2	BBB	Hoes	2	12.50	03/01/86
3	CCC	Shovels	3	21.50	03/01/86
4	AAA	Rakes	2	10.00	03/01/86
5	CCC	Shovels	4	26.50	03/01/86
7	CCC	Shovels	1	7.50	03/01/86
6	AAA	Rakes	2	11.00	03/02/86
8	BBB	Hoes	2	12.50	03/02/86
9	AAA	Rakes	5	23.50	03/02/86

In some cases, you might want to combine the date with another field for sorting. For example, you might want the SALES database to be sorted by date, and within common dates be further sorted by product code (CODE). In this case, you need to convert the date to a Character type, using the DTOC function, like you did with the DATECODE report. From the dot prompt, the indexing command looks like this:

```
INDEX ON DTOC(DATE) + CODE TO DATECODE ◄┘
```

If you want the records in descending order by date, that is, from the most-recent to least-recent date, index on the *inverse* of the date. Specify the DATE field subtracted from a large date, such as 12/31/99:

INDEX ON CTOD("12/31/99") – DATE TO INVDATE ↵

When you list the database, the records will be in descending chronological order:

Record#	CODE	TITLE	QTY	AMOUNT	DATE
6	AAA	Rakes	2	11.00	03/02/86
8	BBB	Hoes	2	12.50	03/02/86
9	AAA	Rakes	5	23.50	03/02/86
1	AAA	Rakes	3	15.00	03/01/86
2	BBB	Hoes	2	12.50	03/01/86
3	CCC	Shovels	3	21.50	03/01/86
4	AAA	Rakes	2	10.00	03/01/86
5	CCC	Shovels	4	26.50	03/01/86
7	CCC	Shovels	1	7.50	03/01/86

Note: The FIND or SEEK command will not work with this index file unless you first subtract the date you are trying to find from CTOD("12/31/99").

REVIEWING DATES AND NUMBERS

In this chapter you have learned a number of techniques for managing dates and numbers:

▬

To sum values in a numeric field, select *Sum* from the **Retrieve** menu. The *Construct a field list* option allows you to sum only certain fields, and the *Build a search condition* option allows you to sum only certain records.

▬

To average values in a numeric field, select the *Average* option from the **Retrieve** menu. As with *Sum,* you can use *Construct a field list* and *Build a search condition.*

▬

To count how many records contain an item of information, select the *Count* option from the **Retrieve** menu.

▬

To subtotal information in a report, highlight the *Groups* menu in the report generator. The database needs to be pre-sorted or indexed on the grouping field(s).

▬

To print a summary report, select the *Summary report only* option under the report generator *Groups* menu.

▬

The dot prompt allows many functions for managing dates, including CDOW (Character Day of Week), CMONTH (Character Month), CTOD (Character to Date Conversion), DAY (Numeric Day of Month), DOW (Numeric Day of Week), DTOC (Date to Character Conversion), MONTH (Numeric Month), and YEAR (Year of Date).

Managing Multiple Data Files

The techniques we've discussed so far are useful for managing a simple database. However, many larger business applications require that information be divided into separate databases. In this chapter, we'll look at reasons for dividing information into separate databases, as well as techniques for managing information in separate files.

AN ACCOUNTS RECEIVABLE DATABASE DESIGN

Some business applications require multiple databases because any given record in one database might have several items of information related to it. Furthermore, the number of related items might be totally unpredictable (for example, the number of items charged by a given customer during the course of a year). Let's take a look at an example of a database that should be broken into two separate databases.

Figure 9.1 shows a single, poorly designed database for storing accounts receivable. Each record stores a customer's name, address, charge amount, and billing date.

LNAME	FNAME	ADDRESS	AMOUNT	DATE
Adams	Andy	123 A St.	50.00	1/1/86
Adams	Andy	123 A St.	100.00	1/9/86
Adams	Andy	123 A St.	75.00	3/3/86
Miller	Michele	P.O. Box 2345	221.66	2/12/86
Watson	Wilbur	670 Baldy View	21.22	3/3/86
Adams	Andy	123 A St.	66.22	4/7/86
Miller	Michele	P.O. Box 2345	888.90	4/1/86
Zeepers	Zeppo	261 Ocean View Dr.	99.99	4/1/86
Miller	Arnold	455 Madison Ave	61.55	4/1/86

Figure 9.1: Poor Design for Storing Accounts Receivable Data

The database shown in Figure 9.1 is a very poor design for the application because of the following problems:

1. The database wastes disk space by repeating name and address for each transaction. These repetitions are particularly space-consuming in a database with 10,000 or more records!

2. The database creates extra work for input operators who must type the repeated information each time a new record is added. (For example, each time Andy Adams orders another item, his name and address have to be re-entered into the database.)

3. Because names and addresses would be entered each time a new record is added, the likelihood of typographical errors is high, and therefore the likelihood of billing errors is also high.

A better way to store these data would be to break the information into two databases, as shown in Figure 9.2. Notice that names and addresses are stored only once in the CUSTLIST.DBF database (like the MAIL.DBF database you created earlier), and individual financial *transactions* are stored in a separate database named CHARGES.DBF.

Notice that both the CUSTLIST.DBF and the CHARGES.DBF databases have a field called CUSTNO (customer number). This field (often called a *common field*) is used to *relate* the two databases. Even though you don't see Andy Adams's name and address on any transaction in the CHARGES database, you can tell which transactions belong to him by simply looking for records that have 1001 as the customer number.

The common field that relates the two databases is an important one. For example, had you tried to relate the two databases by last name, then any charge to an individual named Miller would cause problems because there are two different Millers in the CUST-LIST.DBF database. Granted, you could relate the two databases by last and first names, but then what if there are two John Does? You could use the address as a tiebreaker, but by this point, you're back to the repetition problem in the CHARGES database.

First Database: CUSTLIST.DBF

CUSTNO	LNAME	FNAME	ADDRESS	CITY
1001	Adams	Andy	123 A St.	Los Angeles
1002	Miller	Michele	P.O. Box 2345	Burbank
1003	Watson	Wilbur	670 Baldy View	Pomona
1004	Zeepers	Zeppo	261 Ocean View Dr.	Ramona
1005	Miller	Arnold	455 Madison Ave	Newark

Second Database: CHARGES.DBF

CUSTNO	AMOUNT	DATE
1001	50.00	1/1/86
1001	100.00	1/9/86
1001	75.00	3/3/86
1002	221.66	2/12/86
1003	21.22	3/3/86
1001	66.22	4/7/86
1002	888.90	4/1/86
1004	99.99	4/1/86
1005	61.55	4/1/86

Figure 9.2: Accounts Receivable Data Split into Two Databases

The customer number is the ideal common field because it does not take up much disk space. It is also very easy to assign each customer a unique number. It is important that each record has a unique customer number to relate it to the transactions in the CHARGES.DBF database.

When a database has a field such as CUSTNO (customer number) where each record has a unique value, the field is referred to as a *key field*. It is the key field that relates the CHARGES.DBF database to the CUSTOMER.DBF database. Let's try some exercises with a couple of databases that could be used to help manage an accounts receivable system. First, highlight *Create* on the Assistant menu screen, and select the *Database file* option. Name the database CUSTLIST. Define the structure shown below.

Structure for database: CUSTLIST.DBF

Field	Field Name	Type	Width	Dec
1	CUSTNO	Numeric	4	0
2	LNAME	Character	12	0
3	FNAME	Character	10	0
4	ADDRESS	Character	20	0
5	CITY	Character	15	0
6	STATE	Character	2	0
7	ZIP	Character	5	0
8	PHONE	Character	13	0

Next, add a few hypothetical customers to the database. Assign each customer a unique customer number, as in this sample database:

CUSTNO	LNAME	FNAME	ADDRESS	CITY	ST ZIP	PHONE
1000	Adams	Andy	123 A St.	San Diego	CA 92122	(123)555-1000
1001	Schumack	Susita	1096 Crest Dr.	Encinitas	CA 92024	(123)555-8903
1002	Norris	Nancy	P.O. Box 1234	La Jolla	CA 91191	(123)555-9910
1003	Davies	David	432 Oaktree Ln.	Los Angeles	CA 92210	(123)555-2323
1004	Teasdale	Rhonda	P.O. Box 2802	Leucadia	CA 92211	(123)555-1212

Next, you'll want to create an index file of customer numbers to help manage the related files. Highlight the *Organize* option and select *Index*. Enter the field name CUSTNO as the key expression when requested, and name the index file CUSTLIST.

Next, create a database file for storing individual billing transactions, using *Create* and *Database file* menu options. Name the file CHARGES, and structure it like this:

Structure for database: CHARGES.DBF

Field	Field Name	Type	Width	Dec
1	CUSTNO	Numeric	4	0
2	PRODUCT	Character	15	0
3	QTY	Numeric	4	0
4	UNIT_PRICE	Numeric	12	2
5	DATE	Date	8	0
6	BILLED	Logical	1	0

Notice that the CUSTNO field in both databases has exactly the same name, data type, and width. *Note:* It is essential for the common field between two databases to have the identical name, type, and width; otherwise, there is no guarantee that the records from the two files will link correctly.

You might also notice that the CHARGES.DBF database has a field with the Logical data type. This data type is always one character wide, and can contain one of two possible conditions: True (.T.) or False (.F.). In this sample database, the Logical field is used to mark records as either having been billed (True) or not billed (False). (When entering data into these fields, you just type **F** or **T** without the dots.)

After you've created the CHARGES.DBF database, add a few sample records to it:

Record#	CUSTNO	PRODUCT	QTY	UNIT_PRICE	DATE	BILLED
1	1001	Floppy Disks	10	2.11	03/12/86	.F.
2	1002	8 Mhz Clock	2	16.39	03/15/86	.F.
3	1001	Color Card	1	101.00	03/31/86	.F.
4	1000	Turbo Board	1	550.00	04/01/86	.F.
5	1004	Video Cable	10	16.00	04/15/86	.F.
6	1002	RAM Disk	1	1100.00	04/11/86	.F.
7	1003	8 Mhz Clock	1	16.39	04/15/86	.F.
8	1000	RAM Disk	1	1100.00	04/18/86	.F.
9	1003	Tape Backup	1	1250.00	04/20/86	.F.
10	1003	40 Meg. Disk	1	450.00	04/20/86	.F.

To help set up the relationship between the two databases, and to keep the CHARGES.DBF records in customer number order, create an index file named CHARGES.NDX by highlighting the *Organize* option and selecting *Index*. Enter CUSTNO as the key expression for the index file and CHARGES as the index file name.

Now, keep in mind that for general file maintenance such as adding new records or editing existing data, you'll want to treat these as two separate databases. That is, you'll open either database and the appropriate index files by highlighting *Set Up* and selecting the *Database file* option from the Assistant menu screen. Then use the *Append, Edit, Browse, Delete,* and *Pack* menu options or dot-prompt commands to handle each database.

However, there will be times when you'll want to retrieve information simultaneously from both databases. In that case, you may want to set up a dBASE III PLUS *View*.

SETTING UP A VIEW OF TWO FILES

A *View* allows you to relate two separate databases to one another through a common field. Then you can select particular fields to display on the screen or in a report. You can create many different Views for databases, and thereby view your data from different "angles."

Opening Multiple Databases

For this example, let's suppose that you want to view billings, but you want to see the name and address of the customer for each transaction. In this case, you'll be working primarily with the CHARGES.DBF database (because you're interested in billings), but will need to get related information (names and addresses) from the CUSTLIST.DBF database. Here is how to open the database and index files you'll need before setting up a View:

    √ Highlight the *Create* option.
    √ Select *View*.
    √ Select a drive.
    √ Type **ACCTREC** as the name for the view, press ◄┘.
    √ From the menu of database files, select CHARGES.DBF.
    √ From the menu of index files, select CHARGES.NDX.
    √ Press → to leave the index files submenu.
    √ Select CUSTLIST.DBF as the second file for this View.
    √ Select CUSTLIST.NDX from the index file submenu.

Triangles will appear on-screen as you select the files.

Specifying the Relationship

When you have selected the databases, you must tell dBASE which field relates the databases. To do so, first use → to highlight the *Relate* option that appears after your selections from the menu.

dBASE shows the names of files that you've opened.

The order in which you open these databases is important. In this case, you are primarily interested in billings, but you also want to "pull" the name and address from the CUSTLIST.DBF database. So, you select CHARGES.DBF, the most important database, first.

dBASE will then show a list of files that can be related to CHARGES.DBF (only CUSTLIST.DBF in this example). Press Return to select CUSTLIST.DBF. Next, at the bottom of the screen, dBASE will ask that you define the common field. Press F10 to display the fields submenu, and select CUSTNO. Press Return again. Your screen displays the names of your two databases, your selected file, and this relationship statement:

Relation Chain: CHARGES.DBF—>CUSTLIST.DBF

Selecting Fields to View

Now you can select which fields from the two databases you want to see in this View. Use → to highlight the *Set fields* option. Select CHARGES.DBF to see a submenu of these field names:

▶ **CUSTNO**
▶ **PRODUCT**
▶ **QTY**
▶ **UNIT_PRICE**
▶ **DATE**
▶ **BILLED**

Notice that each field has a ▶ symbol next to it, indicating that it has already been selected. To use all of these fields, just press → to leave the submenu.

Next, select CUSTLIST.DBF from the menu, and you'll see a submenu of fields from CUSTLIST. You only need LNAME and FNAME for this example, so use ↓ and Return to "unselect" the other fields. The ▶ symbol is removed from the unselected fields. Figure 9.3 shows how the screen looks when only two fields remain selected from the CUSTLIST.DBF database.

Now you can use → to select the *Exit* option and select *Save*. The View which we've just created will be stored on disk under the file name ACCTREC.VUE. (dBASE automatically assigns the .VUE extension.)

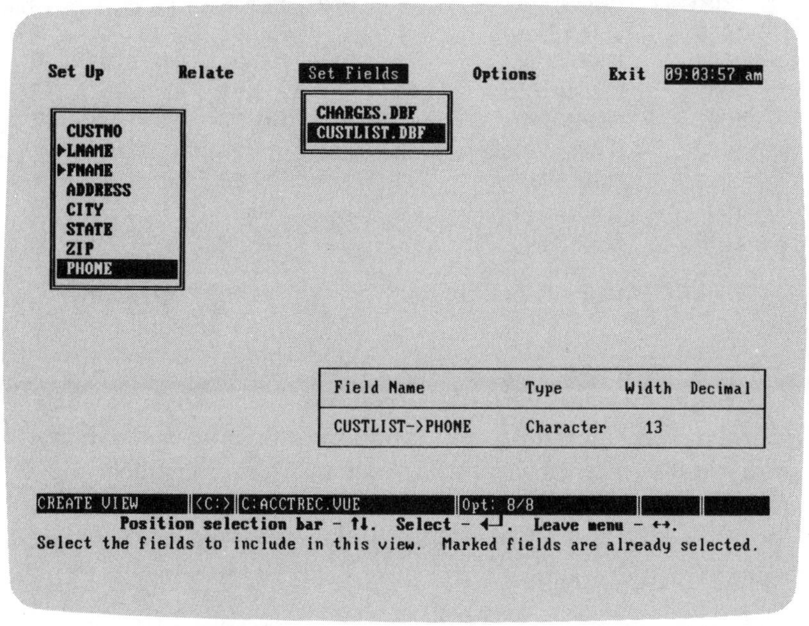

Figure 9.3: Two Fields Selected for Viewing

Opening a View

To use the View, follow these steps from the Assistant menu screen:

√ Highlight the *Set Up* option.
√ Select *View* from the submenu.
√ Select the drive, then ACCTREC.VUE.

Nothing much seems to happen; only the Assistant menu appears. However, if you highlight *Retrieve* and select the *List* and *Execute the command* options, the contents of the two databases will appear on the screen just as though they were from a single database:

CUSTNO	PRODUCT	QTY	UNIT_PRICE	DATE	BILLED	LNAME	FNAME
1000	Turbo Board	1	550.00	04/01/86	.F.	Adams	Andy
1000	RAM Disk	1	1100.00	04/18/86	.F.	Adams	Andy
1001	Floppy Disks	10	2.11	03/12/86	.F.	Schumack	Susita
1001	Color Card	1	101.00	03/31/86	.F.	Schumack	Susita
1002	8 Mhz Clock	2	16.39	03/15/86	.F.	Norris	Nancy
1002	RAM Disk	1	1100.00	04/11/86	.F.	Norris	Nancy
1003	8 Mhz Clock	1	16.39	04/15/86	.F.	Davies	David
1003	Tape Backup	1	1250.00	04/20/86	.F.	Davies	David
1003	40 Meg. Disk	1	450.00	04/20/86	.F.	Davies	David
1004	Video Cable	10	16.00	04/15/86	.F.	Teasdale	Rhonda

Note: Your data will wrap around on the screen.

You can treat the View file as you would any single database. (However, for appending and editing records, it's best to work with the files independently.) For example, if you highlight the *Retrieve* option, and select the *List* and *Construct a field list* options, dBASE will display all the fields from the View on the fields submenu. For this example, select these fields in this order:

CUSTNO
LNAME
FNAME
QTY
UNIT_PRICE

When you execute the command, these results appear on your screen:

Record#	CUSTNO	LNAME	FNAME	QTY	UNIT_PRICE
4	1000	Adams	Andy	1	550.00
8	1000	Adams	Andy	1	1100.00
1	1001	Schumack	Susita	10	2.11
3	1001	Schumack	Susita	1	101.00
2	1002	Norris	Nancy	2	16.39
6	1002	Norris	Nancy	1	1100.00
7	1003	Davies	David	1	16.39
9	1003	Davies	David	1	1250.00
10	1003	Davies	David	1	450.00
5	1004	Teasdale	Rhonda	10	16.00

A much more interesting report can be developed using the report generator with two databases open in a View, as we'll discuss next.

PRINTING A REPORT
FROM TWO DATABASES

With the View open, you can design an interesting report using data from both database files. As usual, highlight the *Create* option and select *Report*. Select a disk drive, and assign ARREPT as the file name.

For the page formatting, you can simply assign this report name:

Page title	**Accounts Receivable Summary Report**
Page width (positions)	**80**
Left margin	**8**
Right margin	**0**
Lines per page	**58**
Double space report	**No**
Page eject before printing	**Yes**
Page eject after printing	**No**
Plain page	**No**

From the *Groups* menu, enter this *Group on expression* statement:

    STR(CUSTNO,4) + ": " + TRIM(LNAME) + ",   " + FNAME

The expression used to group is wider than the screen allows, but the screen will scroll as you type the expression. You can use ^PgDn and ^PgUp to zoom in and out of the highlighting to get more room. Type **Customer** as the Group heading. Your screen will look something like this:

Group on expression	**STR(CUSTNO,4) + ": " + TRIM(LNAME) + ", " + FNAME**
Group heading	**Customer**
Summary report only	**No**
Page eject after group	**No**
Sub-group on expression	
Sub-group heading	

You could have just used CUSTNO as the group expression, which would group (subtotal) records by customer number. However, the group heading would show only the customer number as well. Therefore, simultaneously add the customer number, last name, and first name to the group expression, which will make all three fields appear at the top of each subtotaled group.

Notice the use of the STR function in the grouping expression. CUSTNO is Numeric data type, and LNAME and FNAME are both Character data types. As we've discussed before, data types must be identical in a grouping expression which uses the plus (+) sign. Therefore, I've used the STR (STRing) function to change CUSTNO into Character data for the grouping expression. (Character data are also called *character strings,* or just *strings* for short. The STR function gets its name from the word STRing, because it converts a number to a character string.) The number 4 tells dBASE that the converted number should be four characters long. To separate the customer number from the customer name, add a literal colon and a couple of spaces enclosed in quotation marks (": "). The TRIM function makes sure that the customer name does not come out looking like this in the report:

Adams   Andy

Use a literal comma and space enclosed in quotation marks (", ") to separate the last and first names, so they look like this in the report:

Adams, Andy

Most of the individual columns for the report were defined using usual techniques from the *Columns* option. The arrow (—>) portion of each column definition is supplied automatically by dBASE when you use the F10 menu to select fields for the *Contents* of the column. The CHARGES—> symbol tells dBASE to take the DATE field from the CHARGES database.

To define the first column, highlight the *Columns* option, select *Contents,* press F10, and select DATE from the field submenu. Then enter the heading **Date**:

Contents   CHARGES—>DATE

Heading	Date
Width	8
Decimal places	
Total this column	

Press PgDn and define the second column of the report:

Contents	CHARGES—>PRODUCT
Heading	Product
Width	15
Decimal places	
Total this column	

Press PgDn to define the third column:

Contents	CHARGES—>QTY
Heading	Qty
Width	4
Decimal places	0
Total this column	Yes

Define the fourth column:

Contents	CHARGES—>UNIT_PRICE
Heading	Unit Price
Width	12
Decimal places	2
Total this column	Yes

Finally, the fifth column tells us something new: the total price of the transaction. This expression includes the quantity times the unit price. Because this column contains an expression rather than a field name, it has to be typed rather than selected from the fields submenu (F10). Notice that the CHARGES—> database is defined for each field, and the asterisk (*) is used for multiplication. Type the field content exactly as shown below. (*Note:* The arrow consists of a hyphen followed by a greater-than sign.)

Contents	CHARGES—>QTY*CHARGES—>UNIT_PRICE
Heading	Total Sale
Width	14
Decimal places	2
Total this column	Yes

When you have defined the report format, these column specifications will appear at the bottom of your screen:

Report Format
```
>>Date        Product                Qty    Unit Price       Total Sale
mm/dd/yy      XXXXXXXXXXXXXX         ####    ##########.##    ############.##
```

Finally, highlight the *Exit* option and select *Save* to save the ARREPT.FRM report format.

To view the report, highlight **Retrieve** from the Assistant menu screen, and select *Report*. Select a drive and the ARREPT.FRM report format. Select *Execute the command*. The report will look like Figure 9.4 when it's printed.

> If you create a report format with a view open, you must always remember to open that view before printing that report in the future.

MODIFYING A VIEW

To change a View, highlight the **Modify** option from the main menu bar, and select *View*. Specify a drive and a View file name, and you'll be back to the View menu. From there, just use arrow keys to highlight menu options and make changes. Use the *Exit* and *Save* options to save the changes, or *Exit* and *Abandon* to delete the current changes and keep the original View.

CLOSING A VIEW

When you quit dBASE, the View will be closed automatically. You can also close a View from the dot prompt. While the Assistant menu is on-screen, press Esc to call up the dot prompt. Then type this command:

    CLOSE DATABASES ↵

Enter this command

    ASSIST ↵

to bring back the Assistant menu. You'll need to use *Set Up* to open a new database or View, because no database, index, or View files will be open.

> If you forget to close a view, and attempt to reopen a single file that's already in the view, you'll see the error message *"File is already open."* Use the CLOSE DATABASES command to close the view; then you can open any single database file that you wish.

Summary Report for Accounts Receivable

Date	Product	Qty	Unit Price	Total Sale
**Customer 1000: Adams, Andy				
04/01/86	Turbo Board	1	550.00	550.00
04/18/86	RAM Disk	1	1100.00	1100.00
** Subtotal **				
		2	1650.00	1650.00
** Customer 1001: Schumack, Susita				
03/12/86	Floppy Disks	10	2.11	21.10
03/31/86	Color Card	1	101.00	101.00
** Subtotal **				
		11	103.11	122.10
** Customer 1002: Norris, Nancy				
03/15/86	8 Mhz Clock	2	16.39	32.78
04/11/86	RAM Disk	1	1100.00	1100.00
** Subtotal **				
		3	1116.39	1132.78
** Customer 1003: Davies, David				
04/15/86	8 Mhz Clock	1	16.39	16.39
04/20/86	Tape Backup	1	1250.00	1250.00
04/20/86	40 Meg. Disk	1	450.00	450.00
** Subtotal **				
		3	1716.39	1716.39
** Customer 1004: Teasdale, Rhonda				
04/15/86	Video Cable	10	16.00	160.00
** Subtotal **				
		10	16.00	160.00
*** Total ***				
		29	4601.89	4781.27

Figure 9.4: Accounts Receivable Report (ARREPT) Printed from Two Databases

ENTERING COMMANDS

You can manage multiple databases directly from the dot prompt
as well. Here are a few examples using the CUSTLIST.DBF and
CHARGES.DBF databases. First, to start with a clean slate, close all
open databases and index files by entering this command:

    CLOSE DATABASES ↵

Next, to open two databases simultaneously, use the SELECT
commands with the letters A through J, or the numbers 1 through
10. For example, to open both the CUSTLIST.DBF and
CHARGES.DBF databases, with their respective index files, enter the
commands:

    SELECT A ↵
    USE CHARGES INDEX CHARGES ↵
    SELECT B ↵
    USE CUSTLIST INDEX CUSTLIST ↵

With both files open, you can now set up a relationship between
the A and B files based upon the common field CUSTNO. Use
these commands:

    SELECT A ↵
    SET RELATION TO CUSTNO INTO CUSTLIST ↵

There are some differences between a View and simply opening
two files simultaneously. For example, if you enter the list command

    LIST ↵

you'll only see data from the currently selected database
(CHARGES.DBF). (Entering the command SELECT B will make
CUSTLIST.DBF the currently selected database, and LIST would
show its data.)

Record#	CUSTNO	PRODUCT	QTY	UNIT_PRICE	DATE	BILLED
4	1000	Turbo Board	1	550.00	04/01/86	.F.
8	1000	RAM Disk	1	1100.00	04/18/86	.F.
1	1001	Floppy Disks	10	2.11	03/12/86	.F.
3	1001	Color Card	1	101.00	03/31/86	.F.
2	1002	8 Mhz Clock	2	16.39	03/15/86	.F.

6	1002	RAM Disk	1	1100.00	04/11/86	.F.
7	1003	8 Mhz Clock	1	16.39	04/15/86	.F.
9	1003	Tape Backup	1	1250.00	04/20/86	.F.
10	1003	40 Meg. Disk	1	450.00	04/20/86	.F.
5	1004	Video Cable	10	16.00	04/15/86	.F.

To display records from the unselected database, you need to use a letter and arrow before the field name. For example, when the A file is selected, use B—> in front of the field names from the B file:

SELECT A ⏎
LIST CUSTNO, B—>LNAME, B—>FNAME, QTY, UNIT_PRICE, (QTY*UNIT_PRICE) ⏎

Notice that this LIST command contains a *calculated field*, (QTY*UNIT_PRICE), which displays the total of the sales transaction. The results look like this:

Record#	CUSTNO	B—>LNAME	B—>FNAME	QTY	UNIT_PRICE	(QTY*UNIT_PRICE)
4	1000	Adams	Andy	1	550.00	550.00
8	1000	Adams	Andy	1	1100.00	1100.00
1	1001	Schumack	Susita	10	2.11	21.10
3	1001	Schumack	Susita	1	101.00	101.00
2	1002	Norris	Nancy	2	16.39	32.78
6	1002	Norris	Nancy	1	1100.00	1100.00
7	1003	Davies	David	1	16.39	16.39
9	1003	Davies	David	1	1250.00	1250.00
10	1003	Davies	David	1	450.00	450.00
5	1004	Teasdale	Rhonda	10	16.00	160.00

To get a quick calculation of the last column in the display, simply enter this command:

SUM QTY*UNIT_PRICE ⏎

dBASE displays

10 records summed
QTY*UNIT_PRICE
4781.27

You can also print the report from the dot prompt, but you'll have to make a change using the MODIFY REPORT command.

Earlier in this chapter, you entered this *Group on expression:*

    STR(CUSTNO,4)+": "+TRIM(LNAME)+", "+FNAME

This expression must be changed to

    STR(CUSTNO,4)+": "+TRIM(B—>LNAME)+", "+B—>FNAME

because without the View in effect, LNAME and FNAME need to be defined as fields from the SELECT B database file. (Other reports created from a View might need similar modifications.)

Once a report format exists with fields from the two (or more) databases, you can use the REPORT FORM command from the dot prompt:

    REPORT FORM ARREPT TO PRINT ↵

This command prints a copy of the ARREPT.FRM report.

If at any time when working from the dot prompt you become confused about what files are open, selected, and so forth, you can just enter this command:

    DISPLAY STATUS ↵

dBASE displays a status report that looks something like this:

    Currently Selected Database:
    Select area: 1, Database in Use: C:CHARGES.DBF Alias: CHARGES
       Index file: C:CHARGES.NDX Key: CUSTNO
       Related into: CUSTLIST
       Relation: CUSTNO
    Select area: 2, Database in Use: C:CUSTLIST.DBF Alias: CUSTLIST
       Index file: C:CUSTLIST.NDX Key: CUSTNO

This status report tells you that the CHARGES.DBF and CHARGES.NDX files are open in Select area 1 (same as SELECT A). Furthermore, CHARGES.DBF is the currently selected database, and is related to CUSTLIST, based on the CUSTNO field.

In Select area 2 (B), the CUSTLIST.DBF database is open, with the CUSTLIST.NDX database.

To close all open databases and index files, enter this command at the dot prompt:

    CLOSE DATABASES ↵

AN INVENTORY DATABASE DESIGN

In this section, we'll discuss another design requiring multiple databases and new techniques for managing data. Some of the more advanced techniques in this section are not accessible from the Assistant menu, so we'll do this entire section directly from the dot prompt.

If you are using a computer with two floppy disks, you should make sure that you have a work disk in Drive B. Then enter this command at the dot prompt before you begin the following exercises:

SET DEFAULT TO B ⏎

This will ensure that all files are stored and accessed on the disk in Drive B.

Master File and Transaction Files

Inventory systems usually involve multiple databases as well. The relationship among these databases is often called a *Master File-Transaction File* relationship. To simplify managing the data, inventory information is most easily divided into three separate databases: one for sales, one for purchases (or new stock), and a master inventory database. Envision the relationship among these databases, as shown in Figure 9.5.

The Sales and New Stock files are called transaction files, because they record information about individual sales and purchase transactions. The inventory file is called the master file, because it contains the current status of each item in stock. In this section, we'll see how to *update* the current status of the master file from the contents of the transaction files.

An Inventory System

First, let's create the master inventory file and give it the file name MASTER. Enter this command at the dot prompt:

CREATE MASTER ⏎

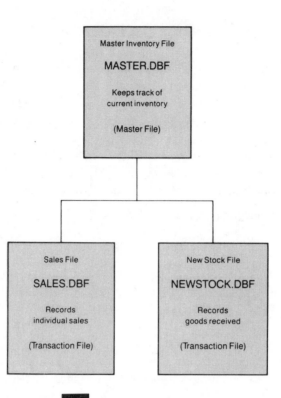

Figure 9.5: Inventory Databases

Give the MASTER file this structure:

Structure for database: MASTER.DBF

Field	Field Name	Type	Width	Dec
1	CODE	Character	5	
2	TITLE	Character	15	
3	QTY	Numeric	5	
4	PRICE	Numeric	5	2
5	REORDER	Numeric	5	

When dBASE asks if you want to input data records now, answer **Y**es and type the following data:

CODE	TITLE	QTY	PRICE	REORDER
AAA	Rakes	30	3.50	25
BBB	Hoes	30	4.50	25
CCC	Shovels	30	5.00	25

Then enter these commands:

```
USE MASTER ←┘
LIST ←┘
```

Three records appear:

Record#	CODE	TITLE	QTY	PRICE	REORDER
1	AAA	Rakes	30	3.50	25
2	BBB	Hoes	30	4.50	25
3	CCC	Shovels	30	5.00	25

The first record tells you that product code AAA is rakes, that you have 30 in stock, that the purchase price is $3.50, and that you reorder when the stock on hand gets below 25. You have 30 hoes in stock (product code BBB), each costing $4.50, and you reorder when stock gets below 25. Product code CCC is shovels. You have 30 in stock, each costing $5.00. Reorder when stock is below 25.

Now let's create a database to keep track of new stock received. Call it NEWSTOCK with this command:

```
CREATE NEWSTOCK ←┘
```

Structure it like this:

Structure for database: NEWSTOCK.DBF

Field	Field Name	Type	Width	Dec
1	CODE	Character	5	
2	QTY	Numeric	5	
3	PRICE	Numeric	12	2
4	DATE	Date	8	

Say **Y**es when dBASE asks "Input data now? (Y/N)". Assume that you've just received two orders from wholesalers, one order of ten rakes, each costing $4.00, and another order for six shovels, each costing $4.50. Furthermore, let's assume that you received them on March 1, 1986. To add these new items to NEW-STOCK, type the following data:

CODE	QTY	PRICE	DATE
AAA	10	4.00	03/01/86
BBB	6	4.50	03/01/86

When dBASE asks for data from Record #3, press Return and the dot prompt will appear. So if you now

```
USE NEWSTOCK ↵
LIST ↵
```

you'll see your new stock listed in database format:

Record#	CODE	QTY	PRICE	DATE
1	AAA	10	4.00	03/01/86
2	BBB	6	4.50	03/01/86

Now you need to come up with a method to update the master inventory so that it reflects the new goods received.

Updating Databases with UPDATE

The dBASE UPDATE command allows you to update the contents of one database based upon information from another. You can specify that the update either add, subtract or replace entire fields. This is best explained with an example. Suppose that you want to add the new stock items to the MASTER file. Furthermore, if there is a change in the price for an item, you want the MASTER file to record the new price. In that case, replace the existing price in the MASTER file with the price in the NEWSTOCK file.

Let's review the contents of both files first. If you

```
USE MASTER ↵
LIST ↵
```

the original inventory appears:

Record#	CODE	TITLE	QTY	PRICE	REORDER
1	AAA	Rakes	30	3.50	25
2	BBB	Hoes	30	4.50	25
3	CCC	Shovels	30	5.00	25

That is, you have 30 rakes in stock, at a wholesale price of $3.50. You have 30 hoes, wholesale priced at $4.50. You have 30 shovels, wholesale priced at $5.00. Now let's

```
USE NEWSTOCK ←┘
LIST ←┘
```

to see new items in stock:

Record#	CODE	QTY	PRICE	DATE
1	AAA	10	4.00	03/01/86
2	BBB	6	4.50	03/01/86

You've received ten product AAA (rakes) at $4.00 each. You've also received six product BBB (hoes) at $4.50 each. So add these items to your inventory, and note that the wholesale price of rakes has increased from $3.50 to $4.00. Here is the procedure.

First, identify a *key field,* one that relates the contents of the MASTER file with the NEWSTOCK file. Both files must have this field in common. In this example, CODE is the key field, because you want dBASE to add ten items of product code AAA to the MASTER file, and six of product code BBB.

Second, you must open both the MASTER and NEWSTOCK files simultaneously. Use the SELECT command to do so. For this example, open the MASTER file in a work area labeled A, and the NEWSTOCK file in a work area labeled B. Here are the correct commands:

```
SELECT A ←┘
USE MASTER ←┘
SELECT B ←┘
USE NEWSTOCK ←┘
```

Now, specify the MASTER file by selecting work area A. Then use the UPDATE command to perform the update. Here are the commands:

```
SELECT A ←┘
UPDATE ON CODE FROM NEWSTOCK REPLACE QTY WITH;
    QTY + B—>QTY, PRICE WITH B—>PRICE ←┘
```

These commands mean, "Update the MASTER file from the data in NEWSTOCK using CODE as the comparison (key) field; replace the QTY field with its current value plus the value of the QTY field in NEWSTOCK (QTY + B—>QTY), and replace the PRICE with the PRICE from the NEWSTOCK file (B—>PRICE)." The B—> symbol is used to specify data from the NEWSTOCK file opened in work area B. (The arrow symbol is formed by typing a hyphen followed by a greater-than sign.)

As soon as the update procedure is complete, list the contents of the MASTER file:

LIST ⮐

You'll see these records:

1	AAA	Rakes	40	4.00	25
2	BBB	Hoes	36	4.50	25
3	CCC	Shovels	30	5.00	25

There are now 40 rakes (AAA) in stock, because you've received 10. The price of rakes is now $4.00, as opposed to $3.50, because you REPLACED PRICE. There are now 36 hoes (BBB) in stock because you received 6. The price of hoes is still $4.50. Shovels (CCC) were not affected, because the NEWSTOCK file did not have any information about shovels.

Now, let's discuss updating the MASTER file from the SALES database. As stated in the dBASE manual, the FROM (transaction) file in an UPDATE command must be sorted and indexed by the key field. You can see that these are certainly not sorted by the key field, CODE. If you

USE SALES ⮐
LIST ⮐

you'll see these records:

1	AAA	Rakes	3	15.00	03/01/86
2	BBB	Hoes	2	12.50	03/01/86
3	CCC	Shovels	3	21.00	03/01/86
4	AAA	Rakes	2	10.00	03/01/86
5	CCC	Shovels	4	26.50	03/01/86
6	AAA	Rakes	2	11.00	03/02/86
7	CCC	Shovels	1	7.50	03/02/86
8	BBB	Hoes	2	12.50	03/01/86
9	AAA	Rakes	5	23.50	03/02/86

You can use INDEX in this case, so let's try it.

```
INDEX ON CODE TO SALES ↵
LIST ↵
```

Now the inventory is sorted by product code:

1	AAA	Rakes	3	15.00	03/01/86
2	AAA	Rakes	2	10.00	03/01/86
3	AAA	Rakes	2	11.00	03/02/86
4	AAA	Rakes	5	23.50	03/02/86
5	BBB	Hoes	2	12.50	03/01/86
6	BBB	Hoes	2	12.50	03/01/86
7	CCC	Shovels	3	21.00	03/01/86
8	CCC	Shovels	4	26.50	03/01/86
9	CCC	Shovels	1	7.50	03/02/86

Now open the MASTER and SALES files, along with the SALES index file to perform the update. First, let's cancel all previous SELECT assignments by typing this command:

```
CLEAR ALL ↵
```

Now select the MASTER file as A, and the SALES file and index as B:

```
SELECT A ↵
USE MASTER ↵

SELECT B ↵
USE SALES INDEX SALES ↵
```

To perform the update, reselect the MASTER file, and perform the update, subtracting the quantities in the SALES file from the quantities in the MASTER file.

```
SELECT A ↵
UPDATE ON CODE FROM SALES REPLACE QTY WITH;
    QTY – B—>QTY ↵
```

To see the effect, LIST the MASTER file:

```
LIST ↵
```

dBASE displays:

Record#	CODE	TITLE	QTY	PRICE	REORDER
1	AAA	Rakes	28	4.00	25
2	BBB	Hoes	32	4.50	25
3	CCC	Shovels	22	5.00	25

There are now 28 rakes in stock because you've sold 12. There are 32 hoes because you've sold 4, and 22 shovels because you've sold 8. dBASE subtracted the appropriate quantities from the MASTER file based upon the quantities and product codes in the SALES file.

Now, to see which items need to be reordered, type this command:

LIST FOR QTY < REORDER ↵

The result is

Record#	CODE	TITLE	QTY	PRICE	REORDER
3	CCC	Shovels	22	5.00	25

The amount of shovels in stock (22) has fallen below the reorder point (25).

Now, to keep future exercises in order, let's "unassign" the SELECT commands by typing this command:

CLOSE DATABASE ↵

You now have a managerial problem on your hands. The MASTER file is accurate, but SALES and NEWSTOCK still have data in them. If you were to add new records to these transaction databases and do another update, the MASTER file would then be incorrect. The UPDATE command would add or subtract these items a second time from the MASTER file. Therefore, you must come up with a managerial scheme for getting rid of data you've already updated. If you wished to update the MASTER file daily, a good approach might be to do the following:

1. Use the NEWSTOCK and SALES files during the course of the day to record goods received and sold.

2. At the end of the day, print a REPORT of all sales and goods received from the SALES and NEWSTOCK files for a permanent record.

3. UPDATE the MASTER file from the SALES and NEWSTOCK files.

4. DELETE and PACK (or ZAP) all records from the SALES and NEWSTOCK files, so future updates are not confused with previous updates.

The disadvantage to this approach is that you lose all the data from the SALES and NEWSTOCK files. Here's a better approach which leaves the SALES and NEWSTOCK files intact. Let's use NEWSTOCK as the example. Suppose that on March 2 you receive 10 rakes at $4.00 each. Let's

```
USE NEWSTOCK ←┘
APPEND ←┘
```

and add the following information:

```
CODE   :AAA :
QTY    :10   :
PRICE  :4.00     :
DATE   :03/02/86:
```

When you LIST, you'll see the new record added to the list

Record#	CODE	QTY	PRICE	DATE
1	AAA	10	4.00	03/01/86
2	BBB	6	4.50	03/01/86
3	AAA	10	4.00	03/02/86

When you do another UPDATE, you won't want Records #1 and 2 to be used again. So move only the newest entry to a file named TEMP:

```
COPY TO TEMP FOR DTOC(DATE) = "03/02/86" ←┘
```

If you now

```
USE TEMP ←┘
LIST ←┘
```

you'll see

Record#	CODE	QTY	PRICE	DATE
3	AAA	6	4.00	03/02/86

Now you can update the MASTER file from TEMP without worrying about updating Records #1 and 2 again. That is, you can

```
SELECT A ◄┘
USE MASTER ◄┘
SELECT B ◄┘
USE TEMP ◄┘
SELECT A ◄┘
UPDATE ON CODE FROM TEMP REPLACE QTY WITH;
    QTY + B—>QTY, PRICE WITH B—>PRICE ◄┘
```

Note: Remember to sort or index the TEMP file first. Since there was only one record in your TEMP file, you had no need to sort or index it first.

When you LIST the MASTER file now, you'll see

1	AAA	Rakes	38	4.00	25
2	BBB	Hoes	32	4.50	25
3	CCC	Shovels	22	5.00	25

Ten rakes have been added to the inventory. Your NEW-STOCK file still contains records of all goods received.

REVIEWING MULTIPLE DATABASES

In this chapter you have learned many techniques for managing multiple databases:

▬

Data are often divided into separate databases to avoid unnecessary repetitions, as in the example of customer names and addresses in one database and individual sales transactions in another.

■

A *common field* is required to link two databases. The common field should have the same name, data type, and width in both databases.

■

In one database, each record usually contains some unique identifying code. This code is called the *key field* and is used to link multiple databases. Examples of key fields include customer numbers, part numbers, and account numbers.

■

To set up a View between two files, select *View* from the *Create* menu and assign a name to the View. Identify the database and index file names, the common fields, and fields to view using menu options.

■

To open an existing View, highlight the *Set Up* option from the main menu bar and select *View*.

■

To print a report from two databases, open the View and create the report using the *Create* and *Report* options.

■

To modify an existing View, highlight the *Modify* option from the Assistant menu, and select *View*.

■

The SELECT and SET RELATION commands allow you to open up to ten databases simultaneously and set up relationships between them.

■

Inventory systems often use multiple databases in a *Master File-Transaction File* relationship.

■

The dBASE III PLUS UPDATE command, available only from the dot prompt, allows you to update the values in a Master file with values in a Transaction File.

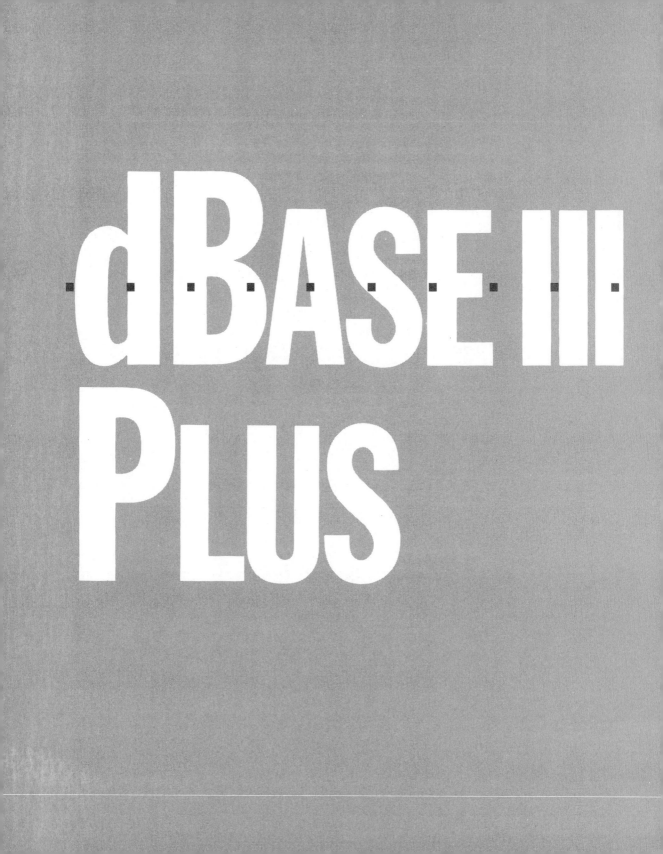

File
Maintenance
and
Performance

I n this chapter, we'll discuss options from the Assistant menu which are generally used for applications involving many or large database files. This will be a "catch all" chapter for options and techniques used with the Assistant menu. After this chapter, you'll learn more about the dot prompt and the dBASE programming language.

THE MENU TOOL KIT

If you highlight the *Tools* option from the Assistant menu, you'll see these options:

Set drive
Copy file
Directory
Rename
Erase
List structure

Import
Export

These options help you manage files and make backups of important data. Let's take a closer look at each of these options.

Set Drive

When selected, the *Set drive* option displays a menu of disk drives (**A:, B:, C:**). The drive you select becomes the *default drive* where dBASE looks for all database, index, report format, and other files. This option works the same as the SET DEFAULT command from the dot prompt.

Copy File

The *Copy file* option allows you to make a copy of any file and is particularly good for making backups. Once selected, this option will display a menu of existing files on the directory. You select a file to copy. Then you'll see a menu of disk drives (**A:**, **B:**, **C:**). After you select a disk drive, a prompt will ask that you enter a name for the copy. Type any valid file name and include a three-letter extension if you wish.

Let's look at a couple of examples for making backups. Suppose that you want to make a backup copy of your MAIL.DBF database. You could select *Copy file* and MAIL.DBF as the file to copy. Then, enter the name MAIL.BAK as the file to copy to. When completed, the MAIL.BAK file will be identical to the MAIL.DBF file. If something happens to MAIL.DBF, you have a backup copy stored under the file name MAIL.BAK. You should repeat the backup process occasionally so that the copy is a reasonable facsimile of the original database.

If you have a hard disk, you can use this method to make backup copies onto floppy disks. Select the *Copy file* option and the file that you want to copy. Make sure that there is a disk in Drive A, and then select **A:** as the drive to copy to. Create a file name for the copy. Because the copied file is going to a different disk drive, you can use the same name as the original file or add an extension that indicates the date of your backup (MAIL.FEB).

The *Copy file* option is useful, but it is not a substitute for the DOS COPY and BACKUP commands. If you plan on using a computer often, it will be worth your time to learn about the DOS COPY command. The DOS BACKUP command is particularly useful if you use a hard disk.

Directory

The *Directory* option lets you see the names of existing files on a disk. When selected, it displays these options:

.dbf	**Database Files**
.ndx	**Index Files**
.fmt	**Format Files**
.lbl	**Label Files**
.frm	**Report Files**
.txt	**Text Files**
.vue	**View Files**
.qry	**Query Files**

```
.scr      Screen Files
.*        All Files
```

You can move the highlighting to the type of file you wish to view, and press Return to select the option. dBASE will display all the files with the file-name extension requested. (*Note:* You can also view All files using the last option.)

Rename

The *Rename* option allows you to change the name of an existing file. However, you should avoid changing the file-name extensions (.DBF, .NDX, and so forth) because they are used to identify the types of files. Like the *Copy file* option, this option displays a list of existing files and asks that you select one to rename. Then you simply type the new name for the file.

Erase

The *Erase* option allows you to remove a file from the disk drive permanently. You should use this option with caution because once a file is deleted, it cannot be recalled.

List Structure

This option displays the structure of the currently open database—a useful, quick reminder of field names in a database, particularly when working from the dot prompt. (The equivalent dot-prompt command is also LIST STRUCTURE.) For example, selecting *List structure* while the MAIL.DBF database is in use would display this structure:

```
Structure for database: MAIL.DBF
Number of data records:   5
Date of last update : 03/05/86
Field    Field Name    Type        Width    Dec
   1     LNAME         Character     15
   2     FNAME         Character     10
```

3	ADDRESS	Character	25
4	CITY	Character	15
5	STATE	Character	5
6	ZIP	Character	10
7	PHONE	Character	13
★ ★ Total ★ ★			94

Import and Export

The *Import* and *Export* options allow you to exchange data from a PFS:FILE database. See Appendix A for a complete discussion of interfacing dBASE III PLUS with other software systems.

DATA CATALOGS

Data catalogs are valuable for hard-disk users who have to manage many files on a single directory. They also help you to keep files organized and make it easier to work with general applications. For example, you could set up a catalog for your mailing list that only provides access to the index files, reports, and screens that are relevant to the MAIL.DBF database.

Even though you can access a catalog from the Assistant menu, you must create it from the dot prompt. So, press Esc until the dot prompt appears.

To start a catalog, enter the SET CATALOG command along with a name for the catalog. For this example, we'll create a catalog named MAILLIST. If you are using a floppy-disk system, type these commands:

```
SET DEFAULT TO B ↵
SET CATALOG TO MAILLIST ↵
```

If you are using a hard-disk system, enter this command:

```
SET CATALOG TO MAILLIST ↵
```

dBASE will see that no such catalog exists and will display the prompt:

Create new catalog? (Y/N)

Answer **Yes**. Then dBASE will ask that you

Enter title for file MAILLIST.CAT:

Type the title **Mailing List Manager**, and press Return. dBASE will then inform you that the

File catalog is empty.

Let's put some files into the catalog now. To put a database file into the catalog, type this command:

USE MAIL ←┘

dBASE asks that you

Enter title for file MAIL.DBF:

Type this title:

Names and Addresses Database →

To put the MAIL index files into the catalog, enter this command:

SET INDEX TO NAMES,ZIP ←┘

To put the ADDNAMES.FMT screen format into the catalog, enter this command:

SET FORMAT TO ADDNAMES ←┘

dBASE will ask that you

Enter title for file ADDNAMES.FMT:

Type this title:

Screen to Enter and Edit Data ←┘

To add a report to the catalog, use the MODIFY REPORT command. For example, to put BYNAME.FRM into the catalog, enter this command:

MODIFY REPORT BYNAME ←┘

dBASE will, of course, give you an opportunity to modify the report. Because the purpose of this exercise is only to place the BYNAME.FRM report format in the catalog, you need not make any changes to the report. Just highlight the *Exit* option and select *Save*. dBASE will ask that you

Enter title for file BYNAME.FRM:

Type this title:

Directory Listing ⏎

In general, when you use the SET CATALOG TO command to open a catalog, you can use these commands to add files, and the titles you provide, to the catalog:

COPY
CREATE
INDEX
MODIFY
SET FORMAT
USE

To stop recording files to be included in the catalog, enter this command:

SET CATALOG OFF ⏎

This will keep new files from being added to the catalog, but the catalog will still be active in the sense that menu selections will display only cataloged files.

To completely close a catalog so that all files once again become accessible, enter the SET CATALOG TO command without a file name:

SET CATALOG TO ⏎

Now, let's get back to the Assistant menu and see what effect this catalog has. Type

ASSIST ⏎

to bring back the Assistant menu. Then, highlight the *Set Up* option and select *Catalog*. Select a drive and MAILLIST.CAT from the submenu.

Nothing much appears to happen until you begin selecting items to work with. If you highlight *Set Up* and select *Database file* to open a database, only MAIL.DBF appears on the screen as an option, along with the title you previously entered:

Database file
MAIL.DBF
Names and Addresses Database

Select MAIL.DBF and answer **Yes** to the "Is the file indexed?" prompt. The screen will display only the index files associated with this data catalog:

NAMES.NDX
ZIP.NDX

If you select the *Format for Screen* option from the *Set Up* menu, only ADDNAMES.FMT will appear as an option. So, as you can see, a catalog allows you to define groups of related files. That means you can have all of your mailing list files in one catalog, your inventory in another, and accounts receivable in another.

An active catalog can also be useful when you are working from the dot prompt. The *catalog query* option (?), will display only files in the current catalog. For example, the command

SET CATALOG TO ? ⏎

calls up a menu of all existing catalogs and allows you to pick one. Once you select a catalog, you can use the **?** option in place of a file name in any command including MODIFY, REPORT, LABEL, SET INDEX, and USE. For example, entering the command

USE ? ⏎

displays a menu of database files in the catalog. The command

SET INDEX TO ? ⏎

displays a list of index files in the catalog. The commands

REPORT FORM ? ⏎

and

SET FORMAT TO ? ⬚

display catalog options for report and screen format files.

Data catalogs are just one method of organizing files. You can also develop menu-driven systems through the dBASE programming language and with the dBASE III PLUS applications generator.

REUSING QUERIES

As you continue working with dBASE III PLUS, you may find it tedious to repeatedly use the *Build a search condition* option when you want to access specific records. For example, suppose that you have a database named SAMPLE.DBF which contains these records:

Record#	CUSTNO	PRODUCT	QTY	UNIT_PRICE	DATE	BILLED
1	1001	Floppy Disks	10	2.11	03/12/86	.T.
2	1002	8 Mhz Clock	2	16.39	03/15/86	.T.
3	1001	Color Card	1	101.00	03/31/86	.T.
4	1000	Turbo Board	1	550.00	04/01/86	.T.
5	1004	Video Cable	10	16.00	04/15/86	.T.
6	1002	RAM Disk	1	1100.00	04/11/86	.T.
7	1003	8 Mhz Clock	1	16.39	04/15/86	.T.
8	1000	RAM Disk	1	1100.00	04/18/86	.T.
9	1003	Tape Backup	1	1250.00	04/20/86	.T.
10	1003	40 Meg. Disk	1	450.00	04/20/86	.T.
11	1003	Floppy Disks	5	2.11	05/12/86	.F.
12	1004	8 Mhz Clock	1	16.39	05/15/86	.F.
13	1003	Color Card	1	101.00	05/31/86	.F.
14	1001	Video Cable	2	16.00	06/15/86	.F.
15	1001	8 Mhz Clock	2	16.39	05/15/86	.F.
16	1001	RAM Disk	1	1100.00	05/18/86	.F.
17	1004	Tape Backup	2	1250.00	06/20/86	.F.

Furthermore, you only want to work with unbilled accounts (records that contain BILLED = .F.). You can repeatedly specify BILLED = .F. in all your commands, or you can set up and save a Query. Use the CHARGES.DBF database to try an on-line Query.

Creating a Query Form

To create a Query, first be sure that CHARGES.DBF and its index files are open. Then, highlight the *Create* option and select *Query*. A prompt will ask that you enter a name for the query form. Follow the usual rules for creating file names (eight letters maximum, no spaces or punctuation). For this example, enter the file name NOTBILLD. The screen displays a blank *query form*.

To fill in the query form so that only records with the BILLED field equal to False are accessed, follow these steps:

✓ Select *Field Name*.
✓ Select BILLED from the submenu.
✓ Select *Operator*.
✓ Select *Is False*.

As you can see, filling in the query form is much like creating a search condition with Assistant menu options. The query form is now completed so that it looks like Figure 10.1.

Saving a Query Form

Once you've filled in the query form, highlight the *Exit* option and select *Save*. You'll be returned to the Assistant menu.

Activating a Query

You can activate a Query by following these steps from the Assistant menu screen:

✓ Highlight the *Set Up* option.
✓ Select *Query*.
✓ Select NOTBILLD.

Once activated like this, dBASE will operate as though only the records specified in the Query exist. For example, if you highlight

```
 Set Filter            Nest          Display         Exit  10:19:13 am

   Field Name         BILLED
   Operator           Is
   Constant/Expression False
   Connect

   Line Number        1


  ┌──────┬────────┬──────────────┬──────────────────────┬─────────┐
  │ Line │ Field  │ Operator     │ Constant/Expression  │ Connect │
  ├──────┼────────┼──────────────┼──────────────────────┼─────────┤
  │  1   │ BILLED │ Is           │ False                │         │
  │  2   │        │              │                      │         │
  │  3   │        │              │                      │         │
  │  4   │        │              │                      │         │
  │  5   │        │              │                      │         │
  │  6   │        │              │                      │         │
  │  7   │        │              │                      │         │
  └──────┴────────┴──────────────┴──────────────────────┴─────────┘

 CREATE QUERY    <C:> C:NOTBILLD.QRY        Opt: 3/5
        Position selection bar - ↑↓.  Select - ↵.  Leave menu - ↔.
        Enter an expression or constant for the filter condition.
```

Figure 10.1: Query Form to Access Unbilled Accounts

Retrieve, select *List* and *Execute the command*, only these records will be displayed:

Record#	CUSTNO	PRODUCT	QTY	UNIT_PRICE	DATE	BILLED
11	1003	Floppy Disks	5	2.11	05/12/86	.F.
12	1004	8 Mhz Clock	1	16.39	05/15/86	.F.
13	1003	Color Card	1	101.00	05/31/86	.F.
14	1001	Video Cable	2	16.00	06/15/86	.F.
15	1001	8 Mhz Clock	2	16.39	05/15/86	.F.
16	1001	RAM Disk	1	1100.00	05/18/86	.F.
17	1004	Tape Backup	2	1250.00	06/20/86	.F.

If you select *Report* from the *Retrieve* menu, only these records will be displayed in your report. You can only BROWSE and EDIT records where BILLED = .F. while this Query is activated. In other words, you can work on these records without having to recreate search conditions for every command.

Closing a Query

Unfortunately, there is no simple way from the Assistant menu to deactivate a Query. To close a Query, leave the Assistant menu by pressing Esc, and enter this command at the dot prompt:

SET FILTER TO ↵

to close the query file. You can then enter the command

ASSIST ↵

to return to the Assistant menu and access your database without the filtering effects of the query form.

Modifying a Query Form

To change an existing query form, highlight the *Modify* option from the Assistant menu and select *Query*. Select the appropriate Query from the menu. You can modify the Query with the same options menu that you used to create the original query form.

Advanced Querying Techniques

Query forms can include the dollar ($) operator for *embedded character searches,* as we discussed earlier. Query forms may also contain parentheses which help refine the logic of a search. For example, take a look at the Query in Figure 10.2.

Notice that this Query specifies

CUSTNO > 1001 .AND. BILLED = .F. .OR. DATE > = 05/01/86

or, in English, "Display records where the customer number is greater than 1001, and where the BILLED field is .F. or the date is greater than 05/01/86." If you LIST with this Query, these records will be displayed:

Record#	CUSTNO	PRODUCT	QTY	UNIT_PRICE	DATE	BILLED
11	1003	Floppy Disks	5	2.11	05/12/86	.F.
12	1004	8 Mhz Clock	1	16.39	05/15/86	.F.

```
┌──────────────────────────────────────────────────────────────────┐
│ ▌Set Filter▐        Nest          Display        Exit ▐01:41:56 am▌│
│ ┌────────────────────────────────────────────────────┐           │
│ │▐Field Name        CUSTNO                          ▌ │           │
│ │ Operator          More than                          │           │
│ │ Constant/Expression 1001                             │           │
│ │ Connect           .AND.                              │           │
│ │                                                      │           │
│ │ Line Number       1                                  │           │
│ └────────────────────────────────────────────────────┘           │
│                                                                    │
│ ┌──────┬─────────┬────────────────────┬─────────────────┬────────┐│
│ │ Line │ Field   │ Operator           │ Constant/Expression│Connect││
│ ├──────┼─────────┼────────────────────┼─────────────────┼────────┤│
│ │ 1    │ CUSTNO  │ More than          │ 1001            │ .AND.  ││
│ │ 2    │ BILLED  │ Is                 │ False           │ .OR.   ││
│ │ 3    │ DATE    │ More than or equal │ 05/01/86        │        ││
│ │ 4    │         │                    │                 │        ││
│ │ 5    │         │                    │                 │        ││
│ │ 6    │         │                    │                 │        ││
│ │ 7    │         │                    │                 │        ││
│ └──────┴─────────┴────────────────────┴─────────────────┴────────┘│
│                                                                    │
│ ▌MODIFY QUERY  ▐<C:> C:TEST1.QRY         ▐Opt: 1/5▌               │
│     Position selection bar - ↑↓.  Select - ◄┘.  Leave menu - ↔.   │
│            Select a field name for the filter condition.          │
└──────────────────────────────────────────────────────────────────┘
```

Figure 10.2: Complex Query without Parentheses

13	1003	Color Card	1	101.00	05/31/86	.F.
14	1001	Video Cable	2	16.00	06/15/86	.F.
15	1001	8 Mhz Clock	2	16.39	05/15/86	.F.
16	1001	RAM Disk	1	1100.00	05/18/86	.F.
17	1004	Tape Backup	2	1250.00	06/20/86	.F.

Although you specified in the query form that the customer number must be greater than 1001, you see records with customer numbers equal to 1001. That's because the .OR. condition lists records with dates greater than or equal to 05/01/86, regardless of the customer number.

Now, take a look at this filter condition:

CUSTNO > 1001 .AND. (BILLED = .F. .OR. DATE >= 05/01/86)

Notice the use of parentheses which block off the .OR. portion of the Query. The parentheses cause the .OR. condition to be evaluated first. Therefore, in order to be displayed by this condition, a given record must either have .F. in the BILLED field, or a date greater than or equal to May 1, 1986. If a record meets either of those criteria, it then must *further* meet the criterion of customer number > 1001 to be included. Therefore customers with numbers less than or equal to 1001 are rejected by this Query.

You insert parentheses into query forms using the *Nest* option from the menu. When you select *Nest,* the screen displays a menu:

Add:
    Start: 0
    End: 0
Remove:
    Start: 0
    End: 0

To place parentheses in a query form, select the *Start* option under *Add:,* and specify the line number where the parentheses should begin. (The line number appears in the left column of the query form.) Then, select the *End* option, and indicate the line where the parentheses should end. Figure 10.3 shows the sample Query with parentheses added to lines 2 and 3. Notice that the parentheses appear on the lines that separate portions of the query form.

After adding the parentheses, you can save and activate the query form in the usual manner. A list of records accessed by the modified query form appears on your screen:

Record#	CUSTNO	PRODUCT	QTY	UNIT_PRICE	DATE	BILLED
11	1003	Floppy Disks	5	2.11	05/12/86	.F.
12	1004	8 Mhz Clock	1	16.39	05/15/86	.F.
13	1003	Color Card	1	101.00	05/31/86	.F.
17	1004	Tape Backup	2	1250.00	06/20/86	.F.

The *Remove* option under the *Nest* menu allows you to remove existing parentheses from a query form. The *Display* option from the *Query* menu will immediately display the first record in the database that meets the Query condition. Pressing PgDn will display other records that meet the search condition. This option allows you to check the validity of your Query before saving it via the *Exit* option.

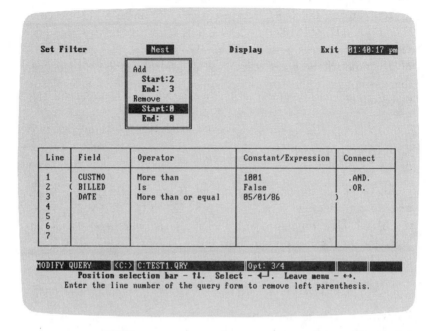

Figure 10.3: Complex Query with Parentheses

MAXIMIZING SEARCH PERFORMANCE

For any given search or query in a database, there will probably be several ways to accomplish the same goal. However, your search method significantly affects the time dBASE requires to find your records. One of the most important factors affecting the speed of a search is the use of the FOR (*Build a search condition*) and WHILE (*Build a scope condition*) options. Let's look at an example.

Suppose that you are using a database with the same structure as MAIL.DBF, but there are about a thousand records in the database. Of these, suppose that ten people have the last name Miller. How long does it take to pull out and view all the Millers in this database? Well, that depends on how you perform the search.

You can use the *Build a search condition* option to build the condition LNAME = 'Miller'. Then it will take about forty seconds to view all the records with a *List* or *Report* option. However, most of that time will be spent reading all of the records in the database that do not have the last name Miller, only to reject them from the display.

Seeking Indexed Records

An index file of last names for the database can speed this process up considerably. First, if the NAMES.NDX index is active for the MAIL.DBF database, and if it is the Master index, you can highlight the *Position* option from the Assistant menu and select *Seek*. Then enter

"Miller" ⬅

(Be sure to include the quotation marks.) The *Seek* option will immediately access the first Miller in the database. Because the database is already in alphabetical order, dBASE can quickly find the other Millers listed beneath the first one:

Mason	**Marcia**	**123 Baker St.**	**San Clemente**	**CA**
⬥ **Miller**	**Muriel**	**P.O. Box 123**	**La Jolla**	**CA**
Miller	**Peter**	**1086 De Mayo**	**Del Mar**	**CA**
Miller	**Wendy**	**5441 Elm St.**	**Eugene**	**OR**
Miller	**Albert**	**High Point Lane**	**Scarsdale**	**NY**
Miller	**Fred**	**1 Hamptom Ct.**	**Greenwich**	**CT**
Miller	**David**	**P.O. Box 2802**	**Boston**	**MA**
Miller	**Aaron**	**544 Oak St.**	**Encinitas**	**CA**
Miller	**Susita**	**186 Crest Dr.**	**Portland**	**ME**
Miller	**Cynthia**	**Tara**	**Atlanta**	**GA**
Miller	**Bill**	**Via Granada**	**Rancho**	**WA**
Moses	**Robert**	**321 Adams**	**San Diego**	**CA**

Building a Scope Condition

Now, to keep dBASE from scanning through a thousand records to pull out all the Millers, you can tell dBASE to just keep displaying records as long as (WHILE) the last name is Miller. Follow these steps:

  ✓   Highlight *Retrieve.*
  ✓   Select *List.*
  ✓   Select *Build a scope condition.*
  ✓   Select LNAME.
  ✓   Select = .
  ✓   Type **Miller.**

You have built a command just as you would using the *Build a search condition* option. Notice, however, that the command you've built is

Command: LIST WHILE LNAME = "Miller"

rather than

Command: LIST FOR LNAME = "Miller"

When you select *Execute the command,* you'll notice another difference. It only takes dBASE around three seconds to display the Millers, rather than forty seconds. Of course, if this database contained 10,000 names, the time difference would be even more dramatic.

Although the *Build a scope condition* option is much faster than the *Build a search condition* option, it can only be used under the very specific circumstances described in this example. The WHILE command means, "Starting at the current record, keep accessing until the condition is no longer true." If the records are not sorted or indexed, and if you do not use the *Seek* option first, then the *Scope condition* will not work properly. Later in this book, we'll use the WHILE option in dBASE programs to gain maximum speed from a fully automated mailing list system.

Other Accessing Options

The Assistant menu offers other techniques for accessing records in a database, but these are generally used only with small databases where record numbers are easily memorized. We'll discuss these options briefly because they are of limited value in managing data.

The *Position* menu includes the *GoTo* and *Skip* options. When you select *GoTo*, dBASE asks you to enter a record number. You simply type a record number and press Return. dBASE will "point" to that record. If you then select *Display* from the **Retrieve** menu, or select *Edit* or *Browse* from the **Update** menu, the record whose number you entered will appear on the screen.

When you select the *Skip* option, dBASE will ask that you enter some number. dBASE will then move the record pointer by the number of records that you enter. For example, if you enter **10**, the record pointer will skip down ten records. If you enter **−1**, then the record pointer will skip back one record.

On the **Retrieve** menu, along with the *Build a search condition* and *Build a scope condition,* there is an option to *Specify Scope.* When you select this option, a submenu displays the options summarized in Table 10.1.

Option	Effect
Default Scope:	Has basically no effect. Change the default scope by selecting *Specify Scope* from the menu.
ALL	Specifies all records in the database.
NEXT	Asks for a number (n) and displays the next n records. For example, selecting *Next* and typing **20** displays the next twenty records (about a screenful).
RECORD	Allows you to define a particular record by its number.
REST	Displays records from the current pointer position to the end of the file.

Table 10.1: Specify Scope Menu Options

Let me reiterate that these menu options are of limited value in managing large databases. However, you may want to become familiar with them for your smaller searching and querying jobs.

Starting with the next chapter, we're going to start learning to program using the dBASE language and leave the Assistant menu once and for all. We'll begin with a discussion of a new way of storing information: memory variables in random access memory (RAM).

REVIEWING FILE MAINTENANCE AND PERFORMANCE

In this chapter you have learned how to maintain files and find records quickly:

■

To perform basic file maintenance, highlight *Tools* from the main menu bar, and select one of these options: *Set drive, Copy file, Directory, Rename, Erase, List structure, Import,* or *Export.*

■

To group files by a particular type of application, use the SET CATALOG command at the dot prompt, or use the *Set Up* and *Catalog* options from the Assistant menu.

■

To create Queries that you can save and reuse, complete the query forms using the *Query* option under the *Create* or *Modify* menus.

■

To activate a Query, select the *Query* option under the *Set Up* menu.

■

For maximum speed in searching a database, open an index file of the field that you want to search. Use the *Seek* option from the *Position* menu. Then use the *Build a scope condition* option under the *Retrieve* menu to build a WHILE condition.

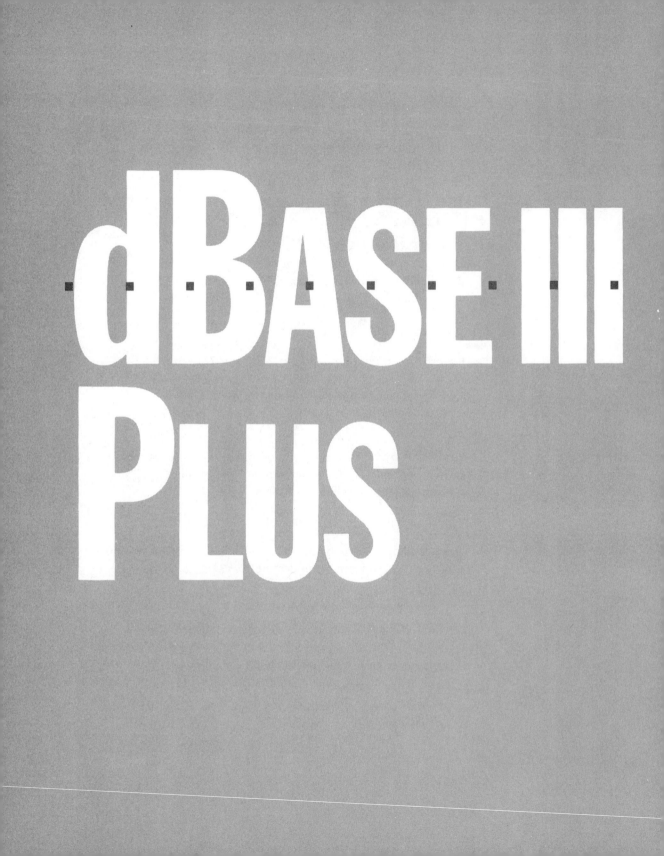

Understanding Memory Variables

A computer's main memory is called *Random Access Memory*, or *RAM*. All of this memory is available when the computer is turned on; whatever was stored in RAM is lost when you shut off the power. With dBASE III PLUS, you can store data in temporary RAM similar to the way that you store data in database fields on disk. Data in RAM are stored in *memory variables*. Memory variables are temporary storage places for pieces of information that you are using to solve a problem. With dBASE III PLUS, you can store 256 of these variables. The name that you create for a memory variable can be up to ten characters long.

Let's start to understand memory variables by examining the arithmetic capabilities of RAM. Beginning with this chapter, we'll work with the dBASE dot prompt, so press the Esc key to leave the Assistant menu and bring up the dot prompt.

MANAGING DATA IN RAM

Using RAM memory in your computer is much like using any pocket calculator. You ask dBASE to calculate some numbers, and it displays the answers. Let's put the computer's main memory (RAM) to work now. Next to the dot prompt, type this command:

```
? 1 + 1 ↵
```

dBASE responds with

```
2
```

the sum of 1 plus 1. Let's give it a tougher problem. Let's ask dBASE to

```
? 25/5 ↵
```

It responds with

```
5.00
```

the quotient of 25 divided by 5. Not bad. dBASE is performing as well as a $5.00 calculator.

Now you can give it an even tougher problem. Suppose that

you need to know what the cost of an item selling for \$181.93 is if you must pay 6% sales tax. That is, you need to know how much 181.93 + 6% of 181.93 is. Type

   ? 181.93 + (.06*181.93) ⏎

dBASE tells you that the total cost is

   192.8458

The four decimal places give you more accuracy than necessary for most applications, but it beats paper and pencil.

   You can also work with non-numeric data (called *character strings* or just *strings*) in RAM, too. For instance, if you type

   ? 'Hi' + 'there' ⏎

you get the result

   Hithere

Notice that when you "added" two strings, they were linked together rather than summed. At first you might think that dBASE was naturally clever enough to figure this out on its own, but it was not dBASE's idea. Rather, it was the fact that you enclosed *Hi* and *there* in apostrophes that told dBASE to link rather than sum. So does this mean that if you enclose the ones in 1 +1 in apostrophes, it will also link rather than sum? Try it. Type

   ? '1' + '1' ⏎

and, yes, dBASE responds with

   11

two ones linked together, not summed. The apostrophes told dBASE to treat the ones as character strings, not as numbers. This leaves you another possibility: Hi + there (no apostrophes). Type

   ? Hi + there ⏎

dBASE informs you that it can't perform this operation:

   Variable not found

```
   ?
? Hi  +  there
Do you want some help? (Y/N)_
```

It looks like these apostrophes carry quite a bit of meaning in RAM. There is a very good reason for this, as you'll see in a moment. For now, keep in mind that if you want to do math with numbers, do not use apostrophes (1 + 1). If you want to link strings together, you must use apostrophes (? 'Hi' + 'there'). Now let's explore the reason for the error that occurred when you attempted to ? Hi + there (no apostrophes).

STORING DATA TO MEMORY VARIABLES WITH STORE

How do you store data in memory variables? First, pick a name for the memory variable, and ask dBASE to store some information in it. A *variable* in the computer sense is exactly the same as a variable in the mathematical sense. That is, if you know that the variable X equals 10 and that the variable Y equals 5, then you know that X + Y = 15. The same is true with computers. To store a value (such as 10) to a variable (such as X), you use the STORE command. Name your first variable X, and store 10 under that name:

STORE 10 TO X ⏎

dBASE displays the brief message

10

Now create another variable name, Y, and store 5 under that name:

STORE 5 TO Y ⏎

dBASE displays

5

When you ask dBASE for the sum of X + Y, like this:

? X + Y ⏎

It should respond with 15, which it does:

15

While the variables are invisible to you right now, you can take a look at them by typing this command:

DISPLAY MEMORY

dBASE displays your variable names and what you've stored in them:

```
X       pub N   10                      (    10.00000000)
Y       pub N    5                      (     5.00000000)
   2 variables defined,      18 bytes used
   254 variables available, 5982 bytes available
```

It informs you that two memory variables exist: X and Y. Furthermore, you know that each is Numeric, and that the value of X is 10 and the value of Y is 5. Since they are Numeric, you can do basic math with them. For example, you can subtract them:

? X − Y ⏎

You get the result

5

which is the difference of $10 - 5$. To multiply them, type

? X * Y ⏎

You get the product

50

which is 10 times 5. If you want to divide the numbers stored in the memory variables, type

? X / Y ⏎

You get the quotient

2.00

the answer to 10 divided by 5.

You are not limited to simple equations. For example, if you want to get the answer to X plus Y times X, type

? X + Y * X ↵

The result is

60

dBASE automatically follows the standard order of precedence in math computation. That is, when an equation involves both multiplication and addition, the multiplication is performed first. You can alter the order of computations by using parentheses:

? (X + Y) * X ↵

You get the result

150

In this case, addition was performed first. At this point, you have stored data in two memory variables, X and Y. So if you ask dBASE to

? A + B ↵

You get an error message

Variable not found
  ?
? A + B
Do you want some help? (Y/N)

because you've asked dBASE to sum A and B, variables that you have not yet used for storing data.

If you again examine the memory variables by typing

DISPLAY MEMORY ↵

you see that you have numbers stored in X and Y:

| X | pub N | 10 | (| 10.00000000) |
| Y | pub N | 5 | (| 5.00000000) |

Earlier you got a syntax error when you asked dBASE to ? Hi + There because memory variables HI and THERE do not exist. Of course, you could create a couple of memory variables called HI and THERE. That is, you can

> STORE 'Hello' TO HI ⤶

and then

> STORE ' yourself' TO THERE ⤶

Now you can type the command

> ? HI + THERE ⤶

and dBASE will respond with

Hello yourself

That is, the contents of memory variables HI and THERE linked together. Why are they linked? Let's see what you have stored in your memory variables.

> DISPLAY MEMORY ⤶

Now you have four memory variables:

```
X       pub N   10                      (   10.00000000)
Y       pub N   5                       (    5.00000000)
HI      pub C   "Hello"
THERE   pub C   " yourself"
```

Memory variables HI and THERE are of the Character type. You told dBASE that they were Character types by putting apostrophes around them when you stored them (STORE 'Hello' TO HI). Notice an important difference between fields and memory variables here. When you define types of data in fields, you specify **C** or **N** when you CREATE the database. In memory variables, dBASE automatically assumes that data stored without apostrophes (STORE 10 TO X) are numbers, and data stored with apostrophes (STORE 'Hello' TO HI) are characters.

If you wish to link the words *Hi* and *there* rather than asking for the contents of the memory variables HI and THERE, use apostrophes:

    ? 'Hi' + ' there' ⏎

This gives the on-screen result

Hi there

The apostrophes told dBASE that you literally wanted to link the words *Hi* and *there*. To use the same principle with X and Y, ask dBASE to

    ? X + Y ⏎

you get

    15

as the answer, the sum of Numeric variable X (10) plus Numeric variable Y (5). On the other hand, if you use apostrophes,

    ? 'X' + 'Y' ⏎

you get

    XY

This is literally an X and a Y linked together.

   The important aspect of memory variables you should remember is that they are not permanent like database data are. RAM memory is temporary. Disk storage is permanent. When you QUIT dBASE and turn off the computer, your databases are still safe and sound on disk. However, memory variables are erased completely. Memory variables are available as a sort of computer scratch pad, as you will see in the coming chapters.

MATH FUNCTIONS

   Besides simple addition, subtraction, multiplication, and division, dBASE III PLUS can work with exponents and logarithms. The symbols ^ or ** can be used as an exponent symbol. For example, to see the result of three squared, ask dBASE to display $3 \wedge 2$

   ? 3^2 ⏎

dBASE responds with

   9.00

To see the value of three cubed, using the ∗∗ option, type

   ? 3∗∗3 ⏎

dBASE responds with

   27.00

To see the cube root of 27, raise 27 to the 1/3 power:

   ? 27^(1/3) ⏎

dBASE responds with

   3.00

The SQRT function will display the square root of any positive number. For example, to see the square root of 81, type this command:

   ? SQRT(81) ⏎

dBASE responds with

   9.00

You can use memory variables in place of numbers, of course. For example, you can store 81 to a memory variable called Z:

   STORE 81 TO Z ⏎

Then ask for the square root of Z:

   ? SQRT(Z) ⏎

dBASE displays the square root of 81:

   9.00

The ROUND and INT (integer) functions are used to control the number of decimals displayed. For example, store the number 1.234567 to a memory variable called TEST:

STORE 1.234567 TO TEST ↵

To see the number rounded to two decimal places, use the ROUND function:

? ROUND(TEST,2) ↵

dBASE displays

1.230000

The comma two (,2) in the ROUND function specifies two decimal places. To see the same number rounded to four decimal places, use the command

? ROUND(TEST,4) ↵

dBASE displays

1.234600

To see the integer (whole number) portion only, you can round to zero decimal places

? ROUND(TEST,0) ↵

which displays

1.000000

Similarly, the INT (integer) function will display the number without decimal places

? INT(TEST) ↵

which displays

1

There is a difference between rounding and using the INT function, however. For example, if you store 1.9999 to a variable called TEST

> STORE 1.9999 TO TEST ⏎

and print TEST rounded to zero decimal places

> ? ROUND(TEST,0) ⏎

you get the number rounded up to 2

2.0000

However, the INT function *truncates* the decimal portion without rounding. So if you print the integer portion of TEST

> ? INT(TEST) ⏎

you get

1

For those of you who use logarithms in your work, dBASE III PLUS provides the EXP and LOG functions. For example, to view the natural exponent (e) of 1, type this command:

> ? EXP(1) ⏎

dBASE responds with

2.72

To see the natural logarithm of 2.72, type the command

> ? LOG(2.72) ⏎

and dBASE displays

1.00

If you need more decimals, just use them in the number you're working with. For example, the command

> ? EXP(1.00000000) ⏎

displays

2.7182818

You can store values to memory variables without the use of the STORE command if you like. If you use only a variable name, followed by the equal sign, and then some data to store, this will have the same effect as the STORE command. For example, the command

    X = −123

stores the number −123 to variable X. To prove this, type the command

    ? X

and dBASE displays

    −123

The ABS function changes a negative number to a positive number. For example, the command

    ? ABS(X)

displays

    123

In later chapters, you'll have a chance to work with additional dBASE III PLUS functions. Starting with the next chapter, you'll explore one of dBASE's most powerful features: command files.

REVIEWING MEMORY VARIABLES

In this chapter you have learned about creating and storing memory variables in RAM:

Memory variables are stored in Random Access Memory (RAM).

To store a memory variable, use the STORE command with a variable name up to ten characters long.

▬

Optionally, you can store a memory variable with the equal (=) sign: MYNAME = "Joe".

▬

You can perform basic math on numbers using the addition (+), subtraction (−), multiplication (*), and division (/) operators.

▬

Character strings are usually surrounded by quotation marks, while numbers and variable names are not.

▬

To display all active memory variables, enter the command DIS-PLAY MEMORY at the dot prompt.

▬

dBASE III PLUS includes a number of basic math functions including (but not limited to) exponent (^), square root (SQRT), exponent (EXP), natural logarithm (LOG), and absolute value (ABS).

Creating Command Files

A *command file* is a disk file that contains a series of commands. You record commands in files because it is more convenient having dBASE execute a batch of commands than typing each command at the dot prompt. The potential of command files goes far beyond saving time, however, as you will see in this chapter. A command file is actually a *computer program,* and from now on we'll use these words interchangeably.

A computer program is similar to the program you receive when you go to the theater. The theater's program displays the series of events and the order in which these events will occur. Likewise, the computer program presents a series of commands to the computer in a specified order. Of course, the computer program is more difficult to read than the theater program because it is not in plain English. It is written in a computer language. In this book, our programs will be written in dBASE, the computer language that is already familiar to you.

The basic procedure for working with command files goes something like this. First, you create the command file using the MODIFY command. Then you run the command file by asking dBASE to DO the command file. If you find mistakes in the command file, you have to edit it. Correcting these errors in a command file is called *debugging.* Let's deal with creating command files first.

CREATING COMMAND FILES WITH MODIFY

For your first command file, you'll create a program to print mailing labels. This process might seem a bit redundant (dBASE III PLUS has a LABEL FORM command to print labels), but a mailing labels program is an ideal example for explaining the basics of programming: loops and decision making. Later, you'll use the same skills to create more practical programs such as menus.

Let's write a mailing labels command file now. We'll call this command file LABELS, and store it on the same disk as the MAIL.DBF database. The command to create a new command file, or edit an existing one, is MODIFY COMMAND plus the name of the command file. So from the dot prompt, enter this command:

MODIFY COMMAND LABELS ←⏎

dBASE displays the prompt

Edit: LABELS.PRG

and gives you a blank screen on which to write the command file. Let's go ahead and type it. Make sure that you type it exactly as it appears here:

```
? TRIM(FNAME),LNAME ←⏎
? ADDRESS ←⏎
? TRIM(CITY)+',  '+STATE+ZIP
```

If you make errors while you're typing the program, you can move the cursor around to make changes. The cursor control keys are the same as those in the EDIT and APPEND modes and are displayed at the top of the screen. When you have typed it exactly as shown, save it by pressing ^W or ^End.

You have just written your first command file and stored it on the data disk as LABELS.PRG. (As you've probably guessed, dBASE added the .PRG, which stands for *program*.) Now let's run the program.

RUNNING COMMAND FILES WITH DO

First, let's tell dBASE to use MAIL.DBF as the database:

USE MAIL ←⏎

Now to run the command file, tell dBASE to

DO LABELS ←⏎

and you'll see one of the records from MAIL.DBF in label format:

Betsy Smith
222 Lemon Dr.
New York, NY 01234

dBASE did all three lines in the command file in the order they were placed. That is, dBASE printed the first name with the blanks trimmed off followed by the last name (? TRIM(FNAME), LNAME). Then it printed the address (? ADDRESS). Finally, dBASE printed the city followed by a comma, the state, and the zip (? TRIM(CITY) + ', ' + STATE + ZIP). This is the first mailing label.

Let's review the steps:

√ Create the command file using MODIFY COMMAND.

√ Name it LABELS.PRG.

√ Save the command file by pressing ^W or ^End.

√ Ask dBASE to DO LABELS.

dBASE executes each of the commands in order. That is, dBASE reads the command file left to right, top to bottom, just as you read English. The results print in the order that you specify.

This is not bad for a first command file, but you can see one major weakness: it only prints one label. To get dBASE to print all the labels in the database, you must set up a *loop* to tell dBASE to go back to the first command and repeat the steps in the command file until each record in the database has been printed in label format.

SETTING UP LOOPS IN PROGRAMS WITH DO WHILE AND ENDDO

dBASE has a pair of commands called DO WHILE and ENDDO which can be used in a program to repeat a series of commands indefinitely. All you have to do is enclose the commands to be repeated between a DO WHILE and an ENDDO command. Every DO WHILE begins a loop, which will be ended by an ENDDO command. You also need to tell dBASE what the condition is for performing the commands inside the loop. Let's give it a try in your LABELS program. First, ask dBASE to

   MODIFY COMMAND LABELS ↵

dBASE will redisplay LABELS.PRG and let you make some changes:

   ? TRIM(FNAME),LNAME
   ? ADDRESS
   ? TRIM(CITY)+', '+STATE+ZIP

To make dBASE print labels for every person in the mailing list, you need to put these commands inside a loop. Press ^N to make room for a new line, and add the DO WHILE command at the top of the program. You will also need to add a SKIP command to have dBASE skip down to the next name in the database as it performs the commands in the loop. Then add ENDDO to end the loop. Finally, a RETURN command will tell dBASE to return to the dot prompt after the program has been executed. The command file should be like this:

   DO WHILE .NOT. EOF( )
   ? TRIM(FNAME),LNAME
   ? ADDRESS
   ? TRIM(CITY)+', '+STATE+ZIP
   SKIP
   ENDDO
   RETURN

Now save the edited version of the command file with ^W or ^End. When the dot prompt reappears, type

   USE MAIL ↵
   DO LABELS ↵

to get

   Betsy Smith
   222 Lemon Dr.
   New York, NY 01234
   Record no. 1
   Ruth Doe
   1142 J. St.
   Los Angeles, CA 91234

Record no. 2
Lucy Smithsonian
461 Adams St.
San Diego, CA 92122-1234
Record no. 3
John Q. Smith
123 A St.
San Diego, CA 92123
Record no. 4
Andy Appleby
345 Oak St.
Los Angeles, CA 92123
Record no. 5

Note: Your labels may come out in a different order. Don't worry; you can easily specify any order using the index files.

If something goes wrong when you try this, check to see if you typed the program exactly as it appears in the book. If your program seems to be running on and on endlessly, press Esc to cancel the run and get back to the dot prompt. Then, you'll need to MODIFY COMMAND LABELS again and correct your program so that it *exactly* matches the LABELS.PRG program in the book.

Now all the names on the database are on the screen in a mailing label format. Let's summarize what you did here. In the command file, you told dBASE to DO WHILE .NOT. EOF( ). In English, this translates to, "Do everything between here and the ENDDO command as long as you haven't reached the EOF( ), end of the database file." The next three lines in the command file then print one label. Then the SKIP command causes dBASE to SKIP down to the next record in the database. The ENDDO command marks the end of the loop, but the loop is repeated because the EOF( ) (end of the file) has not been reached yet. Hence, when another label is printed, dBASE skips down to the next name and address, prints another label, and so forth until all the labels have been printed. At that point dBASE has reached the end of the database. This causes the loop to end and the first command under the ENDDO command to be processed. The RETURN command tells dBASE to return to the dot prompt.

One problem with your mailing labels is that they have record numbers on them. You can get rid of the record numbers by asking dBASE to SET TALK OFF. Let's run the program again. This time, let's first

    USE MAIL ⏎

Then, tell dBASE to get rid of the record numbers with

    SET TALK OFF ⏎

If you have a printer hooked up, you can also

    SET PRINT ON ⏎

Now let's run the LABELS program. Tell dBASE to

    DO LABELS ⏎

and you'll see that the record numbers have been removed:

    Betsy Smith
    222 Lemon Dr.
    New York, NY 01234
    Ruth Doe
    1142 J. St.
    Los Angeles, CA 91234
    Lucy Smithsonian
    461 Adams St.
    San Diego, CA 92122-1234
    John Q. Smith
    123 A St.
    San Diego, CA 92123
    Andy Appleby
    345 Oak St.
    Los Angeles, CA 92123

If you did SET PRINT ON, type the command to

    SET PRINT OFF ⏎

Otherwise, everything that you type on the screen will also go to your printer.

Printing Blank Lines

There's a problem here. Most mailing labels are one inch tall, and the names are spaced evenly on each one. It just so happens that most printers print six lines to the inch, so if you modify your command file to print six lines for each label, each name and address should fit perfectly on one label. So let's

    MODIFY COMMAND LABELS ↵

Now press the ↓ key four times to get the cursor on the SKIP command. Then press ^N three times to make room for three new lines. When you finish, your command file will look like this:

```
DO WHILE .NOT. EOF( )
? TRIM(FNAME),LNAME
? ADDRESS
? TRIM(CITY) + ',   ' + STATE + ZIP

-

SKIP
ENDDO
RETURN
```

Now put in commands to print three blank lines on each mailing label. That is, begin each blank line with a ? command. Your program looks like this now:

```
DO WHILE .NOT. EOF( )
? TRIM(FNAME),LNAME
? ADDRESS
? TRIM(CITY) + ',   ' + STATE + ZIP
?
?
?
SKIP
ENDDO
RETURN
```

Save it with ^W. Now let's

    USE MAIL ↵
    DO LABELS ↵

You'll see the names and addresses properly formatted for one-inch mailing labels:

Betsy Smith
222 Lemon Dr.
New York, NY 01234

Ruth Doe
1142 J. St.
Los Angeles, CA 91234

Lucy Smithsonian
461 Adams St.
San Diego, CA 92122-1234

John Q. Smith
123 A St.
San Diego, CA 92123

Andy Appleby
345 Oak St.
Los Angeles, CA 92123

Much better. The labels have the extra three blank lines between them. You may wonder why you must repeatedly type USE MAIL. The USE command returns the database to its first record. If you *don't* USE the database at this point, you'll get nothing on the screen when you type DO LABELS. Try it:

DO LABELS ⏎

All you get is the dot prompt. Yet you know that there are several records in the database. No labels were printed because dBASE is already at the end of the file. Prove this by typing this question:

? EOF( ) ⏎

dBASE responds with

.T.

which is dBASE's way of saying, "True, I'm at the end of the database." Recall that in your command file, you told dBASE to print labels while it's *not* at the end of the database (DO WHILE .NOT. EOF( )). So that's why you got nothing when you ran the program this time. dBASE returns to the top of the database when you type

GO TOP ⏎

Then type this command to see your labels:

DO LABELS ⏎

It's to your benefit to put the GO TOP command right into the command file. Then you don't have to remember to type it every time you DO LABELS. Add GO TOP to your program by editing the command file with MODIFY COMMAND LABELS. Your command file will look like this.

```
GO TOP
DO WHILE .NOT. EOF()
? TRIM(FNAME),LNAME
? ADDRESS
? TRIM(CITY)+',  '+STATE+ZIP
?
?
?
SKIP
ENDDO
RETURN
```

Then the program will always start with dBASE at the top (first record) of the database. Notice that the GO TOP command is outside and above the loop. This is so that dBASE will start at the first record and continue with the loop. Had you put the GO TOP command inside the loop, the command file would print a label for the first record, skip to the next record, go back to the first record, print that label again, skip to the next record, back to the first record . . . on and on. The command file would print countless mailing labels for the first record in the database.

Making a Loop Easier to Read

Now you have a good mailing label program to use with the MAIL database file. dBASE will understand and execute the commands in this file each time that you tell it to DO LABELS. However, you could spruce it up a bit so that it's easier for the human programmer to read. Take a look at this version of LABELS.PRG:

```
* * * * * * * * * Mailing Labels Program.
GO TOP

DO WHILE .NOT. EOF( )
    ? TRIM(FNAME),LNAME
    ? ADDRESS
    ? TRIM(CITY)+',  '+STATE+ZIP
    ?
    ?
    ?
    SKIP
ENDDO
RETURN
```

Notice the added title and line spacing. Programmers often put titles and comments in their programs as notes to themselves. The comments don't have any effect on the actual program; they're just reminders to the person who wrote the program. To put comments in dBASE programs like this, start the line with an asterisk (*). A lot of asterisks make the line stand out, but only one is necessary.

Also note that there is a blank line between the GO TOP command and the start of the DO WHILE loop. This line emphasizes the loop. Also, all of the commands inside of the DO WHILE loop are indented, which emphasizes the loop. If you want to make your command file look like this one, just MODIFY COMMAND LABELS. Then press ^N to make room for the title. Don't forget to put at least one asterisk in front of the title that you type. Then position the cursor under the GO TOP command, and press ^N. Then position the cursor next to the ?TRIM (FNAME) line, press ^V (INSert ON), and hit the Space bar a few times to indent the line. Do the same for the other lines within the loop. Then save it with ^W. (Incidentally, if you need to delete a line from a command file, you can use ^Y.)

In the next chapter, we'll discuss how to add decision-making capabilities to command files.

REVIEWING COMMAND FILES

Using the LABELS.PRG example, this chapter showed you the basics of dBASE programming:

▬

A *command file* is a computer program written in the dBASE language. It contains step-by-step instructions for dBASE to perform a specific job.

▬

Like other files, store command files on your data disk.

▬

To create or edit a command file (program), enter MODIFY COMMAND, followed by the name of your program, at the dot prompt.

▬

To run a program, enter the DO command followed by the name of the program. dBASE will execute each command in the file without your retyping it.

▬

To tell dBASE to repeat portions of a program, use the DO WHILE and ENDDO commands to create a *loop*.

——

Note: As an alternative to writing your own command files, see Appendix B for an introduction to the dBASE III PLUS Applications Generator.

Making Decisions

The LABELS program you created in the last chapter has one limitation: It always prints out labels for everyone in the database, even though you might want labels for just San Diego residents or the 92122 zip code area. A better label program would allow you to specify only the labels you want printed. In this chapter, you'll learn to build this capability into the LABELS program.

ASKING QUESTIONS

If the command file is going to print certain labels, it needs to know which labels you want. That is, it needs to ask you which labels you want to print. You can make your command files ask questions with the ACCEPT and INPUT commands. When you use either of these commands, you enclose the question to be asked in apostrophes. You also need to provide a memory variable in which to store the answer to the question. To make the memory variable accessible outside of the command file, you need to define it as PUBLIC. We'll discuss PUBLIC variables in more detail later. For now, let's try out the ACCEPT command with a command file called TEST:

    MODIFY COMMAND TEST ↵

When the blank screen appears, type these lines:

    PUBLIC NAME
    ACCEPT 'What is your name?' TO NAME

and save it with ^W. Then DO TEST. You'll see the prompt on-screen:

    What is your name? _

dBASE will leave the prompt on the screen until you type an answer. You can type any answer:

    FRED ASTAIRE ↵

After you press Return, the dot prompt appears because the program is over. If you now ask dBASE to

? NAME ⟵

you'll see

FRED ASTAIRE

If you were to DISPLAY MEMORY now, you'd see that you have a memory variable called NAME, of the Character type, with the contents FRED ASTAIRE. So you've been able to have the command file ask a question, wait for an answer, and remember the answer by storing it to a memory variable.

The INPUT command is very similar to the ACCEPT command, except that it is used when the answer to the question is a number. For example, try making a command file called TEST2 that looks like this:

```
PUBLIC ANSWER
INPUT 'Enter a number' TO ANSWER
```

Save it. Then DO TEST2, and the request appears:

Enter a number _

Type any old number, say **999,** and press Return. The dot prompt reappears. Next type

? ANSWER ⟵

You'll see

999

When you DISPLAY MEMORY, you see that you have a memory variable called ANSWER, and it is Numeric.

You can also use a combination of the dBASE III PLUS @, SAY, GET, and READ commands to accept input from the user at the terminal. The @ SAY commands allow you to place text anywhere on the screen. However, any variable in which you attempt to store data using an @ SAY combination must already exist. For example, at the dot prompt enter this command:

```
YOURNAME = SPACE(10) ◄┘
```

This creates a memory variable called YOURNAME that contains ten blank spaces. (The SPACE function creates the blank spaces, and the = sign stores them to the variable YOURNAME.) Now that the YOURNAME variable exists, you can use it in an @, SAY, GET combination. Clear the screen of any miscellaneous text by entering this command at the dot prompt:

```
CLEAR ◄┘
```

Now enter this command:

```
@ 10,10 SAY "Enter your Name" GET YOURNAME
```

In English, this command means, "On the screen, at row 10, column 10, place the sentence 'Enter your Name,' and then display a prompt for defining the YOURNAME variable." You'll see the "Enter your Name" prompt near the middle of the screen.

Next, enter the command

```
READ ◄┘
```

to tell dBASE to put the cursor into the prompt for the YOUR-NAME variable, and wait for the user to type some data. For this example, type **Alberto,** and press Return.

To verify that the YOURNAME memory variable now contains the data you typed, enter the command

```
? YOURNAME ◄┘
```

or

```
DISPLAY MEMORY ◄┘
```

You'll see that YOURNAME is a Character memory variable containing Alberto.

Unlike ACCEPT and INPUT, the @, SAY, GET combination does not assume a data type. Instead, the data type of the existing memory variable (or field) is used. We'll experiment with this in just a moment.

The WAIT command presents a message and waits for the user to press any key. The variations of the WAIT command are explained in Table 13.1.

Variation	Effect
WAIT	When used as a single command, WAIT presents the message, "Press any key to continue," and waits for a keystroke. It does not store the resulting keystroke.
WAIT TO <MemVar>	When used with TO and a memory variable, WAIT will store the resulting keystroke to a memory variable.
WAIT "message"	You can use your own message with the WAIT command, enclosed in quotation marks, to replace the default "Press any key to continue" message.

Table 13.1: WAIT Command Variations

Let's try a small command file to test the @ and WAIT commands. First, enter the command

    MODIFY COMMAND TEST@ ↵

at the dot prompt. Next, type the program as it is shown in Program 13.1.

```
* * * * * * * * * * * Program to test @ and WAIT commands.
* * * * * * * * * * * First, set up variables.
ANYNUMBER = 0
ANYWORD = SPACE(254)
ANYDATE = DATE( )
* * * * * * * * * * * Next, use @ SAY, GET to read in new data.
CLEAR
@ 2,5 SAY "Enter a Number " GET ANYNUMBER
```

Program 13.1: Program to Test @ and WAIT Commands

```
@ 5,5 SAY "Enter a sentence or two " GET ANYWORD
@ 10,5 SAY "Enter a date " GET ANYDATE
READ
* * * * * * * * * * * * Next, use WAIT to pause before memory display.
@ 15,1
WAIT "Press any key to see memory " TO KEYPRESS
DISPLAY MEMORY
```

Program 13.1: Program to Test @ and WAIT Commands (continued)

Save the command file with the usual ^W command, and then enter this command to run it:

DO TEST@ ↵

Your screen will display prompts for filling in the variables. When you've completed them, the screen will display the "Press any key to see memory" prompt. Figure 13.1 shows this screen with some sample data entered.

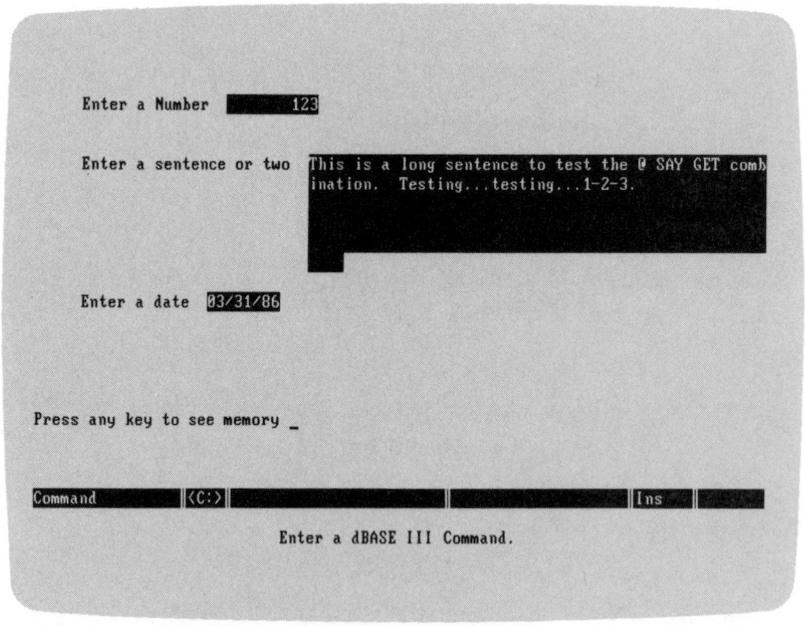

```
    Enter a Number          123

    Enter a sentence or two  This is a long sentence to test the @ SAY GET comb
                             ination.  Testing...testing...1-2-3.




    Enter a date  03/31/86




  Press any key to see memory  _



 Command          <C:>                              Ins
               Enter a dBASE III Command.
```

Figure 13.1: Screen Results of TEST@.PRG

After you press any key to display memory variables, you'll see that the data types are commensurate with the original data types used in the TEST@.PRG command file:

ANYNUMBER	**priv**	**N**	**123 (**	**123.00000000)**
ANYWORD	**priv**	**C**	**"This is a long sentence to test the @**	
			SAY GET combination. Testing . . . testing	
			. . . 1-2-3.	
ANYDATE	**priv**	**D**	**03/31/86**	
KEYPRESS	**priv**	**C**	**" "**	

(Of course, you'll also see any other variables you've created.)

Later in this book, you'll see more examples of the ACCEPT, INPUT, @, and WAIT commands.

MAKING DECISIONS WITH IF AND ENDIF

You can embed some decision making into your command files by using the IF and ENDIF commands. IF, in dBASE, means the same thing that it does in English: "If (a condition is met), then (do something)." Each IF must be accompanied by an ENDIF. Let's look at a practical example.

Start by modifying the LABELS program. Change it so that before it prints labels, it asks which zip code area you want labels for, and only prints labels for individuals who live in the specified zip code area. Here is the first step:

```
MODIFY COMMAND LABELS ←┘
```

This command brings the LABELS program to the screen for you to edit. It should look something like Program 13.2.

```
* * * * * * * * * * * * Mailing Labels Program.
GO TOP
DO WHILE .NOT. EOF()
    ? TRIM(FNAME),LNAME
    ? ADDRESS
    ? TRIM(CITY) + ',   ' + STATE + ZIP
```

Program 13.2: Unedited Mailing Labels Program

```
    ?
    ?
    ?
    SKIP
 ENDDO
 RETURN
```

Program 13.2: Unedited Mailing Labels Program (continued)

Now, just under the title, you need to add three lines. The first, SET TALK OFF, will be used to keep the record numbers off the labels. The second, CLEAR, will clear the screen. Then you'll put in an ACCEPT statement so the command file will ask you a question.

Move the cursor down one line from the title, press ^N three times, and type these three lines:

```
SET TALK OFF
CLEAR
ACCEPT 'What zip code area?' TO AREA
```

The ACCEPT Command will present its question on the screen and wait for an answer. It will store the answer to a memory variable named AREA. Now you need to type two other lines, which will qualify the labels to be printed (IF ZIP = AREA) and end the condition (ENDIF). The first line goes under the DO WHILE command line. The ENDIF goes above the SKIP command. You may want to add blank lines and indent the ? a little further, but it is not necessary to do so. These are just for looks. In Program 13.3, you can see how the command file should look after you make these changes.

```
* * * * * * * * * * * * Mailing Labels Program.
SET TALK OFF
CLEAR
ACCEPT ' What zip code area?' TO AREA
GO TOP
DO WHILE .NOT. EOF( )
   IF ZIP = AREA
      ? TRIM(FNAME),LNAME
```

Program 13.3: Edited Mailing Labels Program

```
            ? ADDRESS
            ? TRIM(CITY) + ',   ' + STATE + ZIP
            ?
            ?
            ?
        ENDIF
        SKIP
    ENDDO
    RETURN
```

Program 13.3: Edited Mailing Labels Program (continued)

Double check that you've typed everything correctly, and then save the command file with ^W. Now, let's try it out. First, USE MAIL if you haven't already done so. Then

DO LABELS ⏎

The first thing that should happen is that the screen clears and the following question appears:

What zip code area? _

Your command file is asking you a question, and it is waiting for an answer. Type **92123** and press Return. Then two labels appear on the screen:

Andy Appleby
345 Oak St.
Los Angeles, CA 92123

John Q. Smith
123 A St.
San Diego, CA 92123

How about that? The command file asked which zip code area you wanted, and then it printed labels for people who live in that area. Now, let's review why it did this. Take another look at the command file in Program 13.3.

When you asked dBASE to DO LABELS, it followed the instructions in your program. It ignored the title because of the leading asterisks, and it cleared the screen (CLEAR). Then it presented the question, "What zip code area?" and waited for an answer. Remember that the ACCEPT command told dBASE to present the question in the apostrophes, and wait for an answer. dBASE waited until you typed your reply, 92123. It stored 92123 to a memory variable called AREA. Then the program began the loop through the database. Prior to printing each label, it checked to see IF ZIP = AREA. That is, it checked to see if the zip code on the record matched AREA, the 92123 zip code you typed in response to the "What zip code area?" question. If they matched, it printed the label. If they didn't match, all the lines between the IF and ENDIF were ignored. Either way, the SKIP command told dBASE to go to the next record. Then ENDDO sent dBASE through another loop, checking to see if the zip code on the next record matched the requested area. It continued this process until it got to the end of the database.

You can DO LABELS again, but this time when it asks

What zip code area? _

type **91234** and press Return. Sure enough, you get

Ruth Doe
1142 J. St.
Los Angeles, CA 91234

This is the only record in your database in the 91234 zip code area.

You can print labels for a broader zip code area by typing a partial zip code. If you DO LABELS and type **92** as the zip code area to print labels for, you'll get all the people in the 92XXX zip code areas:

Andy Appleby
345 Oak St.
Los Angeles, CA 92123

John Q. Smith
123 A St.
San Diego, CA 92123

Lucy Smithsonian
461 Adams St.
San Diego, CA 92122-1234

This feature is useful now, but it wasn't so handy in Chapter 3 when you asked for a list of Smiths and got Smithsonians in there too. dBASE lists these records because 9 and 2 are the first digits of their zip codes.

Let's add the option to send mailing labels to the printer. Ask dBASE to MODIFY COMMAND LABELS, so you can edit it. Now, as shown in Program 13.4, add the new lines set in darker print.

```
* * * * * * * * * * * Mailing Labels Program.
SET TALK OFF
CLEAR
ACCEPT ' What zip code area? ' TO AREA
ACCEPT ' Shall I send labels to the printer? (Y/N) ' TO YN
IF UPPER(YN) = "Y"
   SET PRINT ON
ENDIF
GO TOP
DO WHILE .NOT. EOF( )
   IF ZIP = AREA
      ? TRIM(FNAME),LNAME
      ? ADDRESS
      ? TRIM(CITY) + ',   ' + STATE + ZIP
      ?
      ?
      ?
   ENDIF
   SKIP
ENDDO
SET PRINT OFF
RETURN
```

Program 13.4: LABELS.PRG with Printer Question

When you've made the changes, save the command file with ^W and then DO LABELS. This time you'll see

What zip code area? _

Type **91234** and press Return. You'll see

Shall I send labels to the printer? (Y/N)

The **Y/N** is a clue that the program is expecting a yes or no answer. If you have a printer hooked up to your computer, type **Y**. Otherwise, type **N**. Then the labels for the 91234 zip code area appear, either on the screen or printer, depending on how you've answered the question about the printer. Why is this?

In the command file you've added the command

ACCEPT ′ Shall I send labels to the printer? (Y/N) ′ TO YN

which causes dBASE to present the question on-screen and wait for an answer. The answer is stored in a memory variable called YN. You've also added these lines to the command file:

```
IF UPPER (YN) = "Y"
    SET PRINT ON
ENDIF
```

These lines say, "If the answer is **Y**, set the printer ON." Notice that the command actually checks to see if the uppercase equivalent is a **Y**. This is so that if you answered the question with a lowercase **y**, the printer would still be set ON. Near the bottom of the command file, you've added the line

SET PRINT OFF

so that when the program finishes printing labels, the printer will set back OFF automatically before returning to the dot prompt.

dBASE allows another method of decision making in command files: DO CASE.

MAKING DECISIONS WITH DO CASE

The IF . . . ENDIF clause is useful for allowing a program to make a simple either/or decision. Some programs may have to decide from several possibilities what to do next. The DO CASE

. . . ENDCASE clause ensures that the program can do this. For example, notice in Program 13.5 that the first few lines present four menu options, and then an INPUT statement asks the user for a choice from the menu. Then the program stores that answer in a memory variable called CHOICE.

```
CLEAR
? " 1. Add new names"
? " 2. Print Labels"
? " 3. Edit a record"
? " 4. Exit"
INPUT "Enter choice " TO CHOICE
DO CASE
   CASE CHOICE = 1
      APPEND
   CASE CHOICE = 2
      LABEL FORM TWOCOL
   CASE CHOICE = 3
      BROWSE
   OTHERWISE
      QUIT
ENDCASE
```

Program 13.5: Sample Program Using DO CASE

Beneath the menu is a DO CASE clause, starting with the command DO CASE and ending with the command ENDCASE. Inside the DO CASE clause, the program decides what to do based upon the value of CHOICE. If CHOICE = 1, the program appends. If CHOICE = 2, the program prints labels from a label file called TWOCOL. If CHOICE = 3, the program goes into BROWSE mode. If none of these situations occurs (OTHERWISE), the program quits.

You'll get a chance to use the DO CASE clause with a menu program in the next chapter. For now, let's talk about another form of decision making in programs: macro substitution.

MACRO SUBSTITUTION

Macro substitution is a powerful programming technique used in command files. A *macro* is simply a memory variable name with an ampersand (&) in front of it. When dBASE encounters a macro in a command file, it replaces that macro with the contents of the memory variable. For example, if you have a memory variable called FLD, and you have the word ZIP stored to that name, every time the &FLD macro is encountered in the program, dBASE will automatically substitute the word ZIP.

Let's discuss a practical example. You've set up your labels program so that it asks for a zip code area before it prints labels. However, you may actually want to print labels for a certain city or state. You need to modify the command file so that it asks which field you wish to search on, and also what value to look for. That is, when you run the new version of the command file, you want it to ask

Search on what field?

and then you can type any field name (such as CITY, STATE, or ZIP). Then it will ask

Look for what _ ?

and you can type a characteristic to search for. For example, if you answer the first question with the word CITY, the second question will appear as

Look for what CITY?

and you can type a city. If you were to answer this question with **Los Angeles,** then only labels for Los Angeles residents would be printed. If you answered the first question with **ZIP,** the second question would ask, "Look for what ZIP?" and you could type a zip code to search for. This gives the command file more flexibility.

To allow this flexibility, you must modify the LABELS command file in Program 13.6 to include macros. The three new lines are shown in darker print.

```
* * * * * * * * * * * * Mailing Labels Program.
SET TALK OFF
CLEAR
ACCEPT ' Search on what field? ' TO FLD
ACCEPT ' Look for what &FLD? ' TO COND
ACCEPT ' Shall I send labels to the printer? (Y/N) ' TO YN
IF UPPER(YN) = "Y"
   SET PRINT ON
ENDIF
GO TOP
DO WHILE .NOT. EOF( )
   IF &FLD = '&COND'
      ? TRIM(FNAME),LNAME
      ? ADDRESS
      ? TRIM(CITY) + ',   ' + STATE + ZIP
      ?
      ?
      ?
   ENDIF
   SKIP
ENDDO
SET PRINT OFF
RETURN
```

Program 13.6: Final Version of LABELS.PRG

Once you've changed the program, you can save the command file and then DO LABELS. When you do so, the screen clears and you see

Search on what field?

Let's answer by entering **CITY**. The next question to appear is

Look for what CITY?

and you can answer by typing **San Diego**. Then it asks

Shall I send labels to the printer? (Y/N)

Answer **N** for now. You'll see the mailing labels for the San Diego residents.

John Q. Smith
123 A St.
San Diego, CA 92123

Lucy Smithsonian
461 Adams St.
San Diego, CA 92122-1234

Let's try again. DO LABELS. The LABELS program asks

Search on which field?

Type **STATE**. Then the command file asks

Look for what STATE?

Type **CA**. It asks about the printer, to which you can reply **Y** or **N**, and then prints mailing labels for all California residents. Let's discuss why.

Near the top of the LABELS program, you see these two lines:

```
ACCEPT ' Search on which field? ' TO FLD
ACCEPT ' Look for what &FLD? ' TO COND
```

When you run the program, the first line causes dBASE to display the question, "Search on which field?" and it waits for an answer. If you type **CITY** in response to this question, dBASE stores the word CITY to a memory variable called FLD. Then the next line is executed, but it has a macro in it, &FLD. This causes the contents of the FLD variable to be substituted into this line, so what you see on the screen next to it is the question, "Look for what CITY?" Whatever you answer to this question gets stored to a memory variable called COND. Hence, if you answer this question with **San Diego**, you have two memory variables in RAM. One is called FLD, and it contains the word *CITY*. The other memory variable is called COND, and it contains the words *San Diego*. Although you can name the memory variables anything you like, choosing FLD and COND will remind you of FieLD (to search on) and CONDition (to search for).

Then the command file asks about the printer and begins the DO WHILE loop. Within the DO WHILE loop is the command IF &FLD = '&COND'. Before this line makes a decision to print a label or not, it is going to have to substitute the macros. Hence, the line becomes

    IF CITY = 'San Diego'

and only labels for San Diego residents are printed.

Had you answered the question, "Search on which field?" with **ZIP**, and the question, "Look for what ZIP?" with **92111**, memory variable FLD would contain ZIP, and COND would contain 92111. In this case, when the program needed to make a decision as to whether or not to print a label, the IF statement would become

    IF ZIP = '92111'

Macro substitution is a bit abstract and takes a little getting used to. The only strict rule on macros is that they must be Character-type memory variables.

Usually, when creating command files, you come up with an idea for a program you want, and then you need to figure out just how to write the program. This process is not easy if you are a beginner. In the next chapter, we'll talk about methods that can help you make the transition from an idea to a working program.

REVIEWING DECISION MAKING

In this chapter you've learned about using commands to make decisions in programs:

▬

The ACCEPT command displays a prompt and waits for the user to enter any character data followed by a press on the Return key.

▬

The INPUT command displays a prompt and waits for the user to enter a number, followed by a press on the Return key.

▬

The @, SAY, GET, and READ commands will place a prompt anywhere on the screen and wait for the user to fill in or modify an existing memory variable or field.

▬

The WAIT command displays a prompt and waits for a single keystroke from the user.

▬

The IF . . . ELSE . . . ENDIF commands set up decision clauses in programs.

▬

The DO CASE . . . ENDCASE clause sets up decisions where only one alternative of several is possible.

▬

Macro substitution allows you to build portions of command lines as a program is running, and substitute those portions into the actual command, using the & symbol and a variable name.

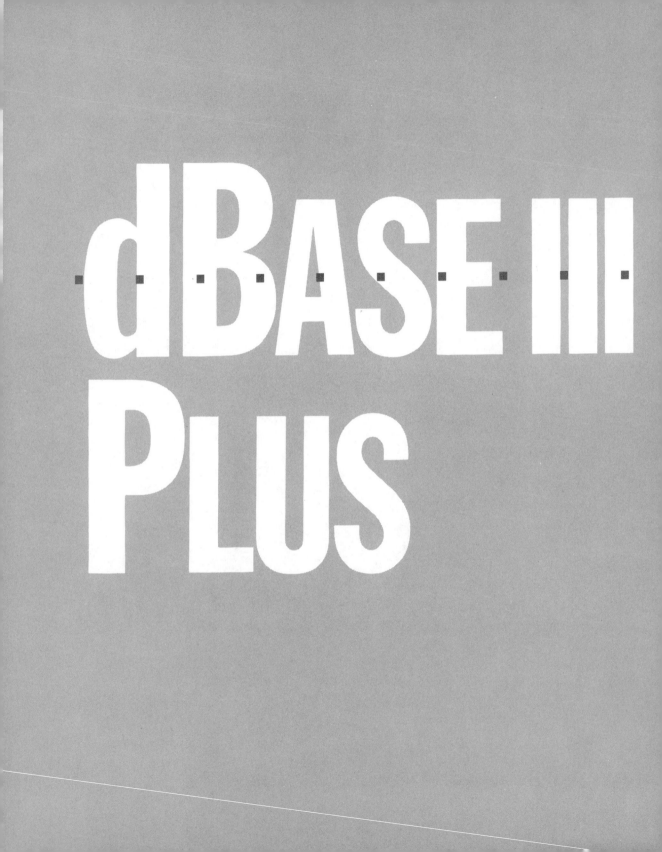

Designing and Developing Programs

When you create a command file (program), you are actually *writing software*. There are five parts to writing dBASE software. First, you design the program by determining its purpose. Second, unless your program will use an existing database, you must design a database structure. Third, to outline the program, you write pseudocode. Fourth, you must write the program. In dBASE you do this by typing MODIFY COMMAND and then typing the program on the screen. Fifth, you run the program to test it. Because you will often make mistakes when you write programs, you need to make corrections to debug the program. Let's examine each of these steps in detail.

STEP 1: OUTLINE THE GENERAL IDEA

It's a good idea to write the general idea of a program on paper first. For example, let's say that you want to develop a fancy mailing list system that's quick and easy to use. The general idea might be something like this:

This system will be designed to manage a mailing list, and will operate from a menu of choices. When first run, the system will display these Mail Menu options:

1. Add new names and addresses.
2. Sort the mailing list.
3. Print names and addresses.
4. Edit data.
5. Exit the system.

The option to print names and addresses will allow you to specify types of individuals to print data for. The system will be completely "menu-driven." That is, once you DO the main command file, jobs like adding new names, sorting, printing mailing labels, and editing will be performed by simply selecting menu options or answering questions on the screen. The system will be completely automated, so that an individual with no knowledge of dBASE III PLUS could still manage the mailing list.

Now that you have the general idea defined, you need to design a database that will support it.

STEP 2: DESIGN THE DATABASE STRUCTURE

Structure the database like this:

Record #	Field Name	Type	Width	Dec
1	LNAME	C	20	0
2	FNAME	C	15	0
3	ADDRESS	C	25	0
4	CITY	C	20	0
5	STATE	C	5	0
6	ZIP	C	10	0
7	PHONE	C	13	0

You've already created a database with this structure, MAIL, so this step is done already.

STEP 3: DEVELOP PSEUDOCODE

It's a little easier to write a program if you first write a reasonable facsimile of it in plain English. Doing so is called writing *pseudocode*. When you write pseudocode, you should try to specify the logic and series of events that will occur in the program, so that when you have to translate the program to actual dBASE language, much of the task is already defined. This isn't particularly easy, of course, because you're not accustomed to thinking like machines. But it's still easier to write a program from pseudocode jotted on a piece of paper than from pure thought. Here's a pseudocoded example of the Mail Menu program for your mailing system:

COMMAND FILE NAME: MENU.PRG
PURPOSE: Present a menu of options for managing the
              mailing list.
PSEUDOCODE:

✓ Set dBASE talk OFF.

✓ Use the mailing list database.

✓ Set menu choice to 0.

✓ Repeat the Mail Menu until option to exit is selected.

✓ Clear the screen.

✓ Display the Mail Menu like this:

Mail Menu
1. ADD new names
2. SORT data
3. PRINT labels
4. EDIT data
5. EXIT the mailing system

✓ Ask which option is desired

✓ If option **1** selected, APPEND new data.

✓ If option **2** selected, SORT by last and first name.

✓ If option **3** selected, PRINT mailing labels.

✓ If option **4** selected, EDIT data.

✓ Redisplay the Mail Menu (as long as option **5** was not selected).

✓ EXIT the mailing system.

Notice that you've defined the logic of the MENU program here. You've also given it a title and mentioned its purpose. If it takes a long time to write the actual program, you can refer back to the pseudocode for reference. Notice that the pseudocode describes the task in English, but it looks like a program, too. This intermediate step makes the next step a little easier. From this point, you can write the actual program using proper dBASE III PLUS commands and syntax.

STEP 4: WRITING THE PROGRAM

Once you have a pseudocoded outline of the program, you need to write the actual program. In dBASE, you use MODIFY

COMMAND for this. Let's now write the actual program. You cannot be as liberal with your sentences as you were in the pseudocode, because dBASE cannot understand English.

Type

MODIFY COMMAND MENU ⟵

which brings you a blank screen to work with. Now you can type the actual MENU program so that it looks like Program 14.1.

```
* * * * * * * * * * * Mailing List System Mail Menu
SET TALK OFF
USE MAIL
STORE 0 TO CHOICE
* * * * * * * * * * * Present Mail Menu
DO WHILE CHOICE < 5
   CLEAR
   ? '    Mail Menu'
   ?
   ? ' 1. Add new names'
   ? ' 2. Sort data'
   ? ' 3. Print labels'
   ? ' 4. Edit data'
   ? ' 5. Exit the mailing system'
   ?
   INPUT ' Enter your choice (1-5) from above: ' TO CHOICE
   * * * * * * * * * Perform appropriate task based on CHOICE
   DO CASE
      CASE CHOICE = 1
         APPEND
      CASE CHOICE = 2
         INDEX ON LNAME + FNAME TO NAMES
         USE MAIL INDEX NAMES
      CASE CHOICE = 3
         DO LABELS
      CASE CHOICE = 4
         EDIT
   ENDCASE
ENDDO
```

Program 14.1: MENU.PRG for Mailing List System

Now let's discuss how the actual program resembles the pseudo-code that you outlined. First, the command file sets the dBASE talk OFF, and uses MAIL as the database. Then, it stores a zero to a memory variable called CHOICE. This is so that the DO WHILE CHOICE < 5 condition will be true when dBASE first enters the loop. Then it clears the screen and displays the Mail Menu using ? commands. Then it displays the question, "Enter your choice (1-5) from above" and waits for an answer. When an answer has been entered, the program performs the desired option. If the choice was **1,** dBASE goes into APPEND mode. If the choice was **2,** dBASE will sort by last name; if the choice was **3,** dBASE will DO our other command file, LABELS, and so forth.

After the selected option has been performed, dBASE will eventually reach the ENDDO command at the bottom of the command file. The loop will repeat, redisplaying the Mail Menu and question. If the choice is **5,** *Exit the Mailing System,* the DO WHILE CHOICE < 5 condition for the loop will cause the ENDDO not to repeat the loop, and the program will end.

STEP 5: RUN AND TEST THE PROGRAM

Step 5 is not simply using the program, because as you probably know by now, you usually make a few mistakes in your program that need correcting. To test your program, of course, you still need to run it, so type this command:

DO MENU ↵

After the screen is cleared, the Mail Menu is displayed:

Mail Menu
1. Add new names
2. Sort data
3. Print labels
4. Edit data
5. Exit the mailing system
Enter your choice (1-5) from above:

If you now type **1,** dBASE will enter the APPEND mode:

```
LNAME   :_                    :
FNAME   :              :
ADDRESS :                        :
CITY    :                  :
STATE   :     :
ZIP     :       :
PHONE   :          :
```

So, anyone who types the command DO MENU can add new data to the database without typing the APPEND command. This is because the program has a line which states CASE CHOICE = 1, and beneath that is the APPEND command. Because CHOICE did = 1, dBASE goes into APPEND mode. You can then add as many names to the mailing list as you wish. When you exit the APPEND mode (by pressing Return instead of typing another name) the Mail Menu reappears:

```
Mail Menu
1.  Add new names
2.  Sort data
3.  Print data
4.  Edit data
5.  Exit the mailing system
Enter your choice (1-5) from above:
```

Why? Because none of the CASE clauses below the APPEND command in the program will be true. dBASE won't do the commands in CASE CHOICE = 2 or CASE CHOICE = 3, and so forth, because CHOICE = 1. When dBASE reaches the ENDDO command, CHOICE is less than 5, so the program loops around up to DO WHILE CHOICE < 5 command, and the menu is redisplayed, and the INPUT question reappears. You could type another option now, and whatever option you select (1-5) will be stored in CHOICE. Then, the appropriate function will take place (APPEND, INDEX, and so forth).

Notice in the command file that if you select option **3,** *Print labels,* dBASE is told to DO a different command file, your LABELS .PRG program. As you may recall, the last line in LABELS is the RETURN command. When one command file calls another, as in this case were MENU calls LABELS, the RETURN command tells dBASE to go back to where it left off in the first program. Therefore, MENU will DO LABELS, and LABELS will print the mailing labels and then RETURN to the next command in MENU.

We're assuming here that your program ran correctly the first time. More likely, it didn't, and you got one of dBASE's many error messages. You usually don't see the errors in a program until you try to run the program. The computer catches them right away. The most common errors that occur in command files are syntax errors, which result from misspelling a command, a field name, or a variable name. Syntax errors also occur if you forget to put spaces between commands, or if you attempt to use a field or memory variable that does not exist.

When dBASE encounters an error in a command file, it will display an error message and usually give you a chance to correct it. Let's look at an example. Suppose that when you asked dBASE to DO MENU, you got the message

```
Variable not found
  ?
CASE CHOCE = 1
Terminate command file? (Y/N)
```

At first glance, you may not see the problem. But on close inspection, you see that the word CHOICE is misspelled. dBASE attempted to find a memory variable called CHOCE, and couldn't. If you answer **Y** to the question "Terminate command file?" dBASE will return to the dot prompt. Then you can MODIFY COMMAND MENU to correct the error.

In the next chapter we'll discuss dBASE III PLUS debugging techniques which can help you find and correct errors in your own custom software systems. Then you'll develop a sophisticated mailing system using many of the techniques you've learned so far, and a few new ones, too.

REVIEWING PROGRAM DESIGN AND DEVELOPMENT

These are the steps to designing and developing a dBASE command file (program):

■ The first step to writing a program is to jot down a general idea of what the program will do.

■ The second step is to design and create the database structure.

■ The third step is to write a plain English version of the program (called pseudocode).

■ The fourth step is to actually write the program, using the pseudocode as an outline.

■ Finally, you need to test and debug the program.

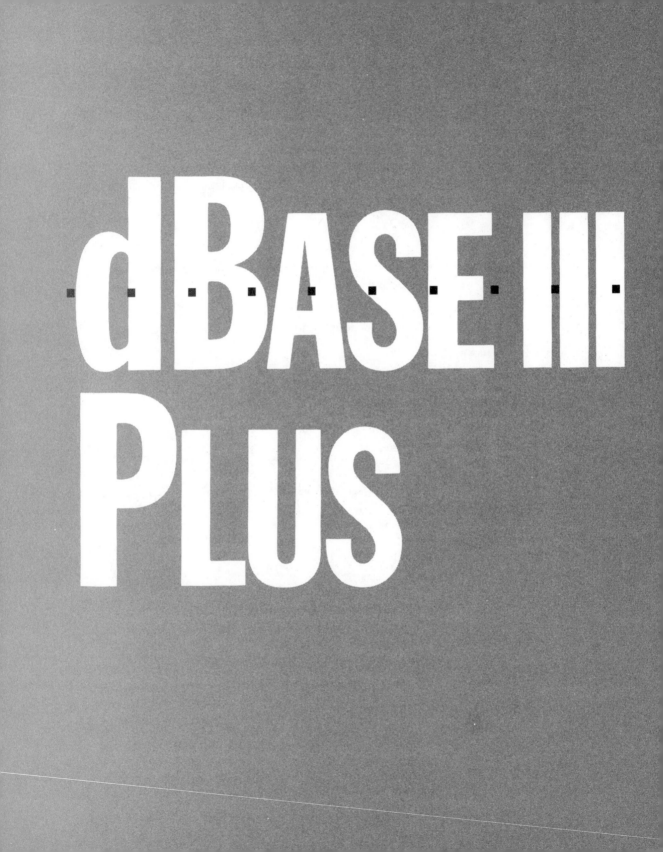

Debugging Techniques

When your programs fail to perform as expected, you often stare at the screen helplessly and think, "Now what do I do?" Some errors are fairly obvious and easy to fix, such as in the misspelling of CHOICE in the last chapter. Sometimes, however, dBASE will display a line as having an error in it, and you don't see the error. At that point, you may need to go deeper into your search for the error. Here are some good techniques that can help.

SUSPENDING A PROGRAM

As soon as dBASE encounters an error in a program, it will stop running the program and display a brief description of the error. You'll be given three choices at that point:

Cancel, Ignore, Suspend (C,I,S)

Selecting *Cancel* terminates the program and returns to the dot prompt. Selecting *Ignore* continues running the program beyond the faulty line. The *Suspend* option temporarily halts the program and returns to the dot prompt. From there, you can investigate possible errors and probably solve the problem.

When you suspend a program, the word "Suspended" appears in the Status Bar in the lower left corner of the screen. You can perform any number of tasks from the dot prompt before you enter the command

RESUME ↵

to get your program running again.

The Escape Key

Pressing Esc at any time while a program is running will stop the program and display the menu of *Cancel*, *Suspend*, and *Ignore* options. Therefore, you need not wait for an error message to analyze a portion of a program. Just press Esc, and select *Suspend* to get the dot prompt.

USING DISPLAY COMMANDS

When dBASE displays an error message, you might not be able to tell exactly where the problem is. You've already learned how to suspend the program. Now let's discuss some options you might try at the dot prompt to debug your program before you run it.

DISPLAY MEMORY

If you get an error message such as "Variable Not Found" or "Data Type Mismatch", there may be a missing memory variable, or an attempt to mix two data types (such as Character and Numeric) in a single expression. You can quickly check all memory variables by suspending the program and entering this command at the dot prompt:

DISPLAY MEMORY ↵

You'll notice that some variables are Private (priv) and others are Public (pub):

```
CHOICE        priv   N   2  (2.00000000)      C:MENU.PRG
TODAYSDATE    pub    D      03/31/86
   2 variables defined,        11 bytes used
 254 variables available,    5989 bytes available
```

Check to make sure that all of the program's variables exist and are of the correct data type. Public variables are those that are available to all programs at all times. Private variables are only used in the program that is currently suspended. In the example above, the variable CHOICE is a private variable, used only in the program MENU.PRG. The variable TODAYSDATE is the Date data type, and is Public.

In general, you do not need to concern yourself with Public and Private variables until you get into more advanced programming. For more information on these memory variables, see the PUBLIC and PRIVATE commands in your dBASE III PLUS manuals.

To make a printed copy of existing memory variables, enter the command shown below.

DISPLAY MEMORY TO PRINT ⏎

DISPLAY STRUCTURE

From the dot prompt you can also enter the command

DISPLAY STRUCTURE ⏎

or

DISPLAY STRUCTURE TO PRINT ⏎

to view the structure of the currently open database. Again, check to make sure that all the fields used by your program are available and are the correct data type. The DISPLAY STRUCTURE output for the MAIL.DBF database would look like this:

```
Structure for database: C:MAIL.DBF
Number of data records: 7
Date of last update : 01/09/85
```

Field	Field Name	Type	Width	Dec
1	LNAME	Character	15	
2	FNAME	Character	10	
3	ADDRESS	Character	25	
4	CITY	Character	15	
5	STATE	Character	5	
6	ZIP	Character	10	
7	PHONE	Character	13	
** Total **			94	

DISPLAY STATUS

The DISPLAY STATUS command provides lots of useful information for the programmer. From the dot prompt, simply enter this command:

DISPLAY STATUS ⏎

dBASE will tell you the names of all open database files and index files, as well as the contents of each index file. The list will look something like the following.

Currently Selected Database:
Select area: 1, Database in Use: C:MAIL.DBF   Alias: MAIL
Index file: C:NAMES.NDX Key: LNAME + FNAME
Index file: C:ZIP.NDX Key: ZIP

You'll also see additional information about the current status of dBASE III PLUS; however, these are less likely to help you to debug a program. (We discussed DISPLAY STATUS in more detail in Chapter 10.) Of course, you can enter the command

DISPLAY STRUCTURE TO PRINT ↵

to print a copy of the structure.

You can also use the SET ECHO, SET STEP, SET TALK, and SET DEBUG options, which we'll discuss in a moment, at the SUSPEND dot prompt. Just remember to type the command RESUME to get your program running again. (*Note:* You cannot use MODIFY COMMAND to change a program in SUSPEND mode. You'll have to press the Esc key, and/or select *Cancel* to get back to the normal dot prompt to use the MODIFY COMMAND editor.)

USING HISTORY COMMANDS

At any time in your work with dBASE III PLUS, you can enter the command:

DISPLAY HISTORY ↵

to view the last twenty commands you've entered at the dot prompt. These twenty commands will not include lines from a command file, unless you perform certain steps first.

First, at the dot prompt you can use the SET HISTORY command to determine how many lines will be recorded. When recording from a program, you may want to increase the default value of twenty to perhaps fifty or more, as in this command:

SET HISTORY TO 50 ↵

Next, before you run your program, enter the command

SET DOHISTORY ON

to ensure that command file lines are recorded in the history file.

When a program error occurs, you can suspend operation, and from the dot prompt enter the command

DISPLAY HISTORY ←┘

or

LIST HISTORY ←┘

to view the last fifty commands. (DISPLAY pauses the screen lines, but LIST does not. You can use the TO PRINT option with either command.)

The SET DOHISTORY ON command will slow down a program's performance dramatically. Therefore, when not debugging, be sure to enter the command

SET DOHISTORY OFF ←┘

at the dot prompt.

DEBUGGING WITH SET OPTIONS

There are several SET options that you can use to help pinpoint an error in a program. The SET commands let you see a program's progress in a line-by-line fashion, so you can watch the logical flow of events. Four SET commands are useful in debugging: TALK, ECHO, STEP, and DEBUG.

SET TALK ON

In the mailing list system command file, you SET TALK OFF at the top of the Mail Menu program. If you eliminate this line from the command file, and SET TALK ON before you DO the command file, dBASE's extraneous messages will be displayed on the screen. These extraneous messages can be useful to you for watching events as they occur in the command file. They may give you clues about errors in your program.

SET ECHO ON

An exaggerated version of SET TALK ON is the SET ECHO ON command. This displays every command line in the dBASE program as it is being processed. Thus, you can see everything that the command file is doing as it is running. It goes by pretty fast, but you can slow it down considerably with SET STEP ON.

SET STEP ON

If you want to follow the logic of your command file as it is running, step by step, leave ECHO ON, and SET STEP ON. Your command file will be processed one line at a time. As each line is processed, you can tell the program to pause, continue, or stop processing. This is great for those hard-to-find bugs that hide in tiny logical crevices.

SET DEBUG ON

The option to SET DEBUG ON can also be very helpful for getting at the hard-to-find errors. When the DEBUG parameter is ON, all the outputs from SET ECHO ON and/or SET STEP ON are sent directly to the printer and are not displayed on the screen. Hence, you can watch your command file perform on the screen without distraction from the ECHO command. On the printer, the actual lines within the command file, as well as their results, will appear as dBASE executes them. You can then study the hard copy of the events that occurred in the program. If other attempts to find the bug failed, this process will usually lead you to the source of the problem. You can place any of the SET commands (TALK, ECHO, STEP, DEBUG) into the program, and thereby isolate areas for debugging.

ANALYZING A HARD COPY OF THE PROGRAM

A printed copy of your program is very useful. To make a printed copy, be sure that the printer is ready. Then use the TYPE command with the name of the command file, including the .PRG extension, to print the program. For example, to print the MENU command file, type this command:

```
TYPE MENU.PRG TO PRINT ↵
```

When you get a hard copy, draw arrows from your DO WHILEs to their respective ENDDOs. Do likewise for IF . . . ENDIF clauses. You may find dangling DO WHILEs that don't have ENDDOs associated with them, or IFs and ENDIFs which are reversed and throwing everything out of whack. Program 15.1 is a printed command file with the DO . . . ENDDOs attached. Notice that each DO matches an ENDDO. Also notice that the arrows do not cross over one another. If the connecting line intersects, you have discovered a bug.

```
* * * * * * * * * * * Count to 5, 10 times
STORE 1 TO OUTLOOP
STORE 1 TO INLOOP
* * * * * * * * * * * Do outer-most loop 10 times
DO WHILE OUTLOOP < 11
    ? 'OUTER LOOP NUMBER : ' + STR(OUTLOOP,2)
    * * * * * * * * * For each outer loop, do 5 inner loops
    DO WHILE INLOOP < 6
        ? INLOOP
        STORE INLOOP + 1 TO INLOOP
    ENDDO (WHILE INLOOP < 6)
    STORE 1 TO INLOOP
    STORE OUTLOOP + 1 TO OUTLOOP
ENDDO (WHILE OULOOP < 11)
```

Program 15.1: Printed Program with Arrows Connecting DO Loops

It's easiest to draw the arrows connecting the smaller, innermost DO loops and IF clauses first. Then work your way outward to the larger loops and IF clauses. After you mark your routines in this way, study the program again. You may find errors in your logic.

Let's try out some debugging aids with a sample program which includes some errors. Using the command

MODIFY COMMAND TEST ↵

you can create and save the command file in Program 15.2. Now when you

DO TEST ↵

the program runs, but simply displays a dot prompt rather than the expected mailing labels for residents of the 92122 zip code area. Let's use the ECHO option to watch the program run.

```
* * * * * * * * * * * * TEST.PRG
SET TALK OFF
USE MAIL
GO BOTTOM
DO WHILE .NOT. EOF()
   IF ZIP = "92122"
      ? TRIM(FNAME), LNAME
      ? ADDRESS
      ? TRIM(CITY) + ",   " + STATE + ZIP
      ?
      ?
      ?
   ENDIF
SKIP
ENDDO
```

Program 15.2: Sample Program with Errors

Type this command:

SET ECHO ON ↵

Then run the program again:

    DO TEST ↵

This time, you can watch dBASE perform each step in the command file:

```
SET TALK OFF
USE MAIL
GO BOTTOM
DO WHILE .NOT. EOF()
   IF ZIP = "92122"
SKIP
ENDDO
```

If the echoed lines go by too fast to read, you can slow them down with the STEP option. Type this command:

    SET STEP ON ↵

Then run the program again:

    DO TEST ↵

This time, dBASE will process only one line and wait for you to press a key before processing the next line. Press any key to see each line until the dot prompt shows again. You'll see a scenario like this one:

```
SET TALK OFF
Press SPACE to stop, S to suspend, or Esc to cancel
USE MAIL
Press SPACE to stop, S to suspend, or Esc to cancel
GO BOTTOM
Press SPACE to stop, S to suspend, or Esc to cancel
DO WHILE .NOT. EOF()
Press SPACE to stop, S to suspend, or Esc to cancel
   IF ZIP = "92122"
Press SPACE to stop, S to suspend, or Esc to cancel
SKIP
Press SPACE to stop, S to suspend, or Esc to cancel
ENDDO
Press SPACE to stop, S to suspend, or Esc to cancel
```

Here you can see that the command file only went through the loop once, rather than enough times to check all the records in the database. Check to see that dBASE is really at the end of the command file. Type this command:

? EOF() ⏎

dBASE responds with

.T.

Hmmmm. Looking back at the command file, you see that one of the earlier lines reads GO BOTTOM. That's causing dBASE to start at the bottom of the file rather than at the top. To fix the error, type this command:

MODIFY COMMAND TEST ⏎

and change the GO BOTTOM to GO TOP, as in Program 15.3.

```
* * * * * * * * * * * * TEST.PRG
SET TALK OFF
USE MAIL
GO TOP
DO WHILE .NOT. EOF()
    IF ZIP = "92122"
        ? TRIM(FNAME),LNAME
        ? ADDRESS
        ? TRIM(CITY) + ",  " + STATE + ZIP
        ?
        ?
        ?
    ENDIF
SKIP
ENDDO
```

Program 15.3: Corrected TEST Program

Save the command file. Before you test it again, disable the ECHO and STEP to see the program run in its natural state:

SET STEP OFF ⏎
SET ECHO OFF ⏎

Then

> **DO TEST** ↵

The program prints out one mailing label:

> **Lucy Smithsonian**
> **461 Adams St.**
> **San Diego, CA 92122-1234**

Now you might want to make sure that the program was only supposed to print one label. You can check to make sure that the loop is repeating by setting ECHO ON again and running the command file. You'll see the command inside the DO WHILE loop repeat several times.

Another way to make sure that the program printed the correct labels is to use the LIST command from the dot prompt to see how many 92122s are in the database. From the dot prompt, type this command:

> **LIST FOR ZIP = '92122'** ↵

dBASE responds with:

Record#	LNAME	FNAME	ADDRESS	CITY	STATE	ZIP
5	Smithsonian	Lucy	461 Adams St.	San Diego	CA	92122

There is only one record in the database with the 92122 zip code. Therefore, the program performed correctly.

Unfortunately, debugging isn't always this easy. Learning to become a good troubleshooter takes as much experience as learning to be a good programmer.

Now let's have a little pep talk on debugging. All programs have bugs. They are big ones at first, but they eventually get refined to very small ones. Even software systems that have been in use for a while have bugs in them. The professional does not take bugs to heart, pout over them, or shake a fist at the CRT's blank stare (at least, not while anyone is looking). The computer can't do what the programmer *means,* and so everything is going to have to be spelled out clearly. The beginner, on the other hand, often feels intimidated, frustrated, or angered by software bugs, which is not good. One should not get one's ego involved with the software (at least, not until it's debugged and running).

The most important skill to develop in writing software is to break down big, complex problems into smaller, workable pieces. The second most important skill is to say exactly what you mean, using the computer's extremely limited vocabulary. Experience will help you to develop these skills. It's actually the debugging experience which will best help you to express yourself in computer language.

When you debug programs, just remember to check for these common programming errors:

√ Confusing character strings and numbers.

√ Dangling DO WHILEs and ENDIFs. Also, crossed loops and IF clauses, which cause an ENDIF to respond to the wrong IF, or an ENDDO to respond to the wrong DO WHILE.

√ Putting a command line in an IF . . . ENDIF clause when the command actually belongs outside the clause. This is a very common error which can ruin the program's results. Likewise, putting a command line inside a loop when it belongs outside the loop can cause infinite loops to occur. Similarly, forgetting to SKIP inside a 'DO WHILE .NOT. EOF()' loop will cause an infinite loop to occur. The loop will just keep rereading the first record.

√ Misspelling a command, memory variable name, or field name. If you create a field called ADDRESS, and later attempt to ? ADRESS or INDEX ON ADRESS, an error is sure to occur. You called the field ADDRESS, and you're telling dBASE to look for ADRESS, which does not exist.

√ Not bothering with design or pseudocode. When you come up with a good idea for a new program, you're tempted to just start typing it into the computer and make it up as you go along. This can lead to a tangled mess of commands in a program that is very difficult to untangle later. A little preplanning can save a lot of confusion.

REVIEWING DEBUGGING TECHNIQUES

In this chapter, you have learned a number of techniques to correct common programming errors:

▬

When an error occurs in a program, you'll be given options to *Cancel* the program, *Ignore* the error, or *Suspend* the program.

▬

Suspending a program allows you to analyze the current status of relevant databases and memory variables.

▬

The RESUME command resumes program execution after a SUSPEND operation.

▬

The SET DOHISTORY ON command stores commands from a program in a history file. The LIST HISTORY and DISPLAY HISTORY commands display the contents of the history file.

▬

The Esc key causes a program to stop running, and presents the *Cancel, Ignore,* and *Suspend* options.

▬

The SET TALK, SET ECHO, SET STEP, and SET DEBUG commands are all useful debugging aids.

▬

The TYPE command allows you to print a hard copy of a command file. Then analyze the logic of your program by drawing arrows to connect DO loops and IF clauses.

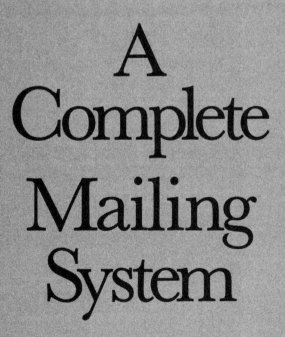

A
Complete
Mailing
System

I n this chapter you'll use the dBASE language to create a
menu-driven mailing system. The term *menu-driven* means that
the person using the programs that you develop need only
run one program. To perform various tasks, the end user will simply select options from a menu. Programmers create menu-driven
systems so that individuals who don't know the commands of a
language can still use the computer. The MENU command file
that you developed in the last chapter is such a program. In this
chapter you will develop a menu command file and four other
programs in a complete software system.

Most of the commands that you'll use will be pretty familiar to
you. The new commands are explained briefly as they are used.
The *Using dBASE III PLUS* manual contains elaborate descriptions
of every command. Refer to the *Commands* and *Functions* portions of
that manual for more technical information when you need it.

Appendix B of this book discusses an altogether different
approach to creating custom systems: You can design your basic
system, and then have the dBASE III PLUS Applications Generator write the programs for you!

In this chapter, however, you're going to integrate all of the
programming skills that you've learned up to this point, learn a
few new tricks, and put together a complete, easy-to-use mailing
system. Although the process is more complicated with a system
than with a single program, we'll still follow the procedure of
designing, describing, pseudocoding, then writing the programs.
(If you would rather not type all the programs discussed in this
chapter, see the Introduction for instructions for buying a disk with
all the programs on it.)

OVERVIEW OF THE
MAIN MENU STRUCTURE

The mailing list system of programs will be specifically designed
for ease of use. Even a complete novice will be able to manage the
mailing system through simple menu selections and answers to on-
screen questions.

Undocumented
Windows

ANDREW SCHULMAN
DAVID MAXEY
MATT PIETREK

Bestseller

"Undocumented Windows will
take a place of honor
on your bookshelf"
[–PC Magazine]

SECOND EDITION

UNDOCUMENTED
DOS

A PROGRAMMER'S GUIDE TO RESERVED
MS-DOS FUNCTIONS AND DATA STRUCTURES

THE
UNDOCUMENTED
PC

A PROGRAMMER'S GUIDE TO I/O, CPUs,
AND FIXED MEMORY AREAS

FRANK VAN GILLUWE

"Undocumented DOS is the
most informative DOS
programming book I have read"
[–Dr. Dobb's Journal]

UNDOCUMENTED
NETWARE

A PROGRAMMER'S GUIDE TO RESERVED
NETWORKING, APIs, AND PROTOCOLS

Available in

August 1994

Addison-Wesley

Your
Undocumented
Information
Source

Addison-Wesley Publishing Company

programs linked by the options of a
gram. Let's take a closer look at the
major components.

he heart of the mailing list system. It
ng that the user sees. When you first
n the command

n Menu
nd Addresses
Labels

Addresses
te Entries
ystem

each of these menu selections will accom-
en all the programs.

nes

and addresses to the database, the user
the Main Menu. Figure 16.1 shows the
ng new data into the mailing system.
ames, the user will automatically be returned

or a Directory

labels or a directory, the user selects option **2**
enu. First, the screen will display the options:

eport Option

bels
Main Menu
r choice : :

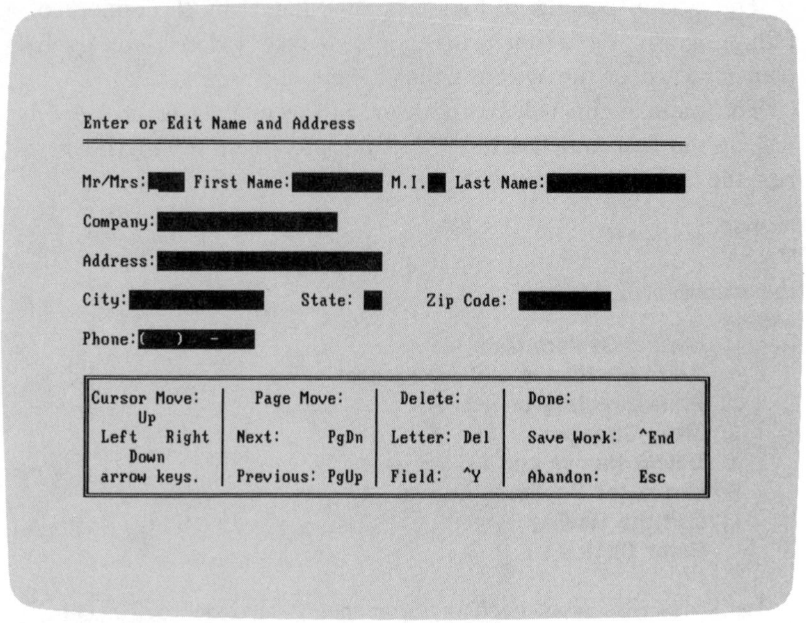

```
Enter or Edit Name and Address
_____

Mr/Mrs:▉▉  First Name:▉▉▉▉▉▉▉  M.I.▉  Last Name:▉▉▉▉▉▉▉▉

Company:▉▉▉▉▉▉▉▉▉▉▉▉

Address:▉▉▉▉▉▉▉▉▉▉▉▉

City:▉▉▉▉▉▉▉      State:▉    Zip Code:▉▉▉▉▉▉

Phone:(▉▉▉) ▉▉-▉▉▉▉

┌─────────────┬──────────────┬──────────────┬──────────────────┐
│Cursor Move: │ Page Move:   │ Delete:      │ Done:            │
│    Up       │              │              │                  │
│ Left  Right │ Next:   PgDn │ Letter: Del  │ Save Work:  ^End │
│   Down      │              │              │                  │
│ arrow keys. │ Previous: PgUp│ Field:  ^Y  │ Abandon:    Esc  │
└─────────────┴──────────────┴──────────────┴──────────────────┘
```

Figure 16.1: Screen for Entering New Names and Addresses

If option *3* is not selected, the screen will then display a menu of options for a sort order:

Select a Sort Order
1. **Alphabetical order by Name**
2. **Zip Code Order**
3. **Original Order**
   Enter your Choice : :

Next the screen displays these options:

Do you want (A)ll records, or (Q)uery?

Selecting *All* (by typing in the letter **A**) displays all records in the database. Selecting *Query* (by typing in **Q**) brings up a query form, as in Figure 16.2.

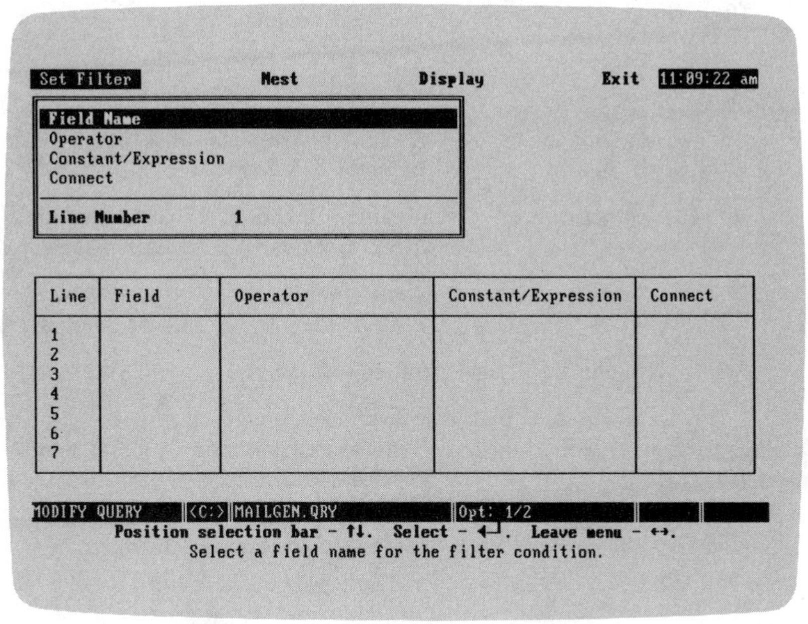

Figure 16.2: Query Form for the Mailing System

Because we've discussed these queries earlier, we won't repeat the details of completing the form now. When the form is filled in to search for particular records (such as STATE = CA) and the user selects the *Exit* and *Save* options from the menu, the program asks

Send report to the printer? (Y/N)

and waits for an answer. Answering **Y** sends the report to the printer; answer **N** displays it on the screen.

A sample of the directory report printed by this system is shown in Figure 16.3.

The mailing labels printed by the system are typical two-column labels, like those you created in Chapter 6.

After the report or mailing labels are printed, the system returns to the Mailing System Main Menu.

```
Page No.      1
01/09/86
```

Mailing System Directory

Adams, Ms. Annabelle A. 2344 Sixth St.	SYBEX International Berkeley, CA 94710	(415)848-8233
Appleby, Mr. Andy K.	American Icebergs 345 Oak St.	(555)453-1212 Los Angeles, CA 92123
Doe, Dr. Ruth A.	Zeerox, Inc. 1142 J. St.	(221)555-9911 Los Angeles, CA 91234
Smith, Mr. John L.	Petaluma Porsche 123 A St.	(555)111-2222 San Diego, CA 92123
Smithsonian, Mrs. Lucy Z.	BonaFide Dog Bones 461 Adams St.	(555)123-4567 San Diego, CA 92122-1234

Figure 16.3: Sample Directory from Mailing List System

Editing the Database

When the user selects option 3 from the Main Menu, the screen asks the user to

Enter last name of person to Edit
or just press Return to Quit :   **:**

Pressing the Return key returns the user to the Main Menu. If the user types a name, but nobody in the database has that name, the computer beeps and the screen displays this error message:

There is no <last name>
Press any key to try again

(*Note:* The incorrect last name that was entered will appear in place of <last name>.)

If the user types a last name, and there is only one record in the database with that last name, the system allows the user to make changes on the editing screen shown in Figure 16.4.

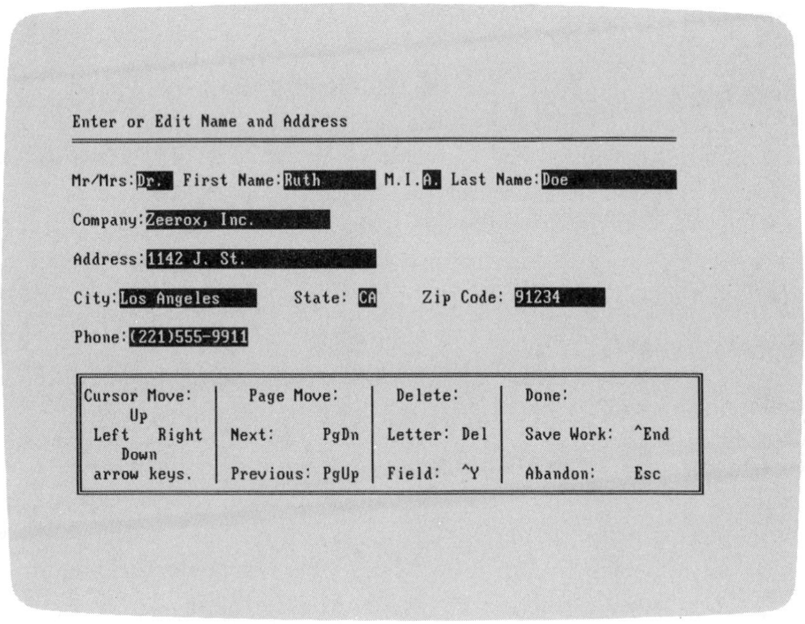

Figure 16.4: Mailing System Editing Screen

If more than one record contains the requested last name, the system checks for more information by displaying the identical names and asking for a record number, as in this example:

Record#	LNAME	FNAME	ADDRESS	CITY
1	Smith	Betsy	222 Lemon Dr.	New York
228	Smith	David	456 Alberston Dr.	Palm Springs
910	Smith	Kay	P.O. Box 1234	New York
75	Smith	Peter	123 A St.	San Diego

Edit which Record # ? : :

Typing one of the record numbers listed in the left-hand column will display that customer's record on the editing screen shown in Figure 16.4.

After editing names and addresses, the user is returned to the Mailing System Main Menu.

Deleting Records

To delete records, the user selects option **4** from the Main Menu. As with the editing option, the program first asks for the last name of the individual to delete. If no such record exists, a warning is issued and the user can try again. If several people with the requested last name are in the database, the system lists these names and asks for a record number. Once a record is identified, the system double checks:

Record#   LNAME   FNAME   ADDRESS   CITY
    1   **Smith**   **Betsy**   **222 Lemon Dr.**   **New York**
Delete this record? (Y/N) : :

The user can answer **Y** or **N**, and continue deleting more records. To stop deleting, the user simply presses Return rather than entering a last name.

Before returning to the Main Menu, the system double-checks before permanently deleting records:

Records to be deleted . . .
Record#   **LNAME**   **FNAME**   **ADDRESS**
    6   ***Doe**   **Ruth**   **1142 J. St.**
    5   ***Smith**   **John**   **123 A St.**
Delete all these? (Y/N) : :

If the answer is **N**o, the system allows the user to recall one of the records displayed by entering its record number. This process is repeated until the user answers **Y**es to the "Delete all these?" prompt, or until there are no records marked for deletion. When the deletion is verified, the system packs the database, thereby permanently removing the records.

Checking for Duplicates

Mailing lists tend to get duplicate names and addresses in them after a period of time, so this system has a built-in option to help find repeated data. To check for duplicates, the user selects option **5** from the Mailing System Main Menu. The program asks whether or not the duplicates should be printed, and then displays a report like the one shown below.

Possible Duplications

Record#	LNAME	FNAME	ADDRESS	CITY
1	Smith	Betsy	222 Lemon Dr.	New York
7	Smith	Betsy	222 Lemon Dr.	New York
9	Smith	Arnold	222 Lemon Dr.	New York
Record#	LNAME	FNAME	ADDRESS	CITY
2	Doe	Ruth	1142 J. St.	Los Angeles
5	Doe	Ruth	1142 J. St.	Los Angeles

Note that the *Check for Duplicate Entries* option only displays records that are similar enough to be duplicates. It does not actually delete any records. The final decision to delete a record is left to the user. The report acts as an aid to locating potential duplicates. Then the user must decide whether or not to delete them using the *Delete* option from the Main Menu.

Exiting the Mailing System

Option **6** from the Main Menu allows the user to exit the mailing system and return to the dBASE III PLUS dot prompt.

DATABASE DESIGN

For the custom mailing system, we'll use a slightly more sophisticated version of the MAIL.DBF database, named MAILDATA.DBF. You can create this database using the CREATE command from the dot prompt.

Note: If you are using a floppy-disk system, be sure to enter the command

SET DEFAULT TO B ⏎

before creating the database, index, report format, label format, screens, or command files discussed in this chapter.

Structure the new MAILDATA.DBF database as shown.

Structure for database: MAILDATA.DBF

Field	Field Name	Type	Width	Dec
1	MR_MRS	Character	4	0
2	LNAME	Character	15	0
3	FNAME	Character	10	0
4	MI	Character	2	0
5	COMPANY	Character	20	0
6	ADDRESS	Character	25	0
7	CITY	Character	15	0
8	STATE	Character	2	0
9	ZIP	Character	10	0
10	PHONE	Character	13	0

The index files for the new MAILDATA.DBF database can be created immediately after creating the database. First, to maintain an alphabetical sort by last and first name, enter the command

INDEX ON UPPER(LNAME + FNAME) TO MAILNAMS ↵

This command creates an index file named MAILNAMS.NDX that contains the last and first names, all in uppercase. Using the UPPER function in this index file achieves consistency in the way that names are stored in the index file. This makes it easier to manage searches later, as you'll see. To organize the records by a zip code order for bulk mailing, with names alphabetized within common zip codes, enter this command:

INDEX ON ZIP + LNAME TO MAILZIPS ↵

The MAILZIPS.NDX file will then maintain the sorted order by zip code.

The mailing system will automatically open and close the index files once you've created them. Should you decide to add or edit records on the MAILDATA database without using the programs in this chapter, be sure to open both index files:

USE MAILDATA INDEX MAILNAMS, MAILZIPS ↵

OVERVIEW OF SCREENS, REPORTS, AND LABELS

The custom mailing system uses new report, label, and screen formats. You will need to set up these formats before you write your programs.

Mailing System Screen

The custom screen for adding and editing data is named MAILSCRN. I used the dBASE III PLUS Screen Painter to create the screen as in Figure 16.5. Of course, you can design your screen however you wish.

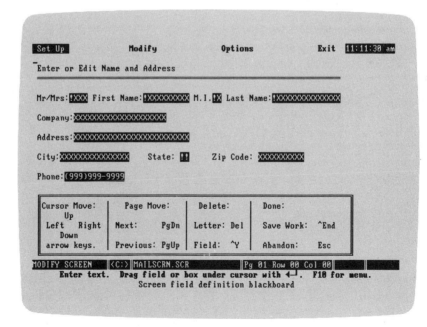

Figure 16.5: MAILSCRN Custom Editing Screen

Mailing System Directory

The report format for the directory is a little tricky, because you need two lines of information for each record in the database. Use the usual MODIFY or CREATE REPORT to build the report format, and name the file NEWDIREC.FRM.

On the first menu in the report generator, set the left margin to zero, and the double-space option to Yes. Enter any title, such as Mailing System Directory used in this example.

Define the first column of the report as below, with a length of 25. (Leave the Heading option blank).

```
TRIM(LNAME) + ", " + TRIM(MR_MRS) + " " + TRIM;
(FNAME) + " " + TRIM(MI) ←┘
```

This makes the first column of the report contain the last name followed by a comma and a space, the title (Mr./Mrs.), the first name, and the middle initial:

Livingston, Dr. Ann B.

Define the second column of the report format like this:

```
COMPANY + ADDRESS ←┘
```

Assign a width of 20 characters to the report column, and again no heading. Since the COMPANY field is already 20 characters long, the ADDRESS will wrap around to the line beneath the COMPANY. Hence, the two fields will be stacked vertically like this:

ABC Incorporated
1234 Pacific Hwy.

The third column is trickier still. We want the PHONE on the top line, and the CITY, STATE, and ZIP on the bottom line. We can assign a width of 30 characters to this column, but we need to ensure that the PHONE field is exactly 30 characters wide so that the CITY, STATE, and ZIP wrap around to the next line. Since the PHONE field is 13 characters wide, we'll add 17 blank spaces to pad it out to 30 spaces. The contents of the third column in the report are

PHONE + SPACE(17) + TRIM(CITY) + ″, ″ + STATE + ″ ″ZIP ⏎

Again, don't assign a heading to the column, and assign a width of 30 characters. When you print the report, each record will be stacked in two lines like this:

Adams, Ms. Anna A.   Sybex International   (415)848-8233
**   2344 Sixth St.   Berkeley, CA 94710**

Mailing System Labels

For mailing labels, use the usual CREATE or MODIFY LABEL commands, and name the label format file MAILLAB.LBL. Assign whatever size you wish, and fill in the Contents menu like this:

```
Label contents 1: MR_MRS,FNAME,MI,LNAME
               2: COMPANY
               3: ADDRESS
               4: TRIM(CITY) + ″, ″,STATE, ZIP
               5:
```

And that wraps up all the screens, reports, and label format files in the system. Before we start writing command files to manage all these files, let's get an overview of what our plan is here.

SOFTWARE STRUCTURE FOR THE MAILING SYSTEM

When designing a custom system with many command files, it's a good idea to take an extra step of drawing a hierarchical structure of how the programs interrelate. The structure for the mailing system is a fairly straightforward one, as shown in Figure 16.6.

The structural hierarchy shows that the system is broken down into major tasks, each representing a single command file. The MAIL.PRG command file is the Main Menu and is the highest in the hierarchy. The remaining command files are lower in the hierarchy, and are accessed directly from the MAIL.PRG command file using the DO command. Any time a lower-level program finishes its

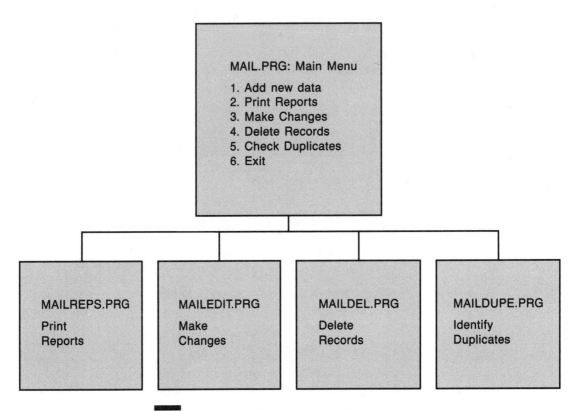

Figure 16.6: Software Structure for the Mailing System

task, it returns control to the calling program, MAIL.PRG.

Dividing a larger system into individual tasks and command files like this simplifies the bigger programming job. It is much easier to reach the goal of developing a large system when the task is composed of much smaller, more easily attained goals. Breaking the big job into smaller sections means that you can design, develop, and test each program in the system independently. Also, developing lots of smaller programs helps to avoid getting entangled in large masses of program code.

Now you can begin writing the five command files that make up the mailing list system.

MAIL.PRG: THE MAIN MENU

You've already developed a menu program (MENU.PRG), so this one will be easy. However, you should not skip the planning stage. Here is the pseudocode for the MAIL.PRG program:

COMMAND FILE NAME: MAIL.PRG
PURPOSE: Present a menu of options for the mailing list system.
PSEUDOCODE:
- ✓ Set up initial dBASE parameters.
- ✓ Open the database and index files.
- ✓ Begin loop for main menu.
- ✓   Clear the screen
- ✓   Display the main menu

> **Mailing System Main Menu**
> **1. Add new Names and Addresses**
> **2. Print Directory or Labels**
> **3. Make Changes**
> **4. Delete Names and Addresses**
> **5. Check for Duplicate Entries**
> **6. Exit the Mailing System**

- ✓   Get user's choice.
- ✓   Branch to the selected task or program.
- ✓ Repeat menu (if exit not requested).
- ✓ Otherwise, return to the dot prompt.

When you have written the pseudocode, you are ready to write the program. Program 16.1 is the complete MAIL.PRG command file. Let's talk about each routine in more detail.

The program begins with some opening comments that display the name of the program and its function. Then several dBASE parameters are set. First, SET TALK OFF keeps extraneous messages from appearing on the screen. Then, SET STATUS OFF turns off the reverse-video Status Bar at the bottom of the screen because it serves no purpose in the mailing system. The SET

DEFAULT TO C command makes a hard disk the default drive. On a floppy-disk system, this line should be changed to SET DEFAULT TO B.

```
*********** MAIL.PRG
*********** Mailing List Management System: dBASE III PLUS.
*---------- Set up initial parameters.
SET TALK OFF
SET STATUS OFF
SET DEFAULT TO C
*---------- Open the database and index files.
USE MAILDATA INDEX MAILNAMS,MAILZIPS
*---------- Begin loop for Main Menu.
CHOICE = 0
DO WHILE CHOICE <> 6
   CLEAR
   TEXT
                    Mailing System Main Menu

            1. Add new Names and Addresses

            2. Print Directory or Labels

            3. Make Changes

            4. Delete Names and Addresses

            5. Check for Duplicate Entires

            6. Exit the Mailing System

   ENDTEXT
   *---------- Get user's choice
   @ 16,20 SAY "Enter choice " GET CHOICE;
      PICTURE "9" RANGE 1,6
   READ

   *---------- Branch to appropriate task or program.
   DO CASE

      CASE CHOICE = 1
         SET FORMAT TO MAILSCRN
         APPEND
         CLOSE FORMAT
```

▬▬

Program 16.1: MAIL.PRG Command File

```
          CASE CHOICE = 2
              DO MAILREPS

          CASE CHOICE = 3
              DO MAILEDIT

          CASE CHOICE = 4
              DO MAILDEL

          CASE CHOICE = 5
              DO MAILDUPE

      ENDCASE

   ENDDO (while choice < > 6)

*---------- Done with program. Return to dot prompt.
SET TALK ON
SET STATUS ON
RETURN
```

Program 16.1: MAIL.PRG Command File (continued)

The next routine in MAIL.PRG looks like this:

```
*------- Open the database and index files.
USE MAILDATA INDEX MAILNAMS,MAILZIPS
```

It opens the MAILDATA.DBF database and the MAILNAMS.NDX and MAILZIPS.NDX index files.

Next a DO WHILE loop, which repeats until the user selects **6** to exit, displays a menu of options. The TEXT and ENDTEXT commands display all lines in between as simple text on the screen or printer. This is a shortcut to using many ? or @ commands. The top of the loop and the menu definition look like this:

```
*------- Begin loop for Main Menu.
CHOICE = 0
DO WHILE CHOICE < > 6
   CLEAR
   TEXT
           Mailing System Main Menu
       1. Add new Names and Addresses
```

```
      2. Print Directory or Labels
      3. Make Changes
      4. Delete Names and Addresses
      5. Check for Duplicate Entries
      6. Exit the Mailing System
   ENDTEXT
```

Next, a small routine waits for the user's menu choice. The @, SAY, GET, and READ commands are used in this example. The PICTURE "9" portion forces the user to enter a number (not a character), and the RANGE 1,6 portion forces a number between 1 and 6. A number outside this range is rejected, and the user is asked to try again. This routine gets the user's input:

```
*-------- Get user's choice
@ 16,20 SAY "Enter choice " GET CHOICE;
   PICTURE "9" RANGE 1,6
READ
```

Next, a DO CASE clause decides what to do, based upon the user's menu selection. If the user selects option **1** to add new records, the program sets the screen format to the MAILSCRN.FMT format file and allows the user to add new records with the APPEND command. When the user finishes, the screen is set back to normal (CLOSE FORMAT), and the menu loop repeats.

Other menu options require branching to external programs, as shown in the DO CASE clause:

```
*--- Branch to appropriate task or program.
DO CASE
   CASE CHOICE = 1
      SET FORMAT TO MAILSCRN
      APPEND
      CLOSE FORMAT
   CASE CHOICE = 2
      DO MAILREPS
   CASE CHOICE = 3
      DO MAILEDIT
   CASE CHOICE = 4
      DO MAILDEL
   CASE CHOICE = 5
      DO MAILDUPE
ENDCASE
```

The bottom of the MAIL.PRG command file marks the end of the DO WHILE loop and the end of the program (when the user selects option **6** to exit). Because dBASE ignores all words to the right of an ENDDO or ENDIF command, you can add programmer comments there, which make good reminders about which ENDDO goes with which DO WHILE, and which ENDIF goes with which IF. Before returning to the dot prompt, the program sets some dBASE III PLUS parameters back to normal, as shown in the closing lines of the MAIL.PRG command file:

```
ENDDO (while choice < > 6)
*--- Done with program. Return to dot prompt.
SET TALK ON
SET STATUS ON
RETURN
```

MAILREPS.PRG: PRINTING MAIL REPORTS

The MAILREPS.PRG command file displays a menu of report choices, a menu of sort orders, an option to display all records or create a query, and an option to display the report on the screen or printer. Here is the pseudocode for the MAILREPS.PRG command file:

COMMAND FILE NAME: MAILREPS.PRG
PURPOSE: Display sort and report options, and print reports.
PSEUDOCODE:

√ Clear screen and ask which report to print.

   1. Directory
   2. Mailing Labels
   3. None: Return to menu

√ If no report requested, return to Main Menu.
√ Display sort order options, and get selection.

1. Alphabetical Order by Name
2. Zip Code Order
3. Original Order

✓ Use appropriate index file based on sort selection.
✓   If alphabetical sort, use MAILNAMES.NDX.
✓   If zip code sort, use MAILZIPS.NDX.
✓   If no sort, don't use an index.
✓ Ask about query options.
✓   If query requested, display query form, allow changes, then filter database.
✓ Ask about the printer.
✓ Print the report.
✓   If directory requested, use NEWDIREC format.
✓   If labels requested, use MAILLAB label format.
✓ Pause screen if printer not selected.
✓ Set filter and index files back to normal.
✓ Return to Main Menu.

When you've written the pseudocode, you are ready to write the program. Program 16.2 is the complete MAILREPS.PRG command file. Let's take a closer look at its routines.

```
* * * * * * * * * * * * MAILREPS.PRG
*---------- Reports Program for Mailing System.

*---------- Clear screen and ask which report.
CLEAR
TEXT

                        Select a Report Option

            1. Directory

            2. Mailing Labels

            3. Return to Main Menu
ENDTEXT

*---------- Initialize variable and ask for report choice.
REPCHOICE = 0
@ 14,20 SAY "Enter your choice (1-3) " ;
    GET REPCHOICE PICTURE "9" RANGE 1,3
```

▬▬
Program 16.2: MAILREPS.PRG Command File

```
READING

*---------- If return requested, return to Main Menu.
IF REPCHOICE = 3
   RETURN
ENDIF

*---------- Ask about sort order.
CLEAR
TEXT

                          Select a Sort Order

                 1.  Alphabetical order by Name

                 2.  Zip Code Order

                 3.  Original Order
ENDTEXT
*---------- Initialize variable and ask for sort choice.
SORTCHOICE = 0
@ 14,20 SAY "Enter your choice (1-3) " ;
   GET SORTCHOICE PICTURE "9" RANGE 1,3
READ

*---------- Use appropriate index file.
DO CASE

   CASE SORTCHOICE = 1
      SET INDEX TO MAILNAMS

   CASE SORTCHOICE = 2
      SET INDEX TO MAILZIPS

   CASE SORTCHOICE = 3
      CLOSE INDEX

ENDCASE

*---------- Ask about query.
CLEAR
QCHOICE = "A"
@ 10,5 SAY ;
   "Do you want (A)ll records, or a (Q)uery? ";
   GET QCHOICE PICTURE "!"
```

Program 16.2: MAILREPS.PRG Command File (continued)

```
READ

*---------- Display query form if requested.
IF QCHOICE = "Q"
   MODIFY QUERY MAILGEN
   SET FILTER TO FILE MAILGEN
ENDIF

*---------- Ask about the printer.
PMACRO = " "
TOPRINT = "N"
CLEAR
@ 10,5 SAY "Send report to printer? (Y/N) ";
   GET TOPRINT PICTURE "!"
READ

*---------- Make a macro if printer requested.
IF TOPRINT = "Y"
   PMACRO = "TO PRINT"
ENDIF

*---------- Now print the report.
DO CASE

   CASE REPCHOICE = 1
      REPORT FORM NEWDIREC &PMACRO

   CASE REPCHOICE = 2
      LABEL FORM MAILLAB &PMACRO

ENDCASE

*---------- If printer was not selected, pause
*---------- before returning to menu.
IF TOPRINT &LT> "Y"
   @ 24,1 CLEAR
   WAIT "Press any key to return to menu . . . "
ENDIF

*---------- When report is done, set filter and
*---------- index files back to normal, and then
*---------- return to Main Menu.
SET FILTER TO
SET INDEX TO MAILNAMS,MAILZIPS
RETURN
```

————

Program 16.2: MAILREPS.PRG Command File (continued)

The MAILREPS.PRG command file opens with some comments, a command to clear the screen, and a menu of report choices displayed with the TEXT . . . ENDTEXT commands. Then an @, SAY, GET, READ combination is used to wait for and store the user's menu choice. These first lines of the command file also store the user's menu selection in a variable named REPCHOICE:

```
* * * * * * * * * * * * MAILREPS.PRG
*---------- Reports Program for Mailing System.
*---------- Clear screen and ask which report.
CLEAR
TEXT
                Select a Report Option
        1.  Directory
        2.  Mailing Labels
        3.  Return to Main Menu
ENDTEXT
*---------- Initialize variable and ask for report choice.
REPCHOICE = 0
@ 14,20 SAY "Enter your choice (1-3) " ;
    GET REPCHOICE PICTURE "9" RANGE 1,3
READ
```

If the user simply requests to return to the menu, the IF clause below sends him back immediately:

```
*---------- If return requested, return to main menu.
IF REPCHOICE = 3
    RETURN
ENDIF
```

Next, a routine displays a menu of sort options, and then a DO CASE clause sets up the appropriate index file (or no index file) for the sort. The routine looks like this:

```
*---------- Ask about sort order.
CLEAR
TEXT
                Select a Sort Order
        1.  Alphabetical order by Name
        2.  Zip Code Order
        3.  Original Order
ENDTEXT
*---------- Initialize variable and ask for sort choice.
```

```
SORTCHOICE = 0
@ 14,20 SAY "Enter your choice (1-3) " ;
   GET SORTCHOICE PICTURE "9" RANGE 1,3
READ
*---------- Use appropriate index file.
DO CASE
   CASE SORTCHOICE = 1
      SET INDEX TO MAILNAMS
   CASE SORTCHOICE = 2
      SET INDEX TO MAILZIPS
   CASE SORTCHOICE = 3
      CLOSE INDEX
ENDCASE
```

Next, the program asks if the user wants to print all the records in the database or to set up a Query. The user's response is stored in a variable named QCHOICE. The PICTURE "!" portion converts the user's answer to uppercase as soon as it is entered. The routine looks like this:

```
*---------- Ask about query.
CLEAR
QCHOICE = "A"
@ 10,5 SAY ;
   "Do you want (A)ll records, or a (Q)uery? ";
   GET QCHOICE PICTURE "!"
READ
```

If the user opts to query the database, a Query form named MAILGEN.QRY is brought to the screen for the user to fill in or edit. When completed, the SET FILTER TO FILE command, as shown in this routine, activates the query form and sets up the filter:

```
*---------- Display query form if requested.
IF QCHOICE = "Q"
   MODIFY QUERY MAILGEN
   SET FILTER TO FILE MAILGEN
ENDIF
```

Next a small routine asks the user if the report should be printed. The user's answer is stored in the variable TOPRINT, as shown in the following.

```
*---------- Ask about the printer.
PMACRO = " "
TOPRINT = "N"
CLEAR
@ 10,5 SAY "Send report to printer? (Y/N) ";
    GET TOPRINT PICTURE "!"
READ
```

If the user opts for the printer, a variable named PMACRO is assigned the words "TO PRINT" which will be used for macro substitution later in the program:

```
*---------- Make a macro if printer requested.
IF TOPRINT = "Y"
    PMACRO = "TO PRINT"
ENDIF
```

Finally, the program prints the requested report, based on the user's original report selection (the REPCHOICE variable). The DO CASE clause decides which report to print. Note the use of the &PMACRO macro. If the user requested that the report be printed, the words TO PRINT will be added to the REPORT or LABEL command lines, thereby printing the output. If the printer was not selected, a blank space will be substituted into the end of the LABEL and REPORT commands, and the output will be directed to the screen. The routine looks like this:

```
*---------- Now print the report.
DO CASE
    CASE REPCHOICE = 1
        REPORT FORM NEWDIREC &PMACRO
    CASE REPCHOICE = 2
        LABEL FORM MAILLAB &PMACRO
ENDCASE
```

To keep the report from disappearing from the screen too quickly (if the report was not printed), the program pauses before returning control to the Main Menu, as shown in this routine:

```
*---------- If printer was not selected, pause
*---------- before returning to menu.
IF TOPRINT <> "Y"
    @ 24,1 CLEAR
```

```
        WAIT "Press any key to return to menu . . . "
    ENDIF
```

Before returning control to the Main Menu, the FILTER is deactivated (so all records become accessible), and the normal index files are reactivated, as shown in this routine:

```
*---------- When report is done, set filter and
*---------- index files back to normal, and then
*---------- return to Main Menu.
SET FILTER TO
SET INDEX TO MAILNAMS,MAILZIPS
RETURN
```

MAILEDIT.PRG: EDITING RECORDS

The MAILEDIT.PRG command file allows the user quick and easy access to records for editing. Program 16.3 shows the MAIL-EDIT.PRG command file, and its pseudocode appears below.

COMMAND FILE NAME: MAILEDIT.PRG
PURPOSE: Locate and modify a record.
PSEUDOCODE:

√ Set up loop for editing records.
√   Ask for last name of person to look up.
√   If no name entered, return to Main Menu.
√   Convert LOOKUP to uppercase to match index file.
√   Try to find requested name.
√   Count how many records have requested name.
√   If no records have that name, ask the user to try again.
√   If several records have that name, get more information.
√   If record identified, display it on custom screen.
√ Allow edits until exit requested.
√ Return to Main Menu.

```
* * * * * * * * * * * MAILEDIT.PRG
* Lookup and Edit Names on the MAILDATA Database.
*---------- Set up loop for editing records.
STILLATIT = .T.
DO WHILE STILLATIT

    *---------- Ask for last name of person to look up.
    CLEAR
    LOOKUP = SPACE(15)
    @ 10,12 SAY "Enter last name of person to edit"
    @ 12,12 SAY "or just press Return to exit ";
       GET LOOKUP
    READ

    *---------- If no name entered, skip all commands
    *---------- between here and Enddo.
    IF LOOKUP = " "
       STILLATIT = .F.
       LOOP
    ENDIF (LOOKUP = " ")

    *---------- Convert LookUp to uppercase to match
    *---------- index file.
    LOOKUP = UPPER(LOOKUP)

    *---------- Try to find requested name, and
    *---------- remember record number.
    SEEK LOOKUP
    RECNUMB = RECNO()

    *---------- Count how many there are.
    COUNT WHILE UPPER(LNAME) = LOOKUP TO HOWMANY

    *---------- If no record has that name,
    *---------- ask the user to try again.
    IF HOWMANY = 0
       @ 20,10 SAY "There is no &LOOKUP"
       @ 22,10 SAY "Press a key to try again"
       ? CHR(7)
       WAIT " "
       RECNUMB = 0
    ENDIF (HOWMANY = 0)
```

▄▄▄

Program 16.3: MAILEDIT.PRG Command File

```
*---------- If more than one record has that last
*---------- name, get more information.
IF HOWMANY > 1
   CLEAR
   RECNUMB = 0
   SEEK LOOKUP
   LIST LNAME, FNAME, ADDRESS, CITY;
      WHILE UPPER(LNAME) = LOOKUP
   @ ROW()+3, 10 SAY "Edit which Record # ? ";
      GET RECNUMB PICTURE "9999"
   READ
ENDIF

*---------- If there is a record number greater than
*---------- zero at this point, edit the record.
IF RECNUMB > 0
   GOTO RECNUMB
   SET FORMAT TO MAILSCRN
   READ
   CLOSE FORMAT
ENDIF

ENDDO (while STILLATIT)

RETURN
```

▬

Program 16.3: MAILEDIT.PRG Command File (continued)

This program demonstrates many basic programming techniques for quickly accessing data through index files. The program starts with the usual opening comments and description. A DO WHILE loop controls a logical variable named STILLATIT, as shown in the first routine:

```
*********** MAILEDIT.PRG
*********** Lookup and Edit Names on the MAILDATA database.
*---------- Set up loop for editing records.
STILLATIT = .T.
DO WHILE STILLATIT
```

Within the loop, the program creates a character variable named LOOKUP, which is exactly fifteen spaces long (the same length as the LNAME field in the MAILDATA.DBF database). An @, SAY, GET, READ combination then asks the user to type the last name of the customer's record to be edited. The user's entry is stored in the LOOKUP variable, as shown in this routine:

```
*---------- Ask for last name of person to look up.
CLEAR
LOOKUP = SPACE(15)
@ 10,12 SAY "Enter last name of person to edit"
@ 12,12 SAY "or just press Return to exit ";
   GET LOOKUP
READ
```

If the user does not enter a name but presses Return, the program is signaled that the user is finished editing, and therefore returns control to the Main Menu. It accomplishes this task by setting the STILLATIT variable (which controls the DO WHILE loop) to False (.F.), and by forcing the program to pass control directly to the ENDDO command (LOOP), as shown in this routine:

```
*---------- If no name entered, skip all commands
*---------- between here and ENDDO
IF LOOKUP = " "
   STILLATIT = .F.
   LOOP
ENDIF (LOOKUP = " ")
```

If the user does not request to exit, then the program looks up the name that the user entered. First, remember that when you created the NAMES.NDX index, you used the UPPER function to convert all names to uppercase for consistency. So here, the program can convert the user's entry to uppercase. Therefore, we need not be concerned about how the user enters the name to look up (e.g. SMITH, Smith, smith, or SmItH), because the program automatically converts everything to uppercase. The LOOKUP variable is converted to uppercase by the following line:

```
*---------- Convert LOOKUP to uppercase to match
*---------- index file.
LOOKUP = UPPER(LOOKUP)
```

Next, the program attempts to quickly find the requested last name in the NAMES.NDX index file (which is always active in this system). The program records the number of the record where the SEEK positions the pointer in a variable named RECNUMB, as shown in the following routine. RECNUMB will come in handy later in the program for quickly getting the pointer back to the record to edit.

```
*---------- Try to find requested name, and
*---------- remember record number.
SEEK LOOKUP
RECNUMB = RECNO( )
```

Next, the program counts how many records contain the requested last name using a COUNT command. Because the database is in alphabetical order by last name, due to the NAMES.NDX index file, the faster WHILE option can be used rather than the slower FOR option. Note that the results of the following COUNT command are stored in a memory variable named HOWMANY:

```
*---------- Count how many there are.
COUNT WHILE UPPER(LNAME) = LOOKUP TO HOWMANY
```

Now the program has to decide what to do next. If the name that the user entered is not in the database, then the program displays an error message, beeps (the ? CHR(7) line), and waits for the user to press any key. The &LOOKUP enclosed in quotation marks is a macro that will display the invalid last name when the program runs. The following IF clause handles the situation when the user enters a name which is not in the database:

```
*---------- If no record has that name,
*---------- ask the user to try again.
IF HOWMANY = 0
    @ 20,10 SAY "There is no &LOOKUP"
    @ 22,10 SAY "Press a key to try again"
    ? CHR(7)
    WAIT " "
    RECNUMB = 0
ENDIF (HOWMANY = 0)
```

If several records contain the last name entered by the user, the program needs more information. So, first it clears the screen, and then it SEEKs the first record in the database with the requested last name. (The COUNT command above moved the pointer, so now it has to be repositioned.) A LIST command lists all individuals with the requested last name (including record number), and an @, SAY, GET, READ combination asks the user to select a record by typing its number. The following IF clause handles this situation:

```
*---------- If more than one record has that last
*---------- name, get more information.
IF HOWMANY > 1
   CLEAR
   RECNUMB = 0
   SEEK LOOKUP
   LIST LNAME, FNAME, ADDRESS, CITY;
      WHILE UPPER(LNAME) = LOOKUP
   @ ROW( )+3, 10 SAY "Edit which Record # ? ";
      GET RECNUMB PICTURE "9999"
   READ
ENDIF
```

By this time, one of two possible conditions exists. Either a record has been identified to edit, and its number stored in the RECNUMB variable, or no record has been defined, and the RECNUMB variable equals zero. If a record has been identified, the program sets up the MAILSCRN.FMT format file and allows the user to edit the record, as shown in the following IF clause:

```
*---------- If there is a record number greater than
*---------- zero at this point, edit the record.
IF RECNUMB > 0
GOTO RECNUMB
   SET FORMAT TO MAILSCRN
   READ
   CLOSE FORMAT
ENDIF
```

When the user stops requesting records to edit, the program falls out of the DO WHILE loop and returns control to the Main Menu, as shown in the closing lines of the program:

```
ENDDO (while STILLATIT)
RETURN
```

MAILDEL.PRG: DELETING RECORDS

The MAILDEL.PRG command file is similar to the MAIL-EDIT.PRG command file, in that it calls up a record for a specific task to be performed by the user. Program 16.4 shows the MAILDEL.PRG command file, and its pseudocode appears below.

COMMAND FILE NAME: MAILDEL.PRG
PURPOSE: Locate and delete a record
PSEUDOCODE:

✓ Set up loop for deleting records.
✓   Ask for last name of person to delete.
✓   If no name entered, return to Main Menu.
✓   Convert LOOKUP to uppercase to match index file.
✓   Try to find requested name.
✓   Count how many people have requested name.
✓   If no records contain that name, ask user to try again.
✓   If several records have that name, get more information.
✓   If record identified, ask for permission to delete it.
✓   If permission granted, mark the record for deletion.
✓ Allow more deletions until exit requested.
✓ Count how many records are marked for deletion.
✓ While there are still records marked for deletion
✓   Display records marked for deletion.
✓   Ask for permission to permanently delete.
✓   If permission not granted
✓   Allow user to recall one record.
✓   Decrement counter of deleted records.
✓   If permission to delete is granted
✓   Pack the database.
✓ Continue displaying and asking for permission until granted.
✓ Return to Main Menu.

* * * * * * * * * * * MAILDEL.PRG
* Lookup and Delete Names on the MAILDATA database.

```
*---------- Set up loop for deleting records.
STILLATIT = .T.
DO WHILE STILLATIT

   *---------- Ask for last name of person to look up.
   CLEAR
   LOOKUP = SPACE(15)
   @ 10,12 SAY "Enter last name of person to delete"
   @ 12,12 SAY "or just press Return to exit ";
      GET LOOKUP
   READ

   *---------- If no name entered, skip all commands
   *---------- between here and Enddo.
   IF LOOKUP = " "
      STILLATIT = .F.
      LOOP
   ENDIF (lookup = " ")

   *---------- Convert LOOKUP to uppercase to match
   *---------- index file.
   LOOKUP = UPPER(LOOKUP)

   *---------- Try to find requested name, and
   *---------- remember record number.
   SEEK LOOKUP
   RECNUMB = RECNO()

   *---------- Count how many there are.
   COUNT WHILE UPPER(LNAME) = LOOKUP TO HOWMANY

   *---------- If no record has that name, warn
   *---------- the user to try again.
   IF HOWMANY = 0
      @ 20,10 SAY "There is no &LOOKUP"
      @ 22,10 SAY "Press a key to try again"
      ? CHR(7)
      WAIT " "
      RECNUMB = 0
   ENDIF (HOWMANY = 0)

   *---------- If more than one record has that
   *---------- last name, get more information.
```

▄▄▄▄

Program 16.4: MAILDEL.PRG Command File

```
IF HOWMANY > 1
   CLEAR
   RECNUMB = 0
   SEEK LOOKUP
   LIST LNAME, FNAME, ADDRESS, CITY;
      WHILE UPPER(LNAME) = LOOKUP
   @ ROW()+3, 10 SAY "Delete which one? ";
      GET RECNUMB PICTURE "9999"
READ
ENDIF


*---------- If there is a record number greater than
*---------- zero at this point, double check then delete.
IF RECNUMB > 0
   GOTO RECNUMB
   CLEAR
   DISPLAY LNAME, FNAME, ADDRESS, CITY
   ?
   WAIT "Delete this record? (Y/N) " TO ANSWER
   *---------- If answer is yes,
   *---------- mark record for deletion.
   IF UPPER(ANSWER) = "Y"
      DELETE RECORD RECNUMB
   ENDIF (ANSWER)
ENDIF (RECNUMB > 0)


ENDDO (while STILLATIT)

*---------- Before exiting, verify deletions and pack.
COUNT FOR DELETED() TO NODELS
OKTOPACK = "N"
DO WHILE OKTOPACK = "N" .AND. NODELS > 0
   CLEAR
   ? "Records to be deleted . . . "
   ?
   DISPLAY LNAME, FNAME, ADDRESS FOR DELETED()
   @ 23,1 SAY "Delete all these? (Y/N) ";
      GET OKTOPACK PICTURE "!"
   READ
   IF OKTOPACK <> "Y"
      *---------- If not ok to pack, recall a record.
      DELREC = 0
      @ 23,1 SAY "Recall which one (by record #)";
```

Program 16.4: MAILDEL.PRG Command File (continued)

```
        GET DELREC PICTURE "9999"
    READ
    *---------- If record number entered, and record
    *---------- is indeed deleted, recall it.
    IF DELREC > 0
       GOTO DELREC
       IF DELETED()
          RECALL RECORD DELREC
          NODELS = NODELS - 1
       ENDIF (deleted)
    ENDIF (DELREC > 1)
 ELSE
    *---------- If ok to pack, do so and show progress.
    SET TALK ON
    PACK
    SET TALK OFF
 ENDIF (OKTOPACK)
ENDDO (OKTOPACK)
RETURN
```

Program 16.4: MAILDEL.PRG Command File (continued)

The basic technique for pinpointing a record to delete is identical to the technique used by MAILEDIT.PRG to locate records. However, when a record is pinpointed, this program does not allow editing. Instead, it simply shows a portion of the record and asks for permission to delete it. If the user enters **Y** to delete the record, the DELETE RECORD command marks the record for deletion, as shown in the following IF clauses:

```
    *---------- If there is a record number greater than
    *---------- zero at this point, double check then delete.
 IF RECNUMB > 0
    GOTO RECNUMB
    CLEAR
    DISPLAY LNAME, FNAME, ADDRESS, CITY
    ?
    WAIT "Delete this record? (Y/N) " TO ANSWER
    *---------- If answer is yes,
    *---------- mark record for deletion.
    IF UPPER(ANSWER) = "Y"
       DELETE RECORD RECNUMB
    ENDIF (ANSWER)
 ENDIF (RECNUMB > 0)
```

The user can delete any number of records in this fashion. Before returning to the Main Menu, the program verifies all deletions by giving the user a chance to reconsider. First the program counts the number of records that are marked for deletion using the COUNT command. The result is stored in a variable named NODELS.

Then, a DO WHILE loop displays the records that are marked for deletion and asks the user, "Delete all these?" If the user answers **N**o, the program allows the user to recall a record (by record number), and then displays the remaining records that are marked for deletion and again allows the user to verify. This process continues until either the user answers **Y**es to the "Delete all these?" prompt, or until there are no more records marked for deletion (NODELS = 0). Once records are verified for deletion, the PACK command removes them from the database permanently. Because it takes some time to pack the database and rebuild the index files, the SET TALK ON command is used to display messages about dBASE's progress during this phase. When packing is complete, the TALK parameter is turned back OFF and control is passed back to the Main Menu, as shown in the closing routine:

```
*---------- Before exiting, verify deletions and pack.
COUNT FOR DELETED( ) TO NODELS
OKTOPACK = "N"
DO WHILE OKTOPACK = "N" .AND. NODELS > 0
   CLEAR
   ? "Records to be deleted . . . "
   ?
   DISPLAY LNAME, FNAME, ADDRESS FOR DELETED( )
   @ 23,1 SAY "Delete all these? (Y/N) ";
      GET OKTOPACK PICTURE "!"
   READ
   IF OKTOPACK <> "Y"
      *---------- If not ok to pack, recall a record.
      DELREC = 0
      @ 23,1 SAY "Recall which one (by record #)";
         GET DELREC PICTURE "9999"
      READ
      *---------- If record number entered, and record
      *---------- is indeed deleted, recall it.
```

```
    IF DELREC > 0
        GOTO DELREC
        IF DELETED( )
            RECALL RECORD DELREC
            NODELS = NODELS - 1
        ENDIF (deleted)
    ENDIF (DELREC > 1)
ELSE
    *---------- If ok to pack, do so and show progress.
    SET TALK ON
    PACK
    SET TALK OFF
    ENDIF (OKTOPACK)
ENDDO (OKTOPACK)
RETURN
```

MAILDUPE.PRG: CHECKING FOR DUPLICATES

The MAILDUPE.PRG command file displays records that have identical zip codes, street addresses, and last names. Pseudocode for the MAILDUPE.PRG command file is shown below:

COMMAND FILE NAME: MAILDUPE.PRG
PURPOSE: Checks for duplicate names and addresses
PSEUDOCODE:

√ Ask about printer.
√ Display opening messages and pre-sort the database.
√ If printer requested, turn it on.
√ Print report title.
√ Loop through the database.
√   Look to ZIP + ADDRESS + LNAME.
√   Skip to next record, and compare ZIP +
√   ADDRESS + LNAME to previous record.
√   If records match
√   Go back to first matching record.
√   Display all records that match.
√ Continue loop through database.

✓ When done with report, handle printer or screen.
✓ Erase temporary index file and
✓   reactivate normal sort orders.
✓ Return to Main Menu.

```
* * * * * * * * * * * MAILDUPE.PRG
* – – – – – Mail System Check for Duplicates Program.

* – – – – – Ask about printer.
CLEAR
TOPRINT = "N"
@ 10,10 SAY "Send duplicates to printer? (Y/N) ";
   GET TOPRINT PICTURE "!"
   READ

* – – – – – Display opening messages and show progress.
@ 15,10 SAY "Pre-sorting for duplicates check . . . "
SET TALK ON
USE MAILDATA
INDEX ON UPPER(ZIP + ADDRESS + LNAME) TO TEMP
SET TALK OFF
CLEAR

* – – – – – If printer requested, turn it on.
IF TOPRINT = "Y"
   SET PRINT ON
ENDIF

* – – – – – Print report title.
CLEAR
? DTOC(DATE()) + SPACE(20) + "Possible Duplications"
?? SPACE(20) + TIME()
?
?

* – – – – – Loop through the database.
GO TOP
DO WHILE .NOT. EOF()
   Compare = UPPER(ZIP + ADDRESS + LNAME)
   SKIP
   IF UPPER(ZIP + ADDRESS + LNAME) = Compare
      SKIP -1
```

Program 16.5: MAILDUPE.PRG Command File

```
        LIST LNAME, FNAME, ADDRESS, CITY WHILE;
          UPPER(ZIP + ADDRESS + LNAME) = Compare
        ?
        ?
      ENDIF (upper zip + . . . )
    ENDDO (not eof)


    *---------- Done with report, handle printer or screen.
    IF TOPRINT = "Y"
      EJECT
      SET PRINT OFF
    ELSE
      @ 23,1
      WAIT "Press a key to return to the menu . . . "
    ENDIF (TOPRINT)


    *---------- Erase temporary index file and
    *---------- reactivate normal indexes.
    CLOSE DATABASES
    ERASE TEMP.NDX
    USE MAILDATA INDEX MAILNAMS,MAILZIPS
```

Program 16.5: MAILDUPE.PRG Command File (continued)

To facilitate checking for duplicate records, the program pre-sorts the database by zip code, address, and last name. That way, any records with that are identical within these three fields will be right next to each other. The sorting is handled with an INDEX command, using an index file named TEMP.NDX. The opening lines of the program ask the user if the resulting report should be printed, and create the TEMP.NDX index file:

```
* * * * * * * * * * * MAILDUPE.PRG
*---------- Mail system Check for Duplicates program.
*---------- Ask about printer.
CLEAR
TOPRINT = "N"
@ 10,10 SAY "Send duplicates to printer? (Y/N) ";
  GET TOPRINT PICTURE "!"
  READ
*---------- Display opening messages and show progress.
@ 15,10 SAY "Pre-sorting for duplicates check . . . "
SET TALK ON
USE MAILDATA
```

```
INDEX ON UPPER(ZIP + ADDRESS + LNAME) TO TEMP
SET TALK OFF
CLEAR
```

If the user requests that the report be printed, the following routine turns the printer on. (*Note:* SET PRINT ON sends all output commands, except @, to the printer. To send @ commands to the printer, use SET DEVICE TO PRINT.)

```
*---------- Of printer requested, turn it on.
IF TOPRINT = "Y"
    SET PRINT ON
ENDIF
```

Next, the program prints the current date and time (the DATE( ), TIME( ) line), and a report title followed by a couple of blank lines:

```
*---------- Print report title.
CLEAR
? DTOC(DATE( )) + SPACE(20) + "Possible Duplications"
?? SPACE(20) + TIME( )
?
?
```

Next a loop is set up that reads every record in the database, starting at the first record (TOP):

```
*---------- Loop through the database.
GO TOP
DO WHILE .NOT. EOF( )
```

Within this loop, the uppercase (used for consistency) equivalent of the address, zip code, and last name are stored in a memory variable named COMPARE:

```
COMPARE = UPPER(ZIP + ADDRESS + LNAME)
```

Next, a SKIP command moves the pointer to the next record, and an IF clause determines whether or not the zip, address, and last name of the new record are identical to the zip, address, and last name of the previous record. (Again, since the database is pre-sorted, identical records must be next to each other.)

```
SKIP
IF UPPER(ZIP + ADDRESS + LNAME) = COMPARE
```

If the two records match, the program skips back to the previous record, and lists all records with identical zip codes, addresses, and last names:

```
SKIP -1
LIST LNAME, FNAME, ADDRESS, CITY WHILE;
    UPPER(ZIP + ADDRESS + LNAME) = COMPARE
  ?
  ?
ENDIF (UPPER ZIP + . . . )
```

This process continues until the end of the file is encountered. If the report was printed, the EJECT command moves the paper in the printer to the next page and turns the printer off. If the report was displayed on the screen, the program pauses to allow the user to view the screen before returning to the Main Menu. These tasks are handled in this routine:

```
ENDDO (NOT EOF)
*---------- Done with report, handle printer or screen.
IF TOPRINT = "Y"
   EJECT
   SET PRINT OFF
ELSE
   @ 23,1
   WAIT "Press a key to return to the menu . . . "
ENDIF (TOPRINT)
```

Finally, before returning to the Main Menu, the following routine closes all open database and index files, erases the temporary index file (TEMP.NDX) from the disk, and sets up the normal NAMES and ZIPS.NDX index files:

```
*---------- Erase temporary index file and
*---------- reactivate normal indexes.
CLOSE DATABASES
ERASE TEMP.NDX
USE MAILDATA INDEX MAILNAMS,MAILZIPS
RETURN
```

REVIEWING THE CUSTOM SYSTEM

In this chapter we've demonstrated a custom system written in the dBASE language. In Appendix B, we'll look at an alternative to writing your own programs, the dBASE III PLUS Applications Generator. The system we developed consisted of the following programs:

▬

MAIL.PRG—Main menu for the mailing list system.

▬

MAILREPS.PRG—Display sort and search options, then print data.

▬

MAILEDIT.PRG—Locate a specific record on the database, and change it.

▬

MAILDEL.PRG—Locate a specific record, and delete it.

▬

MAILDUPE.PRG—List probable duplicates in the database.

Some Useful Tips

B efore ending this book, I'd like to give you some additional useful tips. I suspect that you'll find them handy at some point in your work with dBASE III PLUS.

CHOOSING COLORS

If you use a color monitor, you'll probably want to try out some color combinations for your screen. To do so, enter the command SET next to the dot prompt, and then press Return. Use → to move the highlighting to the *Screen* option. Then you can use ↑ and ↓ to move the highlighting to various options on the screen, and press Return while an option is highlighted to experiment with colors. (The instructions at the bottom of the screen will help.)

Figure 17.1 shows some fancy color settings you might want to try if you have a color monitor. Notice that the colors selected for

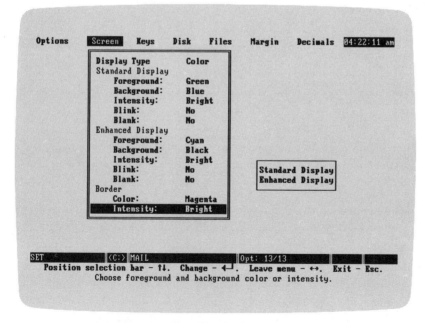

Figure 17.1: Settings for a Color Monitor

the Standard Display are Green and Blue, with Bright Intensity, and the enhanced display is Cyan on Black, also in Bright Intensity. The border is Magenta. This color combination may be a bit garish, so try a few combinations of your own.

When you're done with the SET parameters, press Esc to return to the dot prompt. Of course, to return to the menu, enter the ASSIST command at the dot prompt.

USING ABBREVIATIONS

To speed up typing, dBASE allows you to abbreviate commands to four letters. Therefore, you can type **MODI COMM** rather than

Command	Abbreviation
REPORT FORM BYNAMES	REPO FORM BYNAMES
DELETE RECORD 6	DELE RECO 6
REPLACE ALL LNAME WITH 'Smith'	REPL ALL LNAME WITH 'Smith'
APPEND	APPE
SET DEFAULT TO B	SET DEFA TO B
MODIFY COMMAND LABELS	MODI COMM LABELS
MODIFY STRUCTURE	MODI STRU
DISPLAY STRUCTURE	DISP STRU
DISPLAY MEMORY	DISP MEMO

Table 17.1: Command Abbreviations

MODIFY COMMAND to get the same result. Any command can be abbreviated. Table 17.1 shows some common commands and their abbreviations.

MULTIPLE-PAGE CUSTOM SCREENS

If a database contains many fields and you want to use a custom form, you will probably have to separate the form into *pages*. Figure 17.2 shows a portion of a large sample database named TAXES.DBF.

Structure for database: C:taxes.dbf

Field	Field Name	Type	Width	Dec
1	CLIENT_NO	Character	4	
2	LNAME	Character	15	
3	FNAME	Character	15	
4	MI	Character	1	
5	ADDRESS	Character	20	
6	CITY	Character	20	
7	STATE	Character	2	
8	ZIP	Character	10	
9	PHONE	Character	8	
10	SSN	Character	12	
11	SPOUSESSN	Character	12	
12	OCCUPATION	Character	20	
13	SPOUSEOCC	Character	20	
14	ELECTION	Character	1	
15	SPOUSEELEC	Character	1	
16	SINGLE	Character	1	
17	MARJOINT	Character	1	
18	MARSEPARAT	Character	1	
19	SPOUSENAME	Character	20	
20	HEAD	Character	1	
21	CHILDNAME	Character	20	
22	WIDOW	Character	1	
23	SPDEATHYR	Numeric	2	
24	SELF	Character	1	
25	OVER65	Character	1	
26	BLIND	Character	1	
27	SPOUSE	Character	1	
28	SPOVER65	Character	1	
29	SPBLIND	Character	1	
30	BOX6AB	Numeric	2	
31	BOX6C	Numeric	2	

Figure 17.2: Portion of Sample TAXES.DBF Database

Obviously, even the fields shown will probably not fit on one screen. To handle this situation, you can use the *Create* and *Screen* options from the menu or the CREATE SCREEN command from the dot prompt to create a custom screen. For this example, name it TAXES. Using the arrow keys, you can design the first page of the form as shown in Figure 17.3.

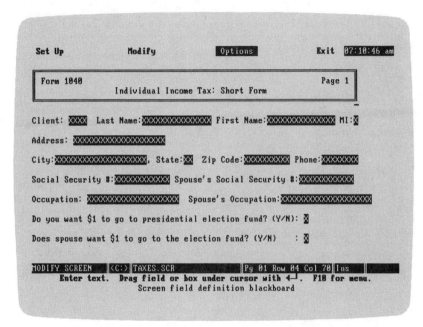

Figure 17.3: First Page of Custom TAXES Screen

When the first screen is defined, you can press PgDn to move to the next page. Now it becomes tricky, because you can't use your eye to find where the next page begins. You need to use a combination of the ^N key (to insert blank lines) and ^Y key (to delete blank lines) to place the cursor to the top of the screen on page 2. When the cursor is at the top of page 2, the Status Bar displays

Pg 02   Row 01   Col 01

At the top of page 2, design the next page of the form. Figure 17.4 shows a second page for the TAXES form. The cursor has been repositioned to the upper-left corner of the screen. The Status Bar shows the starting position of the text on the screen.

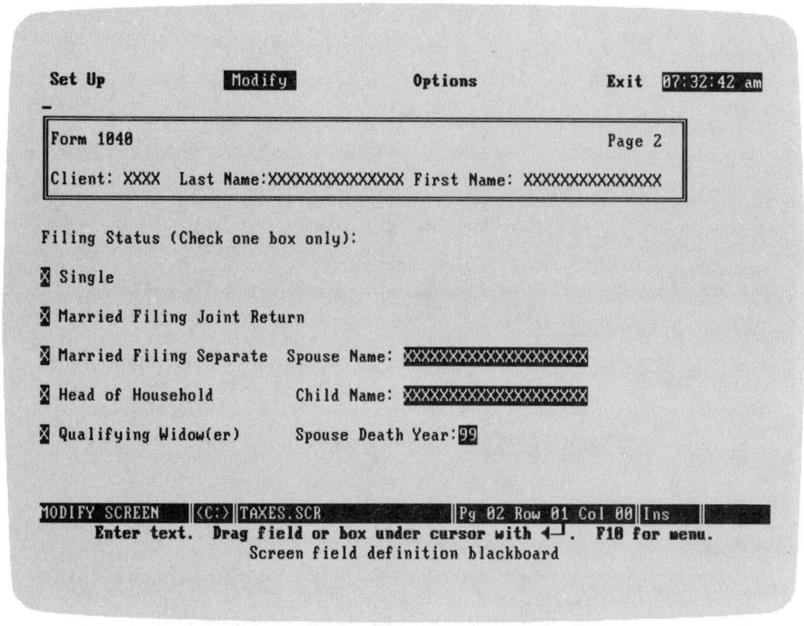

```
 Set Up              Modify            Options            Exit  07:32:42 am
 -
┌──────────────────────────────────────────────────────────────────────┐
│Form 1040                                               Page 2          │
│Client: XXXX  Last Name:XXXXXXXXXXXXXX First Name: XXXXXXXXXXXXXX        │
└──────────────────────────────────────────────────────────────────────┘

 Filing Status (Check one box only):
 X Single
 X Married Filing Joint Return
 X Married Filing Separate   Spouse Name: XXXXXXXXXXXXXXXXXXX
 X Head of Household          Child Name: XXXXXXXXXXXXXXXXXXX
 X Qualifying Widow(er)      Spouse Death Year:99

 MODIFY SCREEN  ‖<C:>‖TAXES.SCR                 ‖Pg 02 Row 01 Col 00‖Ins ‖
        Enter text.  Drag field or box under cursor with ◄┘.  F10 for menu.
                     Screen field definition blackboard
```

Figure 17.4: Second Page of TAXES Screen

Notice that the client number, last name, and first name are repeated on the second page of the form. These fields are for reference and need not be re-entered by the operator. To place these fields on the second page and make them uneditable, first type the field label, and then place the cursor to where you want the field highlighting to start, like this:

Client: _

Press F10 to call up the Assistant menu, and select *Content* under the *Modify* menu. dBASE will show you a list of existing fields. Select the field that you want to place.

To make sure that the field is for display only, move the highlight to the *Action* option and press Return to change it from Edit/ GET to Display/SAY. Press F10 to return to the blackboard and continue designing the form. Field highlightings for Display/SAY fields are not displayed in reverse video.

You can create up to 32 pages for a single custom form using this process. As usual, save your work by highlighting the *Exit* option and selecting *Save*.

Using a Multiple-Page Screen

Once you've saved your custom screen, you can treat it as you would any custom screen. The only difference in control-key commands is that PgUp and PgDn will now scroll from page to page rather than from record to record when entering or editing data.

Fixing a Problem with Boxes

You may encounter a slight problem with boxes on multiple page forms—all of the boxes appear together on the last page of the form. If this problem occurs when you create multiple-page screens, here is a remedy.

From the dot prompt, enter MODIFY COMMAND with the name of the format file (the file name you assigned to the screen, followed by the extension .FMT, as in TAXES.FMT). When you see the format file on the screen (which consists of @, SAY, and GET commands), press PgDn until you get to the bottom of the form, which will show @ and SAY commands with the DOUBLE option:

```
@ 5,12 GET TAXES—>SPOVER65
@ 6,10 SAY "SPBLIND"
@ 6,12 GET TAXES—>SPBLIND
@ 1,0  TO 4, 70   DOUBLE
@ 2,0  TO 6, 70   DOUBLE
```

These @ SAY . . . DOUBLE commands draw the double-line boxes on the forms. You need to put these on each page rather than clumped together at the end of the format file. The READ command embedded throughout the format file marks the end of one page and the beginning of the next.

Simply jot down the @ SAY command for each page (they appear in proper order in the format file) on a piece of paper. Then, type them into their appropriate page positions. For example, these lines show the @ 1,0 TO 4,70 DOUBLE box retyped at the top of page 1 in the form:

```
@ 1,0  TO 4, 70   DOUBLE
@ 2,2  SAY "Form 1040                         Page 1"
@ 3,18 SAY "Individual Income Tax: Short Form"
@ 6,0  SAY "Client:"
```

The second @ SAY . . . DOUBLE command should appear at the top of page 2, below the READ command which marks the bottom of page 1:

```
READ
@ 2,0  TO 6, 70   DOUBLE
@ 3,1  SAY "Form 1040                         Page 2"
@ 5,1  SAY "Client:"
@ 3,9  SAY TAXES—>CLIENT_NO
@ 5,15 SAY "Last Name:"
@ 5,25 SAY TAXES—>LNAME
```

If you use an external word processor, such as WordStar in the non-document mode, you can make these changes to the format file using block commands. However, if you use MODIFY COM-MAND, you'll have to type the @ SAY . . . DOUBLE command at the new position and erase it from its original position. You may have to experiment for a little while to get all the pages exactly how you want them.

MEMO FIELDS

In some cases you might want to store long passages of text as data. For example, suppose that you want to store references to journal articles on a database, including author, title, publication, date, pages, key words, and an abstract. To make room for an abstract of any length, you could make the ABSTRACT field the Memo data type, as shown in this structure:

Structure for database: LIBRARY.DBF
Number of data records: 2
Date of last update: 10/19/84

Field	Field Name	Type	Width	Dec
1	AUTHOR	Character	20	
2	TITLE	Character	20	
3	PUB	Character	20	
4	DATE	Date	8	
5	PAGES	Character	10	
6	ABSTRACT	Memo	10	
7	KEYWORDS	Character	80	

Even though dBASE automatically assigns a width of ten characters to this field, the field can be up to 5,000 characters long.

When you use the APPEND command to add data to the reference database, or EDIT to modify data, the screen displays this data-entry form:

```
AUTHOR              :              :
TITLE               :              :
PUB                 :              :
DATE                :  /  /  :
PAGES               :        :
ABSTRACT            :memo:
KEYWORDS            :                              :
```

To put data into the ABSTRACT field, place the cursor in the field and press ^PgDn. The screen will clear and you'll automatically be in the dBASE word processor. From there you can type your abstract, and use the ^ and the MODIFY COMMAND arrow keys to compose and edit. When you are done typing or editing the abstract, type ^W or ^End to return to the APPEND or EDIT screen.

Data typed into MEMO fields are stored in an auxiliary database with the extension .DBT. For example, if you name the reference file LIBRARY, then the abstracts will be stored on a database called LIBRARY.DBT.

When you use the LIST command to view the records, the

If you copy a database that contains a Memo field to another disk or directory, you must remember to copy both the .DBF and .DBT files (for example, both LIBRARY.DBF and LIBRARY.DBT in this case.)

word "Memo" will be displayed on the listing:

#	AUTHOR		TITLE	PUB
	DATE	PAGES	ABSTRACT	KEYWORDS
1	Adams, A.A.		M68000 Programming	Microsystems.
	04/01/85	111-129	Memo	68000, Programming
2	Stark, Robin D.		Software Design	Jour. of Software Design
	03/01/85	19-27	Memo	Programming, Design, Development

However, if you specify the field names

    LIST OFF AUTHOR,TITLE,PUB,DATE,PAGES,ABSTRACT ↵

then the contents of the ABSTRACT field will be included in the listing:

    Adams, A.A.   68000   Programming Microsystems.
04/01/85   111-129   An in-depth description of programming the 32-bit
M68000 processor at the assembly language level. Includes routines for
custom I/O as well as general purpose applications.

    Stark, Robin D.   Software Design   Jour. of Software Design
03/01/85   19-27   Program design and development considerations
when working in a high-level database management language. Discusses
database and software design as well as modular and structured
programming.

The SET MEMOWIDTH option allows you to control the width of a MEMO field during output. For example, the command

    SET MEMOWIDTH TO 40 ↵

sets a width of forty characters for MEMO field displays. (The default value is fifty.) After setting the memo width to forty, the command

    LIST OFF TITLE, ABSTRACT ↵

displays the data in the following format. (*Note:* The OFF option hides record numbers in LIST displays.)

Title   **Abstract**
68000 Programming   **An in-depth description of programming the 32-bit M68000 processor at the assembly language level. Includes routines for custom I/O as well as general purpose applications.**

Through command files you can gain even more control over MEMO field displays. For example, suppose that you want each record in LIBRARY to look like this sample record when it is printed:

Record no.   :   1
Author   : Adams, A.A.
Title   : M68000 Programming
Publication: Microsystems.
Date   : 04/01/85   Pages: 111-129
Keywords   : M68000, Programming
An in-depth description of programming the 32-bit M68000 processor at the assembly language level. Includes routines for custom I/O as well as general purpose applications.

The command file in Program 17.1 performs this printing task for all of the records in LIBRARY. Note the program's use of a DO WHILE .NOT. EOF() loop to display each record in the database. This program also includes page breaks for the printer.

One slight disadvantage to MEMO fields is that you cannot perform searching functions on them. For example, the command

    LIST FOR "Design" $ABSTRACT ⏎

will generate an error message, because you are attempting to list records with the word *Design* embedded in the Memo field. However, this is usually not a problem. In the sample LIBRARY reference database, you included a KEYWORD field which can be used to store key words. Hence, to view all the references on the subject of design, just type this command

    LIST FOR "Design" $KEYWORDS ⏎

Another limitation to the MEMO field is that it cannot be used

```
* * * * * * * * * * * Print library data.
USE LIBRARY
GO TOP
SET TALK OFF
SET PRINT ON
* * * * * * * * * * * Start line feed counter (LF) at zero.
LF = 0
DO WHILE .NOT. EOF( )
    ? "Author        : ",AUTHOR
    ? "Title         : ",TITLE
    ? "Publication   : ",PUB
    ? "Date          : ",DATE,"                    Pages: ",PAGES
    ? "Keywords      : ",KEYWORDS
    ?
    ? ABSTRACT
    ?
    ?
    LF = LF + 9
    * * * * * * * * * * * If 50 or more lines printed, start on
    * * * * * * * * * * * new page and reset the line counter.
    IF LF > = 50
        EJECT
        LF = 0
    ENDIF (LF > = 50)
    SKIP
ENDDO (while not eof)
SET PRINT OFF
```

Program 17.1: Program to Specify Display of LIBRARY Records

for sorting or indexing. For example, you cannot ask dBASE to

INDEX ON ABSTRACT TO ABS ←

However, it's pretty unlikely that you'd want to index on a
MEMO field. In the LIBRARY example, you'd be more likely to
index on the AUTHOR field for alphabetical listings by author or
the DATE field for listings in chronological order.

COMPLEX SORTS

Combining dates, characters, and numbers in index files for
sorts-within-sorts can be tricky. Generally, whenever you create an

index file with multiple fields, all non-character fields should be converted to Characters data types. Let's look at an example of how the dBASE STR (string) function can help.

In Chapter 8, you created a database called SALES. It contains the following records:

Record #	CODE	TITLE	QTY	AMOUNT	DATE
1	AAA	Rakes	3	15.00	03/01/86
2	BBB	Hoes	2	12.50	03/01/86
3	CCC	Shovels	3	21.00	03/01/86
4	AAA	Rakes	2	10.00	03/01/86
5	CCC	Shovels	4	26.50	03/01/86
6	AAA	Rakes	2	11.00	03/02/86
7	CCC	Shovels	1	7.50	03/02/86
8	BBB	Hoes	2	12.50	03/02/86
9	AAA	Rakes	5	23.50	03/02/86

Suppose that you want to sort this database in order by product code, and in order by quantity within each product grouping. You can index on both CODE and QTY, as long as you convert the QTY field to a string:

```
INDEX ON CODE + STR(QTY,3) TO TEST ←
```

Note that the comma three (,3) in the STR function means, "Convert field to 3-wide." When you list the records, you'll see them in order by product codes, and within each code, they are in ascending order by the quantity sold:

Record #	CODE	TITLE	QTY	AMOUNT	DATE
4	AAA	Rakes	2	10.00	03/01/86
6	AAA	Rakes	2	11.00	03/02/86
1	AAA	Rakes	3	15.00	03/01/86
9	AAA	Rakes	5	23.50	03/02/86
2	BBB	Hoes	2	12.50	03/01/86
8	BBB	Hoes	2	12.50	03/02/86
7	CCC	Shovels	1	7.50	03/02/86
3	CCC	Shovels	3	21.00	03/01/86
5	CCC	Shovels	4	26.50	03/01/86

Now, suppose that you want the records in ascending code order (A-Z), but the quantity in descending order (largest to smallest).

You could accomplish this by indexing on the CODE field plus the inverse of the QTY field. That is, you would subtract the QTY field from some large constant (such as 1000). However, the QTY field still must be converted to a string:

INDEX ON CODE + STR(1000 – QTY,4) TO TEST ↵

A LIST command will now display the records with the product codes in alphabetical order, and descending the quantities sold order within codes:

Record #	CODE	TITLE	QTY	AMOUNT	DATE
9	AAA	Rakes	5	23.50	03/02/86
1	AAA	Rakes	3	15.00	03/01/86
4	AAA	Rakes	2	10.00	03/01/86
6	AAA	Rakes	2	11.00	03/02/86
2	BBB	Hoes	2	12.50	03/01/86
8	BBB	Hoes	2	12.50	03/02/86
5	CCC	Shovels	4	26.50	03/01/86
3	CCC	Shovels	3	21.00	03/01/86
7	CCC	Shovels	1	7.50	03/02/86

You might want to sort these records by date and quantity. For example, suppose that you want the records to be displayed in date order, and descending quantity order. You would need to convert both the date and the inverse quantity to strings:

INDEX ON DTOC(DATE) + STR(1000 – QTY,4) TO TEST ↵

If you list the database

LIST DATE,QTY,CODE,TITLE,AMOUNT ↵

you will see the records sorted by date and quantity:

Record #	DATE	QTY	CODE	TITLE	AMOUNT
5	03/01/86	4	CCC	Shovels	26.50
1	03/01/86	3	AAA	Rakes	15.00
3	03/01/86	3	CCC	Shovels	21.00
2	03/01/86	2	BBB	Hoes	12.50
4	03/01/86	2	AAA	Rakes	10.00
9	03/02/86	5	AAA	Rakes	23.50
6	03/02/86	2	AAA	Rakes	11.00
8	03/02/86	2	BBB	Hoes	12.50
7	03/02/86	1	CCC	Shovels	7.50

Now, you may want something a little different. Suppose that you want the records in month order, disregarding the days, and the quantities in descending order. To do so, you'd want to index on the month and the inverse quantity. Again, both must be converted to character strings:

INDEX ON STR(MONTH(DATE),2) + STR(1000 – QTY,4) TO TEST ↵

Then you would see this list:

Record #	DATE	QTY	CODE	TITLE	AMOUNT
9	03/02/86	5	AAA	Rakes	23.50
5	03/01/86	4	CCC	Shovels	26.50
1	03/01/86	3	AAA	Rakes	15.00
3	03/01/86	3	CCC	Shovels	21.00
2	03/01/86	2	BBB	Hoes	12.50
4	03/01/86	2	AAA	Rakes	10.00
6	03/02/86	2	AAA	Rakes	11.00
8	03/02/86	2	BBB	Hoes	12.50
7	03/02/86	1	CCC	Shovels	7.50

If you add a few records for April with the APPEND command and then LIST, you will see

Record #	DATE	QTY	CODE	TITLE	AMOUNT
9	03/02/86	5	AAA	Rakes	23.50
5	03/01/86	4	CCC	Shovels	26.50
1	03/01/86	3	AAA	Rakes	15.00
3	03/01/86	3	CCC	Shovels	21.00
2	03/01/86	2	BBB	Hoes	12.50
4	03/01/86	2	AAA	Rakes	10.00
6	03/02/86	2	AAA	Rakes	11.00
8	03/02/86	2	BBB	Hoes	12.50
7	03/02/86	1	CCC	Shovels	7.50
12	04/15/86	1000	AAA	Rakes	5000.00
10	04/01/86	99	AAA	Rakes	1234.56
11	04/15/86	57	CCC	Shovels	1777.44

Notice that the quantities go from highest to lowest within each month, but without regard to the particular day of the month. This sort order produces a nice report summarized by month. You could use MODIFY REPORT to create any report format you like, and specify MONTH(DATE) as the Group/Subtotal field.

When you print the report, you'll see the data displayed like this:

```
Page No. 1
11/07/86
DATE          QTY    TITLE      AMOUNT
* * Month number: 3
03/02/86        5    Rakes        23.50
03/01/86        4    Shovels      26.50
03/01/86        3    Rakes        15.00
03/01/86        3    Shovels      21.00
03/01/86        2    Hoes         12.50
03/01/86        2    Rakes        10.00
03/02/86        2    Rakes        11.00
03/02/86        2    Hoes         12.50
03/02/86        1    Shovels       7.50
* * Subtotal * *
               24                139.50
* * Month number: 4
04/15/86     1000    Rakes      5000.00
04/01/86       99    Rakes      1234.56
04/15/86       57    Shovels    1777.44
* * Subtotal * *
             1156               8012.00
* * * Total * * *
             1180               8151.50
```

The data are grouped and subtotaled by month and displayed in descending quantity order within each month.

You can do the same operations with the AMOUNT field, but be sure to specify two decimal places in the STR function for the amount. For example, for ascending amount order, use

INDEX ON STR(AMOUNT,12,2) TO TEST ↵

For descending order, use

INDEX ON STR(999999.99 – AMOUNT,8,2) TO TEST ↵

You should be aware that the index file contains the data in the converted format, so using the FIND and SEEK command will be tricky. You can get around this problem by using one index file of converted fields for displaying records in sorted order, and another index file with unconverted data for SEEK and FIND.

RECORD NUMBERS IN REPORTS

If you'd like to include record numbers in a report, just make one of the columns contain the RECNO( ) function:

Contents	**RECNO( )**
Heading	**Rec.;No.**
Width	**5**
Decimal places	**0**
Total this column	**Yes**

That's all there is to it!

CUSTOM CONFIGURATIONS

The dBASE III PLUS System Disk # 1 contains a file named CONFIG.DB, which you can modify to change the initial default settings in dBASE III PLUS. (When installed on a hard-disk system, the CONFIG.DB file is on the same directory as dBASE itself.) Initially, the CONFIG.DB file contains the commands

STATUS = ON
COMMAND = ASSIST

which ensure that dBASE begins with the Status Bar ON and the Assistant menu displayed. (If you were to remove these two commands, dBASE III PLUS would start with a dot prompt only, like earlier versions of dBASE.)

You can use any word processor (with a non-document mode) or the dBASE MODIFY COMMAND editor to change the CONFIG.DB file to new settings. Key words that you can add to the CONFIG.DB file to alter default settings are listed in Table 17.2.

You can also predefine SET parameters in a CONFIG.DB file. including COLOR. (See the SET descriptions in the *Commands* section of the *Learning and Using dBASE III PLUS* manual that comes with dBASE for a complete technical listing of SET parameters.)

Key Word	Effect
COMMAND	Any command listed with this option is executed the moment dBASE III PLUS begins. Hence, the COMMAND = ASSIST line in CONFIG.DB causes the Assistant menu to appear the moment dBASE III PLUS is started.
BUCKET	The amount of memory allocated for PICTURE and RANGE commands. The default is 2, which stands for 2 * 1024 bytes.
GETS	Specifies the number of @, SAY, GETS that may be active at any one time. The default setting is 128.
MAXMEM	Specifies the amount of memory preserved when dBASE III PLUS executes an external program. The default is 256K bytes.
MVARSIZ	The amount of space allocated for storing memory variables. The default is 6,000 bytes (6K).
PROMPT	The dBASE III PLUS prompt, which appears as a dot (.) by default.
TEDIT	Specifies an external word processor used in place of MODIFY COMMAND.
WP	Specifies an external word processor to use with Memo fields.

Table 17.2: Key Words Used to Change Settings in CONFIG.DB

Here is a sample CONFIG.DB file:

```
COLOR = GR + /B,W + /RB,BG +
DEFAULT = C
PATH = C:\DB\FW
TEDIT = WORD
WP = WS
F9 = "DISPLAY STRUCTURE;"
F10 = "DISPLAY STATUS;"
PROMPT = Command: >
```

This sample CONFIG.DB file has the following effects:

1. The color combination on the screen at start up will be Yellow letters (GR +) on a Blue background (B) for the

standard screen, and White letters (W +) on a Magenta background where reverse video is used. The screen border will be Cyan (BG). The plus sign (+) indicates high intensity. An asterisk (∗) used instead indicates blinking. Other colors and codes are: Black (N), Green (G), Blank (X), and Red (R).

2. The default drive for storing and accessing files is Drive C.

3. dBASE will follow a route when looking for files, due to the PATH command. If a file cannot be found on the DB directory, dBASE will automatically look at the FW directory.

4. When the MODIFY COMMAND command is entered, dBASE will access Microsoft Word rather than the usual dBASE III PLUS editor. (This command requires more than 256K RAM).

5. Using ^PgDn to enter or edit memo fields will access WordStar rather than the dBASE word processor. (This command also requires more than 256K RAM).

6. Function keys F9 and F10 will automatically issue the commands DISPLAY STRUCTURE and DISPLAY STATUS when pressed. The ; presses the Return key after the command is typed.

7. Rather than the dot prompt, dBASE will display Command: >.

8. Neither the Status Bar nor Assistant menu will appear when dBASE is first started because the original STATUS = ON and COMMAND = ASSIST lines have been removed from the CONFIG.DB file.

If you cannot get access to the original dBASE III PLUS manuals in your school or company, you might try SYBEX's *dBASE III PLUS Programmer's Reference Guide*, available at most bookstores.

Your CONFIG.DB file will not have any effect until dBASE is started from the DOS prompt. Therefore, if you create a CONFIG.DB file using the MODIFY COMMAND editor, you'll have to QUIT dBASE, and start it again from scratch to see the effects of the file. For more information on the CONFIG.DB file, see Chapter 1 of the *Using dBASE III PLUS* manual that comes with dBASE.

NETWORK CONSIDERATIONS

Networks are generally created and managed by programmers or very sophisticated users, and therefore a complete discussion of networking is beyond the scope of this book. As a matter of fact, one could easily write an entire book on the subject of networking with dBASE III PLUS. However, we will discuss some general networking capabilities and commands for those who are considering networking with dBASE III PLUS.

The Local Area Network

A Local Area Network (LAN) is a group of computers and peripheral devices—such as hard disks, printers, and plotters—linked together by cables. Generally speaking, the machines are in close proximity to one another, most likely in the same building.

Companies usually network computers to allow many users to have access to the same resources. Another reason to network computers is to save money. For example, a network might consist of one IBM XT with 640K RAM and a 40-megabyte hard disk. Attached to this computer are a letter-quality printer, a plotter, and five IBM PCs with floppy disks. Since the system is networked, each of the less expensive PCs can access the large hard disk, the printer, and the plotter.

Network Administration

In a network, one computer (usually one with at least 640K RAM and a hard disk) is assigned the task of being the *file server.* The computers that are linked to the file server are called *work stations.* The dBASE III PLUS Administrator, which comes with the dBASE III PLUS package, needs to be installed on the *file server* computer. Each work station must have its own copy of the dBASE ACCESS programs. Installation instructions are included in the *Getting Started* manual that comes with the dBASE III PLUS package.

The commands below are available in a networked system:

LIST STATUS: Shows the current activity in the network, including open files and lock settings (described later).

DISPLAY USERS: Displays the work station names of users currently using dBASE in the network.

SET PRINTER: Selects a printer in the network to receive output.

Network Protection

To provide security on a network system, the dBASE III PLUS Network Administrator offers the PROTECT program. There are three levels of protection available with this program, as summarized in Table 17.3.

Security Level	Effect
Log-In	In a log-in security system, each user must enter a user name and a password to gain access to dBASE III PLUS. Keeps unauthorized users completely out of dBASE III PLUS.
Access Control	Different users can be assigned different degrees of access by the network administrator. Users can have any combination of these access *privileges* to records: *Extend* (add new data only), *Delete* (delete records), *Read* (read records), *Change* (edit records). Users may also have any one of these access privileges to a specified field: *Full* (read and write data), *R/O* (read only), *None* (no data access).
Data Encryption	Encrypted data are unintelligible until decrypted by a successful log-in through the dBASE Administrator. Encryption keeps out even those users who know how to display file contents with text editors, debuggers, and other external programs.

Table 17.3: Security Levels Available with PROTECT

Network Programming

Local Area Networks present new challenges to dBASE programmers. For example, suppose that two users access and change the same item of data at precisely the same time? Which change should be saved on the disk? It all depends on how records and files are locked and unlocked.

Several dBASE commands automatically lock an entire file while the command is being carried out. These commands include:

APPEND	**COUNT**	**RECALL ALL**	**TOTAL**
AVERAGE	**DELETE ALL**	**REPLACE ALL**	**UPDATE**
BROWSE	**INDEX**	**SORT**	
COPY	**JOIN**	**SUM**	

As soon as the task is completed, dBASE automatically unlocks the file.

Several dBASE commands and functions allow a programmer to lock and unlock files and records manually. The SET EXCLUSIVE command determines whether a file can be shared by several users simultaneously. The RLOCK( ) (record lock) and FLOCK( ) (file lock) functions can check the lock status of a file or record and change the status of the lock. The FLOCK( ) and RLOCK( ) functions give the programmer control in warding off *collisions* when two or more users attempt to access the same data at the same moment.

The ON ERROR and ERROR( ) commands detect collisions and other errors, and *trap* them. Routines can be set up in the program to RETRY accessing a file to circumvent the error.

Network Requirements

The technical requirements for a network are a computer with at least 640K RAM as the file server, and at least 384K RAM for work station computers. For each three dBASE III PLUS users, you need to purchase the dBASE III PLUS LAN Pack. The LAN Pack requires PC-DOS version 3.1/PC Network Program or a compatible system such as Novell's Advanced NetWare version 1.01 (or higher).

RUNTIME+

For the more advanced dBASE programmers who feel that their custom applications are ready for the world at large, Ashton-Tate offers RunTime+. RunTime+ encrypts command files so that unauthorized users cannot tamper with them. Furthermore, Run-Time+ allows programmers to sell copies of their programs to customers who do not own dBASE III PLUS. Instead, the customer need only buy from Ashton-Tate a special program named dBRUN, which sells for a lower price than dBASE III PLUS. Customers who already own dBASE III PLUS need only buy your encrypted program.

The RunTime+ package is fairly easy to use and is described in the *Programming with dBASE III PLUS* manual that comes with dBASE III PLUS. You should be aware, however, that there are less costly and perhaps more effective ways to encrypt programs and make them available to non-dBASE users. A dBASE III PLUS *compiler* will encrypt your program and make it executable directly from the DOS prompt—which means complete independence from dBASE III PLUS. This, in turn, means that your potential customers need not buy either dBASE III PLUS or dBRUN.

At the time this book was written, the major dBASE III compilers had not announced dBASE III PLUS versions, but they probably will soon. The two best known compilers are Nantucket's Clipper and WordTech by WordTech Systems, Inc.

WHERE TO GO FROM HERE

Here are some suggestions for your continued learning with dBASE III PLUS:

■

Practice. The only way to become fluent in a new language such as dBASE III PLUS is to use it. Create a database and work with it. If you're worried about experimenting with important data, just make a backup of the database first (COPY TO TEMP). Then, if you make a mess of the original data file, just ZAP the records from it and APPEND FROM TEMP.

Refer to the manuals that came with your original dBASE III PLUS package for additional technical information about individual commands and functions. This book was designed to teach you the fundamental concepts of database management and dBASE programming, and is not intended to replace those manuals. You may wish to refer to a more advanced book such as my *dBASE III PLUS Programmer's Reference Guide*, also published by SYBEX and available at most bookstores.

Pace yourself. Don't try to work out problems that are over your head. You'll just end up frustrated. Learning to master the marvelous machine can be very enjoyable if you pace yourself. Work at a comfortable level and experiment to learn more. If you make it fun, you'll learn more in the long run.

Interfacing with Other Software Systems

The dBASE III PLUS COPY and APPEND FROM commands allow you to interact with data from word processors, VisiCalc, Multiplan, and Lotus 1-2-3. The IMPORT and EXPORT commands let you interact with PFS-:FILE data. Many programs, such as Framework, Symphony, Paradox, and R:base 5000 have their own options for interfacing with dBASE data.

INTERFACING WITH PFS:FILE

To import a PFS file into dBASE III PLUS, first make sure the PFS file is readily available on the disk in Drive B, or on your hard disk. Then, enter the command

   IMPORT FROM <filename> TYPE PFS ←┘

substituting the name of the PFS file where <filename> is shown. Also, be sure to use the correct drive. For example, to import a PFS file named ACCOUNTS, stored on Drive B, you would enter the command:

   IMPORT FROM B:ACCOUNTS TYPE PFS ←┘

dBASE III PLUS will separate the PFS file into several manageable files. Each will have the same first name as the PFS file, but a dBASE III PLUS extension. The three files will be a database file (.DBF), a format file for custom screens (.FMT) and a view file for combining the screen and data files (.VUE).

To export data to a PFS file, use the command

   EXPORT TO <filename> TYPE PFS ←┘

where <filename> is the name of the dBASE III PLUS file that you want to export. If the file is on Drive B, use the **B:** drive specification:

   EXPORT TO B:EXPFILE TYPE PFS ←┘

You must open the database (.DBF) file with the USE command before entering the EXPORT command. Also, if the database to be exported has a custom screen associated with it (.FMT file), you should activate that screen before exporting using the SET FORMAT TO command from the dot prompt.

Note that options to Import and Export PFS files are also available from the Tools option under the Assistant menu.

INTERFACING WITH SPREADSHEETS

You can interface dBASE III PLUS data with a variety of spreadsheet packages. To copy a database file to VisiCalc format, USE the database and enter the command

COPY TO <filename> TYPE DIF ←┘

where <filename> is the name of the new file. dBASE will add the extension .DIF to the exported file.

To export data to Multiplan spreadsheets, use the SYLK option with the copy command:

COPY TO <filename> TYPE SYLK ←┘

Again, the file being exported must be in USE before issuing the COPY command. The copied file will not have an extension.

To copy data to Lotus 1-2-3 format, use the .WKS option with the COPY command:

COPY TO <filename> TYPE WKS ←┘

The new file will have the extension .WKS.

For stubborn transfers that are difficult to accomplish, you can experiment with the SDF and delimited options. For example, the command

COPY TO <filename> TYPE SDF ←┘

makes a file in *System Data Format.* This is often called an *ASCII text* file because it contains no special codes. Most spreadsheets can *import* a file stored in system data format if an importing option is available. The file-name extension .TXT will be added to the <filename> automatically, unless you supply another.

The DELIMITED option for copying files might also work for exporting to spreadsheets. We'll discuss the DELIMITED option under interfacing with word processors in this appendix.

To import spreadsheet data, you need to first CREATE a database that has the structure you want for your .DBF file. (Of course, you can use an existing database if you wish.) You then need to USE the database, and use the APPEND FROM, rather than COPY TO option, to import the foreign data.

To import from a text (SDF) file, you would use this syntax:

```
APPEND FROM <filename> TYPE SDF ←
```

You must fully identify the file being imported. For example, to import MAILDATA.TXT from Drive B, you would enter this command:

```
APPEND FROM B:MAILDATA.TXT SDF ←
```

To import data from a VisiCalc DIF file, you would use the command

```
APPEND FROM <filename>.DIF TYPE DIF ←
```

(assuming that the file was stored with DIF as the extension).

To import a Multiplan spreadsheet, you would use this command:

```
APPEND FROM <filename>. TYPE SYLK ←
```

If the Multiplan file has no extension, use a period only in the APPEND FROM file name. For example, to import a Multiplan spreadsheet on Drive B named ACCOUNTS, enter this command:

```
APPEND FROM B:ACCOUNTS. TYPE SYLK ←
```

To import Lotus 1-2-3 worksheets, use the .WKS option with the APPEND FROM command:

```
APPEND FROM ACCOUNTS.WKS TYPE WKS ←
```

Again, be sure to use the **B:** drive designator in a file name if you are using a floppy-disk system. Also, be sure to pay attention to the extension of the file you are importing, and to use that extension in the filename of the APPEND FROM command.

INTERFACING WITH WORD PROCESSORS

You can send dBASE reports to word processing systems for further editing or inclusion in other documents. To do so, design your report using the MODIFY REPORT command in dBASE. Then print the report with the TO <filename> option. You can then load up your word processor, and read the report into the word processing system. Here is a typical scenario using the Word-Star program as the word processor:

```
A> dBASE ←
USE MAIL ←
MODIFY REPORT BYNAME ←
(Define report format)
REPORT FORM BYNAME TO TRANSFER ←
QUIT ←
```

The TO TRANSFER option with the REPORT FORM commands sends a copy of the report to a disk file named TRANSFER.TXT. When you QUIT dBASE, the A> reappeared on the screen. Now you can load up WordStar. Let's say you want to pull the dBASE report into a document called MANUAL.TXT. Type

```
WS MANUAL.TXT ←
```

When the document appears on the screen position the cursor to the place that you want the dBASE report to appear. Then press ^KR. The WordStar program asks, "NAME OF FILE TO READ?" Reply with

```
TRANSFER.TXT ←
```

That's all there is to it. The report which appeared on the screen when you asked dBASE to REPORT FORM BYNAME is now in a WordStar document, and is also in a disk file called TRANS-FER.TXT.

Now, you may want to send your dBASE file to WordStar's MailMerge option for printing form letters. In this case, you need to create a database in MailMerge format. Let's say that you want to send your MAIL database to a MailMerge file from which to print form letters. After loading up dBASE, type

USE MAIL ↤

Then you need to COPY it to another data file in MailMerge readable form. The command is

COPY TO MM DELIMITED ↤

This creates a data file called MM.TXT which the MailMerge file can access to create form letters. Then you would have to create the form letter in WordStar. Recall that your MAIL database contains the fields LNAME, FNAME, ADDRESS, CITY, STATE, ZIP, and PHONE. You would have to QUIT dBASE and load up the WordStar program. Then you could create a document called FORM.LET. Figure A.1 contains a sample form letter which can read the data file you've just created.

The CONVERT program that comes with Release 5 of WordPerfect can convert a mail merge file like MM.TXT in this example to a secondary merge file for printing WordPerfect form letters.

Notice that PHONE was included in the .RV command, even though it is not used in the form letter anywhere. This is essential

```
      .OP
.DF MM.TXT
.RV LNAME,FNAME,ADDRESS,CITY,STATE,ZIP,PHONE
&FNAME& &LNAME&
&ADDRESS&
&CITY&, &STATE&     &ZIP&


Dear &FNAME&,


   How do you like getting these form letters? You probably wouldn't
know the difference if it were not for my dot matrix printer.


            Ta ta for now,


            Zeppo
.PA
```

Figure A.1: Sample MailMerge Form Letter

if the PHONE variable exists. The .RV command is expecting a certain number of fields, so it must have the same number of fields as the data file, regardless of whether or not you plan on using that field in your form letter. Even if you only wanted the first name for your form letter, you would still need to read in all of the fields. If you forget this important tidbit, your form letter might come out in a most unpleasant format.

After you create and save the form letter, you merely need to merge print it using the appropriate MailMerge command. That is, select WordStar option M from the WordStar Main Menu, and when it asks, "NAME OF FILE TO MERGE PRINT?", tell it FORM.LET ◄┘. A letter for each individual in the MAIL database will then be printed. Here is how the first one should come out:

Andy Appleby
123 A St.
San Diego, CA 92123
Dear Andy,
   How do you like getting these form letters? You probably wouldn't know the difference if it were not for my dot matrix printer.
                    Ta ta for now,
                    Zeppo

You could use your LABELS program to print mailing labels for all these individuals, or you could create a WordStar MailMerge document to print names and addresses directly on envelopes, one envelope at a time. Figure A.2 is a MailMerge file (named ENVEL.TXT) to print envelopes from your MM.TXT data file:

```
.MT 0
.OP
.DF MM.TXT
.RV LNAME,FNAME,ADDRESS,CITY,STATE,ZIP,PHONE
                    &FNAME& &LNAME&
                    &ADDRESS&
                    &CITY&, &STATE&    &ZIP&
.PA
```

Figure A.2: MailMerge File to Print Envelopes

After you create and save ENVEL.TXT, you can merge print it in the usual WordStar fashion. However, when the merge print option asks "PAUSE FOR PAPER CHANGE BETWEEN PAGES (Y/N)," be sure to answer **Y.** Then, you can insert each individual envelope, lining it up so that the printer head is right where you want the printing to start. The MailMerge option will print one envelope, eject it from the printer, and wait for you to put in the next envelope.

If you want your form letter to go to certain individuals only, you can specify this in your dBASE COPY command. Let's assume you want your form letters to go to San Diego residents only. With the dBASE dot prompt showing, and the MAIL database in use, type this command:

```
COPY TO MM FOR CITY = 'San Diego' DELIMITED ←┘
```

Only San Diego residents would appear on the MailMerge file, hence only individuals in San Diego would have form letters printed.

If you already have a MailMerge file and want to use some dBASE commands to manage it, you can send a copy of it to dBASE. To do so, you need to load up dBASE and CREATE an empty file with the CREATE command. Structure it so that it has the same fields as your MailMerge file. When dBASE asks, "INPUT DATA NOW?", say **N.** Then USE the newly created database, and

```
APPEND FROM MM.DAT DELIMITED ←┘
```

You can now sort your MailMerge file or do whatever you please with it in dBASE III. (This example assumed that the name of your existing MailMerge file was MM.DAT.) To get the dBASE database back into MailMerge readable form, just USE the dBASE file and

```
COPY TO MM.DAT DELIMITED
```

The Applications Generator

The dBASE III PLUS Applications Generator is a program that writes programs for you. For the beginning dBASE user, the Applications Generator can facilitate learning by providing a structured environment in which to create customized application systems. For the more experienced dBASE user, the Applications Generator can save some programming time. In this appendix, we'll use the Applications Generator by building a system to manage a check register.

COPYING THE APPLICATIONS GENERATOR DISK

The Applications Generator disk that comes with the dBASE III PLUS package contains thirteen program files:

GETDBFNA.PRG	APPSGEN.PRG	GETSCNNA.PRG	SETCOLOR.PRG
QUESTION.PRG	GETAUTHR.PRG	COLOPTS.PRG	GETHEADG.PRG
AUTOAPPS.PRG	GETAPNAM.PRG	GETINDNA.PRG	ADVAPPS.PRG
GENCODE.PRG			

If you are using a computer with two floppy disks, you should make a backup copy of these files. To do so, put a blank, formatted disk in Drive B and the Applications Generator disk in Drive A. Then, at the DOS A> prompt, type this command:

    COPY *.* B: ←

If you are using a hard-disk system, log onto your dBASE directory, and put the Applications Generator in Drive A. From the DOS C> prompt, enter this command:

    COPY A:*.* ←

STARTING THE APPLICATIONS GENERATOR

If you are using a computer with two floppy-disk drives, you need to put your copy of the Applications Generator in Drive B, and run dBASE as usual using System Disk #1 and #2 in Drive A. Press Esc to leave the Assistant menu. Then from the dot prompt enter this command:

SET DEFAULT TO B ⏎

Then enter the command

DO APPSGEN ⏎

On a hard-disk system, just log onto the dBASE directory and and enter this command:

DO APPSGEN ⏎

You'll see these Applications Generator menu options:

1. **CREATE DATABASE**
2. **CREATE SCREEN FORM**
3. **CREATE REPORT FORM**
4. **CREATE LABEL FORM**
5. **SET APPLICATION COLOR**
6. **AUTOMATIC APPLICATIONS GENERATOR**
7. **RUN APPLICATION**
8. **ADVANCED APPLICATIONS GENERATOR**
9. **MODIFY APPLICATION CODE**
0. **EXIT**

You select an option from the menu by typing its number and pressing the Return key. Options **1** through **5** simply access dBASE capabilities that you're already familiar with. When you select option **1,** the screen will ask that you:

Enter the name of the new file:

For this example, type the name **CHECKS** and structure the database as in Figure B.1. (*Note:* If you already have a database that you want to use with the Applications Generator, you can skip this option. The same holds true for options **2, 3,** and **4.**)

Save the database structure, and answer **No** to the "Input data records now?" prompt. You'll be returned to the Applications Generator main menu.

If you want to use a custom screen in your application, select

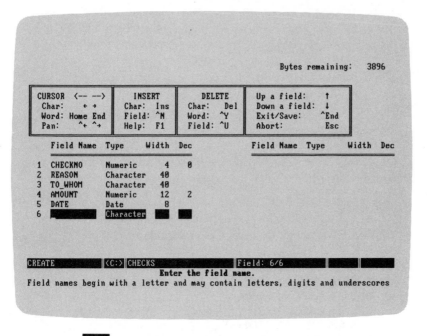

Figure B.1: Database Structure for a Check Register

option **2**. The screen will display this prompt:

Enter screen file name:

Enter a valid file name for the screen, such as CHECKS, and press Return. You'll be at the Screen Painter menu, where you can select the *Select a database* option to define CHECKS as the database. Then select *Load fields*. Figure B.2 shows a custom screen developed for the check register application.

Highlight the *Exit* option and select *Save* after creating the custom screen. You'll be returned to the Applications Generator menu.

Option **3** allows you to design a report for the system, using the dBASE III PLUS report generator. When you select **3**, you'll be asked to provide a name for the report format. Again, use a valid file name, such as CHECKS. You can fill out the report specification to your liking. This sample report specification shows the

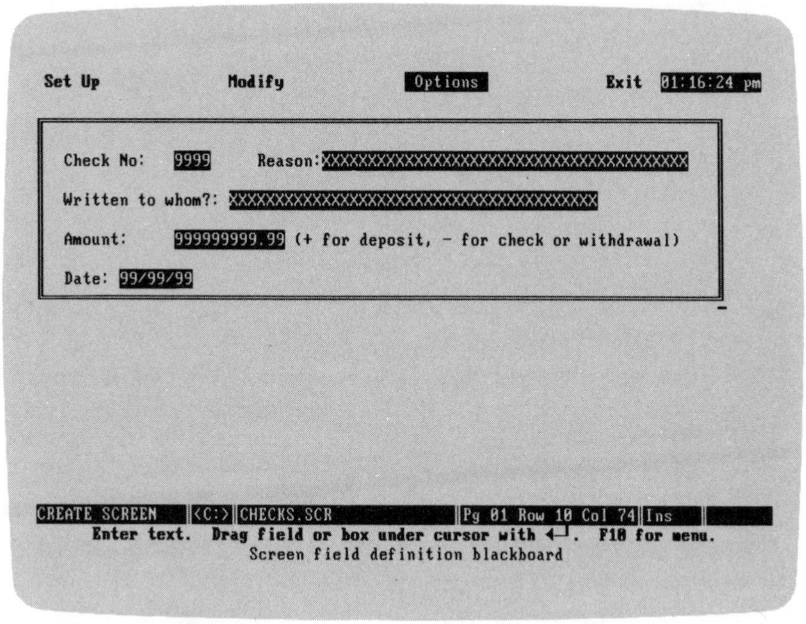

Figure B.2: Custom Screen for the Check Register

REASON and TO_WHOM fields stacked in a single column:

Contents	REASON + TO_WHOM
Heading	Reason and;To Whom Written
Width	30
Decimal places	
Total this column	
Report Format	

>>>>>>>> #	Reason and		Amount	Date
	To Whom Written			
####	XXXXXXXXXXXXXXXXXXXXXXXXX		########.##	mm/dd/yy

Save the report format, and then you'll be returned to the Applications Generator menu.

Selecting option **4** allows you to create a mailing labels format using the *Modify Labels* routine. You won't need labels in this application, so skip this option.

COLORING THE APPLICATION

Option **5** from the Applications Generator menu lets you select colors for the application. Selecting option **5** displays the menu shown in Figure B.3.

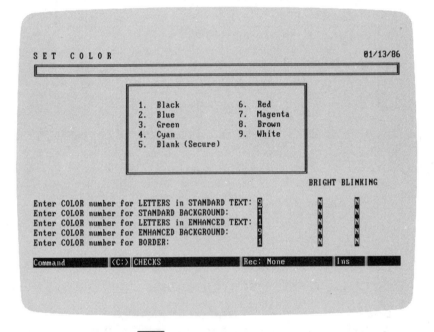

Figure B.3: Color Options Menu

You can move the cursor on the screen and select options to experiment with color combinations. Press ^End when you have defined the colors, and type **S** to save the colors.

AUTOMATIC APPLICATION GENERATOR

Once you've created the database, optional screen, report, and label files, you can select option **6** from the Applications Generator menu. First the screen will ask that you

Enter APPLICATION AUTHOR :

Type your first and last names, and press Return. Next, the screen will ask that you

Enter APPLICATION filename :

Again, a valid file name is required, so enter a title such as REG-ISTER. Next, the screen will ask that you

Enter DATABASE filename :

Type the database name (CHECKS) and press Return. Next the screen will ask that you

Enter INDEX filename :

Again, you can enter the file name CHECKS to create an index file named CHECKS.NDX. The screen will ask that you

Enter index key field :

In this example, you can enter CHECKNO if you want to organize the register by check number, or DATE if you prefer to keep it in chronological order. The Applications Generator will create the index file and ask that you

Enter SCREEN format name :

You created a screen called CHECKS.FMT earlier, so once again type the name **CHECKS** and press Return. The screen will ask that you

Enter REPORT form name :

Once again, enter CHECKS to specify the CHECKS.FRM format you created earlier. The screen will also ask that you

Enter LABEL form name :

Since you did not specify a label format, just press Return.

Finally, the screen will ask that you

Enter APPLICATION MENU HEADING :

For this example, type

CHECKBOOK REGISTER ↵

After a brief delay, the Applications Generator will build and display the command file generated from your input, as shown in Program B.1.

```
* Program....: CHECK.PRG
* Author.......: ZEPPO MONSTER
* Date...........: 01/13/86
* Notice........: Copyright (c) 1986, ZEPPO MONSTER, All Rights Reserved
* Notes.........:
* Reserved...: selectnum
*


SET TALK OFF
SET BELL OFF
SET STATUS ON
SET ESCAPE OFF
SET CONFIRM ON
USE CHECKS INDEX CHECKS

DO WHILE .T.

    * ---Display menu options, centered on the screen.
    * ---Draw menu border and print heading.
    CLEAR
    @ 2, 0 TO 15,79 DOUBLE
    @ 3,22 SAY [C H E C K B O O K   R E G I S T E R]
    @ 4,1 TO 4,78 DOUBLE
    * ---Display detail lines.
    @   7,30 SAY [1. ADD INFORMATION]
    @   8,30 SAY [2. CHANGE INFORMATION]
    @   9,30 SAY [3. REMOVE INFORMATION]
    @ 10,30 SAY [4. REVIEW INFORMATION]
    @ 11,30 SAY [5. PRINT REPORT]
    @ 13,30 SAY '0. EXIT'
    STORE 0 TO selectnum
```

Program B.1: Program Produced with the Applications Generator

```
@ 15,33 SAY '' select ''
@ 15,42 GET selectnum PICTURE ''9'' RANGE 0,5
READ

DO CASE
   CASE selectnum = 0
      SET BELL ON
      SET TALK ON
      CLEAR ALL
      RETURN

   CASE selectnum = 1
    * DO ADD INFORMATION
      SET FORMAT TO CHECKS
      APPEND
      SET FORMAT TO
      SET CONFIRM OFF
      STORE ' ' TO wait_subst
      @ 23,0 SAY 'Press any key to continue . . . ' GET wait_subst
      READ
      SET CONFIRM ON

   CASE selectnum = 2
    * DO CHANGE INFORMATION
      SET FORMAT TO CHECKS
      EDIT
      SET FORMAT TO
      SET CONFIRM OFF
      STORE ' ' TO wait_subst
      @ 23,0 SAY 'Press any key to continue . . . ' GET wait_subst
      READ
      SET CONFIRM ON

   CASE selectnum = 3
    * DO REMOVE INFORMATION
      SET TALK ON
      CLEAR
      @ 2,0 SAY ' '
      ? 'PACKING DATABASE TO REMOVE RECORDS MARKED FOR DELETION'
      PACK
      SET TALK OFF
      SET CONFIRM OFF
      STORE ' ' TO wait_subst
      @ 23,0 SAY 'Press any key to continue . . . ' GET wait_subst
      READ
```

Program B.1: Program Produced with the Applications Generator (continued)

```
      SET CONFIRM ON

   CASE selectnum = 4
   * DO REVIEW INFORMATION
      BROWSE
      SET CONFIRM OFF
      STORE ' ' TO wait_subst
      @ 23,0 SAY 'Press any key to continue . . . ' GET wait_subst
      READ
      SET CONFIRM ON

   CASE selectnum = 5
   * DO PRINT REPORT
      REPORT FORM CHECKS TO PRINT
      SET CONFIRM OFF
      STORE ' ' TO wait_subst
      @ 23,0 SAY 'Press any key to continue . . . ' GET wait_subst
      READ
      SET CONFIRM ON
   ENDCASE

   ENDDO T
   RETURN
   * EOF: CHECK.PRG
```

——

Program B.1: Program Produced with the Applications Generator (continued)

RUNNING THE APPLICATION

To run the newly created application, select option **7,** *Run Application,* from the Applications Generator menu. You'll see these menu options for your custom system:

1. **ADD INFORMATION**
2. **CHANGE INFORMATION**
3. **REMOVE INFORMATION**
4. **REVIEW INFORMATION**
5. **PRINT REPORT**
0. **EXIT**

Selecting option **1** allows you to add new records to the database. Option **2** allows you to make changes to the database using the dBASE EDIT mode. You need to use PgUp and PgDn to locate the record that you want to edit. Option **4** puts you into the BROWSE mode for making changes. Options **2** and **4** allow you to delete records using ^U. Option **3** PACKs the database, thereby permanently removing all records that have been marked for deletion. Option **5** prints the check register report, and **0** exits the check register back to the Applications Generator main menu.

You can also run the generated application directly from the dot prompt. You'll need to have all the CHECKS files (CHECKS .DBF, CHECKS.NDX, CHECKS.FMT, and CHECKS.FRM) together on the same disk or directory. You'll also need the .MEM and .PRG files that the generator created (REGISTER.MEM and REGISTER.PRG). As long as these files are together on the disk, you can run the application with this command:

DO REGISTER ⏎

(In place of REGISTER, substitute the name of any application that you've created.)

ADVANCED APPLICATIONS GENERATOR

To use the Advanced Applications Generator, select option **8** from the Applications Generator main menu. The screen will ask the same questions as for the Automatic Applications Generator, but it will produce a free-form menu that you must complete by typing names for the menu options and their equivalent dBASE commands and formats. You can enter up to nine menu options and commands to go with them. The menu options can be in plain English, but the EXECUTABLE dBASE COMMAND column can only contain valid dBASE commands. If an option uses the APPEND or EDIT command, you can use a custom screen by changing the N in the SCREEN FORMAT column to a **Y**. Figure B.4 shows a sample on-screen application entered on the Advanced Applications Generator menu.

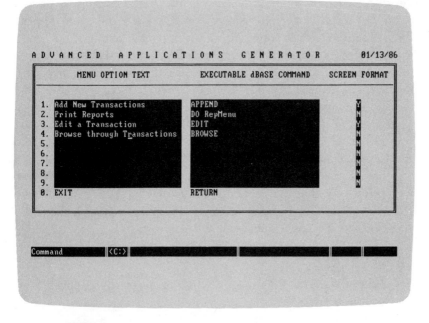

Figure B.4: Sample Advanced Applications Generator Menu

When you've completed the menu, press ^End to save it. You'll be given these options:

(E)xit, (R)edo, (S)ave

Select *Save* to save the application. Select *Redo* to make changes, or *Exit* to completely abandon the work without saving anything. You can run the new application using the same techniques that we've discussed for the Automatic Applications Generator. Figure B.5 shows how the generated menu for the sample application looks on the screen.

MODIFYING APPLICATION CODE

As you become more familiar with dBASE III PLUS, you may find the Applications Generator too simple for your needs. You

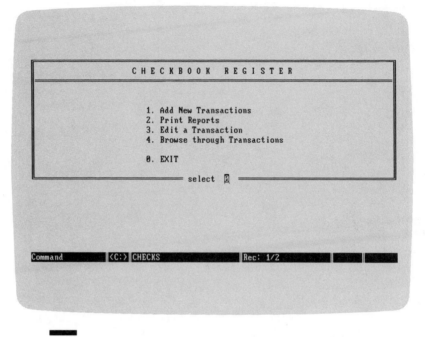

Figure B.5: Menu Generated by the Sample Advanced Application

can, of course, write your own programs from scratch once you've gained enough familiarity with the dBASE language.

As an in-between step, you might want to try modifying the programs generated by the Applications Generator. To do so, select option 9 from the Applications Generator main menu. This will bring up the MODIFY COMMAND editor, which allows you to make changes directly to the generated command file.

dBASE III PLUS Vocabulary

COMMAND	DEFINITION
!	Converts character to uppercase in @, SAY, GET commands (@ 5,5 GET Answer PICTURE "!").
#	Not equal to.
$	Substring function, used for finding a character string embedded within larger character string (LIST FOR 'Lemon' $ADDRESS).
&	Used for macro substitution (IF &FLD = '&COND').
( )	Used for logical and mathematical grouping [?(10 + 10)*5].
*	Multiplies two numbers (?10*10).
**	Exponent symbol. ?99**2 displays 99 squared. X = 1234**(1/3) stores the cube root of 1234 to memory variable X.
;	Splits long command lines into two separate lines.
^	Exponent symbol. ?34^5 displays 34 raised to the fifth power (45435424.00). In text, the ^ symbol usually means, "Hold down the Ctrl key."
+	Adds two numbers or links two character strings.
−	Subtracts two numbers or links two character strings with trailing blanks removed.
.AND.	Two things true simultaneously (LIST FOR 'Oak' $ADDRESS .AND. CITY = 'San Diego').
.NOT.	A condition is not true (DO WHILE .NOT. EOF).
.OR.	One or another of two conditions is true (LIST FOR CITY = 'San Diego' .OR. CITY = 'Los Angeles').
/	Divides two numbers (? 10/5).
<	Less than (LIST FOR LNAME < 'Smith').
< =	Less than or equal to (LIST FOR LNAME < = 'Smith').
=	Equal to (LIST FOR LNAME = 'Smith').
>	Greater than (LIST FOR LNAME > 'Appleby').

COMMAND	DEFINITION
> =	Greater than or equal to [LIST FOR DATE > = CTOD("03/01/86")].
?	Displays the contents of a field, memory variable, or the results of a mathematical equation (? 1 + 1).
??	Displays the contents of a field, memory variable, or expression without starting on a new line [?? SQRT(X)].
@	Formats screen and printer displays (@ 5,1 SAY 'Hi').
ABS	Returns the absolute value of a number [? ABS(-234) displays 234].
ACCEPT	Displays a prompt on the screen and waits for a response. Stores answer to a memory variable as Character data (ACCEPT 'Do you want more?' TO YN).
ALIAS	Allows a database to be accessed through two different names (USE MAIL ALIAS NAMES).
ALL	Refers to all records in the database (DISPLAY ALL, DELETE ALL, REPLACE ALL).
APPEND	Allows us to add new data to our database.
APPEND BLANK	Adds a new record to the bottom of a database, with all fields blank (APPEND BLANK).
APPEND FROM	Reads the records from another database into the database in use. Adds new records to the bottom of database in use (APPEND FROM TEMP).
ASC	Displays the ASCII value of a character [? ASC("A") displays 65].
ASSIST	Aids in the use of dBASE III PLUS by presenting menus (ASSIST).
AT	Shows the position at which one character string starts in another [?AT("B","AABBCC") displays 3 because B appears as the third character in "AABBCC"].
AVERAGE	Computes the average of a numeric field in a database [AVERAGE AMOUNT FOR MONTH (DATE) = 12].
B:	Signifies Drive B for storing data files (CREATE B:MAIL).

COMMAND	DEFINITION
B—>	Refers to a field from a database opened in work area 2 (or B) with the SELECT command. C—> refers to a field opened in work area 3 or C, and so forth (LIST CODE,B—>TITLE, QTY, AMOUNT).
BOF()	Beginning of file. Opposite of EOF() [?BOF()].
BROWSE	Displays a "screenful" of the database and allows us to scan and make changes to the database.
/C	Used with the SORT command to ignore upper-/lowercase in a sort (SORT ON LNAME/C, FNAME/C TO TEMP).
CALL	Executes an assembly language program (binary file) which has been placed into memory with the LOAD command.
CANCEL	Aborts command file execution and returns to the dot prompt (CANCEL).
CDOW	Displays the day of the week as a character (Sunday, Monday, Tuesday) for a Date field or memory variable [?CDOW(DATE)].
CHANGE	Globally edits a specific field in a database (CHANGE FIELD PHONE FOR CITY = "San Diego").
CHR	Displays the ASCII character for a number [? CHR(65) displays "A", ? CHR(7) rings the bell].
CLEAR	Clears the screen.
CLEAR ALL	Closes all the database, index, format, and relational databases. Undoes all SELECT commands (CLEAR ALL).
CLEAR FIELDS	Releases all fields from all work areas originally set with the SET FIELDS command.
CLEAR GETS	Releases GET variables from READ access (CLEAR GETS).
CLEAR MEMORY	Erases all current memory variables.
CLEAR TYPEAHEAD	Empties the typeahead buffer so that old keypresses do not affect current prompts.
CLOSE	Closes open files, of either alternate, database, format, index or procedure types (CLOSE DATABASES).

COMMAND	DEFINITION
CMONTH	Displays the month for a Date field or memory variable as a character (e.g. January) [? CMONTH(DATE)].
COL( )	Displays the current column position of the cursor on the screen [? COL( )].
COMMAND	Creates or edits a command file (MODIFY COMMAND MENU).
CONTINUE	Used with the LOCATE command, to find the next record with a particular characteristic.
COPY	Copies the contents of one database into another database.
COPY FILE	Copies a non-.DBF file to another file (COPY FILE MYPROG.PRG TO MYPROG.BAK).
COPY STRUCTURE	Copies the structure of a database to another database without copying the contents (COPY STRUCTURE TO MAIL2).
COUNT	Counts how many records in a database meet some criterion [COUNT FOR MONTH(DATE) = 12 TO DECEMBER].
CREATE	Allows us to create a database, and define its structure (CREATE MAIL).
CREATE LABEL	Creates a format file for mailing labels (same as MODIFY LABEL) (CREATE LABEL B:TWOCOL).
CREATE REPORT	Creates a custom report format (same as MODIFY REPORT) (CREATE REPORT BYNAME).
CREATE QUERY	Creates a query form and allows the user to fill in a Query.
CREATE SCREEN	Accesses the screen painter for creating custom forms.
CREATE VIEW	Creates a relationship among multiple databases and maintains links.
CTOD	Converts a date, stored as a Character (”01/01/86”) to a Date data type [LIST FOR DATE = CTOD(”01/01/86”)].
/D	Used with SORT to sort from largest to smallest, rather than smallest to largest (SORT ON ZIP/D TO TEMP).
DATE( )	Displays dBASE internal date [? DATE( )].

COMMAND	DEFINITION
DAY	Displays the day of the month for a Date data type as a number [? DAY(DATE)].
DBF	Displays the name of the database file currently in use [? DBF( )].
DEBUG	A debugging aid which displays echoed command lines to the printer (SET DEBUG ON).
DEFAULT	Changes the default drive for storing data files (SET DEFAULT TO B).
DELETE	Marks a record for deletion (DELETE RECORD 7).
DELETED( )	Evaluates to "true" if record is marked for deletion [LIST FOR DELETED( )].
DELIMITED	Copies dBASE databases to other data file formats (COPY TO MM.TXT. DELIMITED).
DIR	Shows files on disk (DIR B:*.PRG displays command file names on Drive B).
DISKSPACE	Returns the amount of space available on the currently logged disk drive [IF DISKSPACE( ) < 200].
DISPLAY	Shows information about a database, or its contents (DISPLAY ALL, DISPLAY STRUCTURE).
DISPLAY HISTORY	Displays the last 20 commands typed at the dot prompt.
DISPLAY MEMORY	Displays all current memory variables (DISPLAY MEMORY).
DISPLAY STATUS	Displays the current status of databases and index files in use, SET parameters, and function key (F1-F10) assignments (DISPLAY STATUS).
DO	Runs a command file (DO MAIL).
DO CASE	Sets up a clause of mutually exclusive options in a command file. Terminated with the ENDCASE command.
DO WHILE	Used with ENDDO to set up a loop in a command file [DO WHILE .NOT. EOF( )].
DTOC	Converts a date field or memory variable to a Character data type [LIST FOR DTOC(DATE) = "01/01/86"].
ECHO	A debugging aid, displays all statements in a command file as processed (SET ECHO ON).

COMMAND	DEFINITION
EDIT	Displays existing data in a record and allows you to change its contents (EDIT 17).
EJECT	Starts the paper in the printer on a new page (EJECT).
ELSE	Performs a set of commands if the criterion in an IF statement is false.
ENDDO	Used with the DO WHILE command to mark the bottom of a loop in a command file.
ENDIF	Marks the end of an IF clause in a command file.
EOF( )	End of File. Used primarily in DO WHILE loops in command files [DO WHILE .NOT. EOF( )].
ERASE	Deletes a specific file from the directory (ERASE TEMP.DBF).
ERROR	Returns a number indicating the error caught by an ON ERROR command.
EXACT	Determines how searches will function (SET EXACT ON).
EXIT	Escapes from a DO WHILE loop without terminating execution of the command file (EXIT).
EXP	Natural exponent of a number [? EXP(1)].
EXPORT	Copies data from a dBASE III database into another file in pfs format.
FIELD	Returns name of a field in a database file [? FIELD(3) displays the name of field number 3 in the currently open database].
FILE	Refers to a disk file. DISPLAY FILES shows disk files.
FIND	Used to look up information in an index file (FIND "Miller").
FKLABEL	Displays the names of function keys on a computer [? FKLABEL( )] would display F1, the name of the key on an IBM keyboard. On another computer, FKLABEL(1) might display another label.
FKMAX	Determines the number of programmable function keys on a given terminal [? FKMAX( ) returns 9 on an IBM keyboard, for programmable function keys F0 through F9].

COMMAND	DEFINITION
FOUND	The FOUND( ) function is True (.T.) when a FIND, SEEK, LOCATE, or CONTINUE command finds the requested record. Otherwise, ? FOUND( ) results in False (.F.).
GET	Used with the READ command to accept field and memory variable data from the screen (@ 5,1 SAY 'Last name' GET LNAME).
GETENV	Returns information about the operating system environment [? GETENV("COMSPEC") might display C:COMMAND.COM, indicating that the COMMAND.COM file is on the root directory of Drive C].
GO BOTTOM	Goes to the last record in a database.
GO TOP	Starts at the first record in a database.
HELP	Provides help on the screen for a command or function [HELP RECNO( )].
IF	Determines whether or not to perform commands in a command file based upon some criteria (IF ZIP = '92122').
IIF	Abbreviated version of the IF command using the syntax: IIF(<this is true>, <do this>, <otherwise do this>) [ROOT = SQRT(IIF (X>0,X,ABS(X))) takes the square root of the absolute value of X if X<0].
IMPORT	Reads data from a PFS:FILE database into dBASE III PLUS format.
INDEX	Creates an index file of sorted data, (INDEX ON LNAME TO NAMES), or uses an existing index to display data in sorted order (USE MAIL INDEX NAMES).
INKEY	Scans the keyboard to see if a key has been pressed, and returns the keypress as an ASCII code between 0 and 255. Does not interrupt program execution to scan the keyboard.
INPUT	Displays a prompt on the screen, and waits for a response. Used with numeric data (INPUT 'How many labels per page' TO PER:PAGE).
INSERT	Puts a new record into a specified position in the database (GOTO 4 ↵ INSERT BEFORE ↵).
INT	Integer portion of a number, with decimal places truncated (not rounded) [? INT(1.99999) displays 1].

COMMAND	DEFINITION
ISALPHA	Determines whether the first letter of a variable is a letter or not. Example: ? ISALPHA("123 A St.") returns .F.
ISCOLOR	Returns .T. if color monitor is use, otherwise returns .F.
ISLOWER	Determines if the first letter of a character string is a lowercase letter [? ISLOWER("alan") returns .T.].
ISUPPER	Determines if the first letter of a character string is uppercase [? ISUPPER("Snowball") returns .T.].
JOIN	Creates a third database based upon the contents of two existing databases (JOIN TO NEWDB FOR CODE = B—> CODE)
LABEL	Prints mailing labels in the format specified in a file created with the MODIFY LABEL command (LABEL FORM TWOCOL TO PRINT).
LEFT	Returns the left portion of a character string [? LEFT("Snowball",4) returns Snow].
LEN	Displays the length of a string [? LEN(TRIM(LNAME))].
LIST	Shows the contents of a database.
LIST FOR	Lists data that have some characteristic in common (LIST FOR LNAME = 'Smith').
LOAD	Places an assembly language (binary) file into memory where it can be executed with a CALL command.
LOCATE	Finds a record with a particular characteristic (LOCATE FOR LNAME 'Smith').
LOG	Calculates the natural logarithm of a number [? LOG(2.72)].
LOOP	Skips all commands between itself and the ENDDO command in a DO WHILE loop (LOOP).
LOWER	Converts upper- to lowercase [? LOWER(NAME)].
LTRIM	Removes leading blanks [? LTRIM(" Hello") displays Hello without leading blanks].
LUPDATE	Returns the date of the last update for the currently open database file [? LUPDATE()].

COMMAND	DEFINITION
M—>	Specifies a memory variable. Useful when a field and memory variable share the same name (? M—>LNAME).
MAX	Returns the higher of two numbers [? MAX(20,40) returns 40].
MEMORY	Displays memory variables in RAM (DISPLAY MEMORY).
MIN	Returns the lower of two numbers [? MIN(20,40) returns 20].
MOD	Returns the modulus (remainder) of two numbers [? MOD(5,3) returns 2].
MODIFY	Used to create or change a COMMAND file, database STRUCTURE, LABEL format, REPORT format, SCREEN, or VIEW file.
MONTH	Returns the month of a Date field or variable as a number (1-12) [LIST FOR MONTH (EXPDATE) = 12].
NDX	Displays the names of active index files (1-7). To display the name of the Master index file, enter the command [? NDX(1)].
OFF	Leaves record numbers out of displays (LIST OFF). Also, turns off parameters (SET PRINT OFF).
ON	Sets dBASE parameters into ON mode (SET PRINT ON).
ON ERROR	Executes a dBASE command when an error occurs.
OS	Returns the name of the operating system in use [? OS( )].
PACK	Permanently deletes records marked for deletion from the database.
PARAMETERS	Command used to define variables passed by a DO WITH command.
PCOL	Displays the current column position of the printer head [? PCOL( )].
PICTURE	Used with the GET command to make templates and define acceptable character types [@ 12,1 SAY 'Phone number' GET PHONE PICTURE'(999)999-9999'].
PRINT	Sends displays to the printer (SET PRINT ON,

COMMAND	DEFINITION
	REPORT FORM BYNAME TO PRINT).
PRIVATE	Specifies memory variables that are automatically erased when a command file terminates (PRIVATE ALL LIKE M∗).
PROCEDURE	An advanced programming technique whereby tasks are broken down into flexible routines accessed throughout a system. The PROCEDURE command names a procedure, SET PROCEDURE opens a procedure file.
PROW	Displays the current row position of the printer head [? PROW( )].
PUBLIC	Specifies memory variables that are not to be erased when command file terminates (PUBLIC CHOICE, LP, X, Y, Z).
QUIT	Exits dBASE III PLUS back to the operating system's A—> prompt.
RANGE	Specifies a range of acceptable values with @, SAY, GET, READ commands (@ 12,5 SAY "Enter choice" GET CHOICE RANGE 1,5).
READ	Used with @, SAY, and GET to read in field and memory variable data from the screen.
READKEY	Returns the key pressed to exit a full screen operation like APPEND, BROWSE, CHANGE, CREATE, EDIT, INSERT, MODIFY, or READ. Keypress is stored as an integer in the range of 0 to 255.
RECALL	Brings back a record marked for deletion (RECALL RECORD 14).
RECCOUNT	Displays the number of records in the open database file [? RECCOUNT( )].
RECNO( )	Record number [LIST FOR RECNO( ) > = 10 .AND. RECNO( ) < = 20 lists all records in the range of records number 10 to 20].
RECORD	Refers to a single record (DELETE RECORD 4).
RECSIZE	Returns the number of bytes in each record in a database [? RECSIZE( )].
REINDEX	Recreates all active index files (REINDEX).
RELEASE	Erases current memory variables (RELEASE ALL).

COMMAND	DEFINITION
RENAME	Changes the name of a disk file (RENAME OLD.DBF TO NEW.DBF).
REPLACE	Changes the current contents of a field with new data. Used in global deletes (REPLACE ALL LNAME WITH 'Smith' FOR LNAME = 'SMITH').
REPLICATE	Replicates a character in a variable up to 255 times [ULINE = REPLICATE("-",80) creates a memory variable named ULINE consisting of 80 hyphens].
REPORT	Allows us to either create a report format (MODIFY REPORT), or display data in report format (REPORT FORM BYNAME).
RESTORE	Recalls memory variables that were saved to disk with the SAVE command back into RAM (RESTORE FROM THOUGHT).
RESUME	Continues running a program that has been temporarily suspended for debugging purposes.
RETRY	Used in networking to retry accessing a record or file that is locked.
RETURN	Returns control from a command file to the dot prompt or another command file.
RETURN TO MASTER	Returns control from a subprogram back to the first-run program, usually the Main Menu program (RETURN TO MASTER).
RIGHT	Takes characters from the right side of a character string [? RIGHT("Snowball",4) displays ball].
ROUND	Rounds a number to a specified number of decimal places [? ROUND(RATE*HOURS),2].
ROW( )	Displays the current row position of the cursor on the screen [? ROW()].
RTRIM	Same as the TRIM function below.
RUN	Executes a program outside of dBASE III PLUS. For example, RUN WS runs the WordStar program (RUN DATE).
SAVE	Stores a copy of memory variables to a disk file (SAVE TO THOUGHT).
SAY	Used with @ to position output on the screen or printer (@ 5,2 SAY 'Hi').

COMMAND	DEFINITION
SDF	Standard Data Format. Copies dBASE files to other database formats (COPY TO BASIC.DAT SDF FOR RECNO( ) < 100).
SEEK	Looks up the contents of a memory variable in an index file [STORE CTOD(''01/01/86'') TO LOOKUP ↵, SEEK LOOKUP].
SELECT	Assigns databases in use to any one of ten work areas numbered 1 through 10, or lettered A through J (SELECT 1, SELECT A).
SET	Displays a menu of SET parameters and allows changes to be made via a menu of options (SET).
SET ALTERNATE	Transfers all screen activity (except @, SAYs) to a data file, after the file name is specified and the alternate is on (SET ALTE TO file, SET ALTE ON).
SET BELL	Determines whether or not the bell sounds when a field is filled on an APPEND, EDIT, or custom screen (SET BELL OFF).
SET CARRY	When the CARRY option is on, a newly appended record automatically receives the contents of the previous record, which may then be edited.
SET CATALOG	Creates catalog files and sets recording of file names either ON or OFF.
SET CENTURY	ON displays the century in date displays, OFF hides the century.
SET DATE	Determines the format for displaying date data. Options are AMERICAN, ANSI, BRITISH, ITALIAN, FRENCH, GERMAN.
SET COLOR	Changes color of screen to blue.
SET CONFIRM	Determines whether pressing the Return key is necessary after filling a screen prompt (SET CONFIRM ON).
SET CONSOLE	When console is off, nothing is displayed on the screen (SET CONSOLE OFF).
SET DOHISTORY	When ON, lines from command files are recorded in the HISTORY file. When OFF, only lines typed in from the dot prompt are recorded.
SET DEBUG	Sends output of an ECHO to the printer when on (SET DEBUG ON).

COMMAND	DEFINITION
SET DECIMALS	Sets the minimum number of decimals displayed in the results of mathematical calculations (SET DECIMALS TO 2).
SET DEFAULT	Determines which disk drive dBASE uses when looking for disk files with the USE, DO, INDEX, SELECT, and other commands that access files (SET DEFAULT TO B).
SET DELETED	Determines whether or not records marked for deletion are displayed with LIST, DISPLAY, ?, REPORT, and LABEL commands (SET DELETED ON hides deleted records).
SET DELIMITER	Determines how field entries are displayed on the screen with APPEND, EDIT, and custom screens (SET DELIMITER TO "[ ]" encloses fields in brackets).
SET DEVICE	Determines whether @, SAY commands display data on the screen or on the printer (SET DEVICE TO PRINTER, SET DEVICE TO SCREEN).
SET ECHO	A debugging aid that displays each line of a command file as it is being processed (SET ECHO ON).
SET ESCAPE	Determines whether or not a command file terminates when Esc is pressed (SET ESCAPE OFF aborts the power of the Esc key).
SET EXACT	Determines how dBASE compares two values either with an exact match or with first letters only. With EXACT off, Smith will match Smithsonian (SET EXACT ON).
SET FIELDS	Determines which fields will be displayed, and which will not.
SET FILTER	Limits display of data to those records which match a criterion (SET FILTER TO LNAME = "Smith" will limit output of LIST, REPORT, LABEL, etc. to Smiths).
SET FILTER TO FILE	Uses the contents of a query (.QRY) file to set up a filter condition (SET FILTER TO NOTBILLD gets filtering information from the NOTBILLD.QRY file. SET FILTER TO with no file name clears all filter conditions).
SET FIXED	Sets the number of decimal places that will appear with all numeric displays. Usually used in

COMMAND	DEFINITION
	conjunction with the SET DECIMALS command (SET FIXED ON).
SET FORMAT	Specifies a custom screen display stored in a format (.FMT) file to be used with EDIT and APPEND command (SET FORMAT TO ADDNAMES, SET FORMAT TO).
SET FUNCTION	Reprograms the function keys (F1-F10) to perform custom tasks. DISPLAY STATUS shows current settings (SET FUNCTION 10 TO 'BROWSE').
SET HEADING	Determines whether field names will be displayed above data in DISPLAY, LIST, SUM, and AVERAGE commands (SET HEADING OFF removes field names from displays).
SET HELP	Determines whether or not the message "Do you want some help?" appears during an error (SET HELP OFF removes the prompt).
SET HISTORY	Specifies the number of commands stored in the HISTORY file, or the status of HISTORY [SET HISTORY TO 50 stores 50 lines in the history file. SET HISTORY OFF stops recording command lines].
SET INDEX	Specifies index file(s) to make active with a database (SET INDEX TO NAMES, ZIPS).
SET INTENSITY	Determines whether or not field entries are displayed on the screen in reverse video (SET INTENSITY OFF removes reverse video).
SET MARGIN	Adjusts the left-hand margin for printer displays (SET MARGIN TO 5).
SET MEMOWIDTH	Determines the width of memo field displays.
SET MENUS	Determines whether or not cursor control commands appear in a menu above APPEND, EDIT, BROWSE, and other displays (SET MENUS ON displays the menus).
SET MESSAGE	Displays a message at the bottom of the screen [SET MESSAGE TO "How are you today?"].
SET ORDER	Selects an index file from a list to make primary.
SET PATH	Specifies directory paths to search for disk files (SET PATH TO \C:DBIII will cause dBASE to search path DBIII on Drive C if file not found on current drive).

COMMAND	DEFINITION
SET PRINT	Determines whether displays will be echoed to the printer (SET PRINT ON causes all screen displays to be printed; SET PRINT OFF returns to normal mode).
SET PROCEDURE	Advanced programming technique whereby subprograms are combined into a single file and assigned procedure names (SET PROCEDURE TO ROUTINES).
SET RELATION	Sets up a relationship between two data files in use, based upon a field that they have in common (SET RELATION TO CODE INTO MASTER).
SET SAFETY	Determines whether or not the message (file name) already exists. overwrite it? appears when a file is about to be overwritten (SET SAFETY OFF disables).
SET STEP	Debugging aid used to limit command file execution to a single line at a time (SET STEP ON).
SET TALK	Determines whether or not dBASE displays a response to various commands. Usually, SET TALK OFF is used in command files to eliminate dBASE messages.
SET UNIQUE	Used with the INDEX command to display an ordered listing of unique field values. Can be used as an aid in checking for duplicates (SET UNIQUE ON).
SET VIEW	Opens a view (.VUE) file.
SKIP	Skips to next record in the database. Can also skip more or less than 1 record (SKIP 10, SKIP − 3).
SORT	Rearranges records on a database into sorted order. Requires that records be sorted to another database (SORT ON LNAME TO TEMP).
SPACE	Generates blanks [LNAME = SPACE(20) creates a memory variable called LNAME that consists of 20 blank spaces].
SQRT	Displays the square root of a number [? SQRT(64), STORE SQRT(64) TO X].
STEP	A debugging aid, pauses after each line in a command file is processed (SET STEP ON).

COMMAND	DEFINITION
STORE	Stores a value to a memory variable (STORE 1 TO COUNTER).
STR	Converts a number to a string. Useful for complex sorting with index files [INDEX ON CODE + SCR(AMOUNT,12,2) TO TEST].
STRUCTURE	Refers to the structure, rather than the contents of a database (DISPLAY STRUCTURE).
STUFF	Allows you to put data into an existing character string without dismantling the original string [? STUFF("HaHoHa",3,2,"Ha") returns HaHaHa—because Ha was stuffed at the 3rd character, replacing 2 characters].
SUBSTR	Isolates a portion of a string [? SUBSTR("ABCDEFG",3,2) displays CD, a substring starting at the third character, 2 characters long].
SUM	Adds a column of fields, and displays the total (SUM AMOUNT).
SUSPEND	Halts execution of a command file and returns control to the dot prompt. The RESUME command restarts execution.
TALK	Sets dBASE's miscellaneous messages on or off (SET TALK OFF).
TEXT	Starts a block of text in a command file, terminated with the command ENDTEXT.
TIME	Displays the current system time [? TIME()].
TOTAL	Summarizes and totals a database to another database. Files must be either presorted or preindexed (TOTAL ON CODE TO SALESUMM).
TRANSFORM	Like a PICTURE statement, lets you define formats for data displayed with the LIST, DISPLAY, REPORT and LABEL commands [LIST TRANSFORM (AMOUNT,"###,###,###.##") displays all amounts in ###,###,###.## format].
TRIM	Removes trailing blanks from a field's contents [LIST TRIM(FNAME),LNAME].
TYPE	Displays the contents of a DOS ASCII file (TYPE MYREPORT.TXT).

COMMAND	DEFINITION
UPDATE	Revises the file in use by adding or replacing data from another database (UPDATE ON CODE FROM SALES REPLACE PRICE WITH B—>PRICE).
UPPER	Converts lowercase letters to uppercase [INDEX ON UPPER(LNAME) TO NAMES].
USE	Tells dBASE which database to work with (USE MAIL).
VAL	Changes character strings to numerics [? VAL(ADDRESS)].
VERSION	Displays the version number of dBASE III PLUS in use [? VERSION( )].
WAIT	Stops execution of a command file, and waits for user to press a key. Key press is stored to a memory variable (WAIT TO DATA).
YEAR	Displays the year of a Date field or variable in 19XX format [LIST FOR YEAR(DATE) = 1986].
ZAP	Permanently removes all records from a database and active index files.

Converting dBASE II Files to dBASE III PLUS Files

I f you have some dBASE II databases and command files that you want to convert to dBASE III PLUS, you can do so very easily with the dCONVERT program.

THE dCONVERT PROGRAM

The dBASE III PLUS Sample Programs Disk contains the program dCONVERT. This program can be used to convert dBASE II databases and command files to dBASE III PLUS. To use it, put the Sample Programs Disk in Drive A, or copy the DCONVERT.EXE program to your hard disk. To run dCONVERT, enter the command DCONVERT from the A> or C> prompt. A menu of options appears on the screen, as shown in Figure D.1.

The *dBASE III PLUS Sample Programs Disk* is one of the disks that comes with the original dBASE III PLUS package.

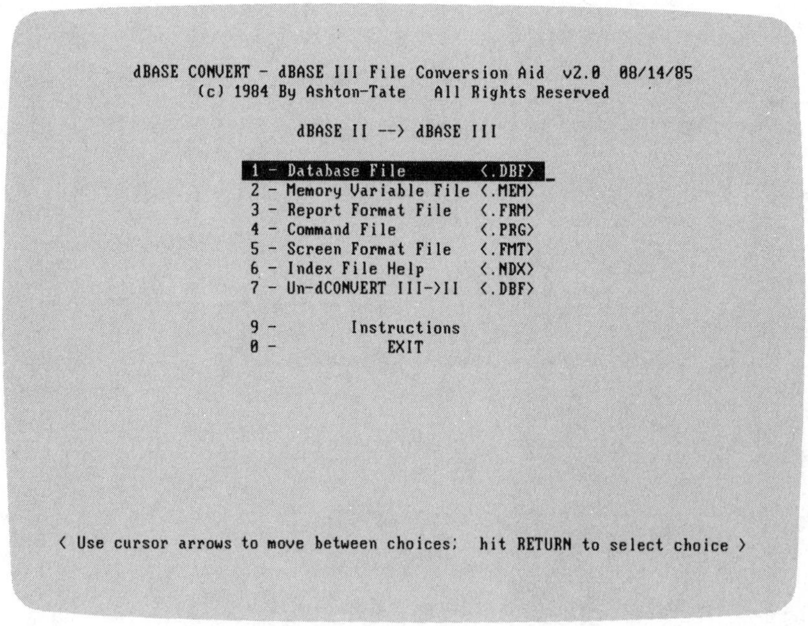

```
     dBASE CONVERT - dBASE III File Conversion Aid  v2.0  08/14/85
          (c) 1984 By Ashton-Tate   All Rights Reserved

               dBASE II --> dBASE III

            1 - Database File        (.DBF)
            2 - Memory Variable File (.MEM)
            3 - Report Format File   (.FRM)
            4 - Command File         (.PRG)
            5 - Screen Format File   (.FMT)
            6 - Index File Help       (.NDX)
            7 - Un-dCONVERT III->II  (.DBF)

            9 -         Instructions
            0 -             EXIT




   < Use cursor arrows to move between choices;  hit RETURN to select choice >
```

Figure D.1: dBASE File Conversion Menu

You can use the arrow keys on the numeric keypad to highlight an option, and then press Return to select the option. Option **9** displays instructions for using dCONVERT.

If you have a computer with two floppy-disk drives, you may want to put the converted files on a separate disk. To do so, first create a blank, formatted disk using the DOS FORMAT command. Then, load the Sample Programs Disk into Drive A, and enter this command:

```
DCONVERT A: B: ◄──┘
```

When the dCONVERT menu appears on the screen, you can remove the Sample Programs disk from Drive A, and put in the disk with the files that you wish to convert. dCONVERT will stay in memory and allow you to convert as many files as you wish. The original files in Drive A will remain unchanged and the modified files will be stored on the disk in Drive B.

CONVERTING DATABASES

Option **1** from the dCONVERT menu will change any dBASE II database to dBASE III PLUS format. When you select this option, dCONVERT will display the names of all .DBF files, and ask you to type the name of the file to convert. After you type the file name, dCONVERT will display the message "Working . . . ", and then it will inform you when it's done.

Since colons are not allowed in dBASE III PLUS field names, they will be replaced with underscore characters. Other than that, the structure and content of the dBASE III PLUS file will be identical to that of the dBASE II file. The converted file will have the same name as the original file. The original file will have the same name, but the extension will be changed to .DBB.

Option **7** from the dCONVERT menu allows you to convert files from dBASE III PLUS to dBASE II. However, the dBASE III PLUS database must fit the rules of dBASE II: 32 fields or fewer, maximum record length of 1,000, and no more than 6,535 records.

CONVERTING INDEX FILES

The easiest way to convert an index file is to convert the .DBF file, then create the index files again with the INDEX ON command. Optionally, you can use dCONVERT to help make the conversion. Select option **6** from the dCONVERT menu, and then enter the name of the index file to convert (NAMES). When the conversion is done, load dBASE III PLUS and use the appropriate dBASE III PLUS database (MAIL). Then run the program created by dCONVERT, which has the same name as the index file, and the extension .RX. To convert the NAMES index file, type the command DO NAMES.RX from the dot prompt. The NAMES.RX command file will reindex the file for you.

CONVERTING REPORT FORMATS

Option **3** from the dCONVERT menu allows you to convert dBASE II REPORT FORM (.FRM) files to dBASE III PLUS format. Simply select the option and specify the name of the format file to convert. From the dBASE III PLUS dot prompt, use the REPORT FORM command to display the report. Then, you can use MODIFY REPORT to make changes to the report.

CONVERTING MEMORY FILES

If you use .MEM files (disk files with memory variables stored in them), use option **2** from the dCONVERT menu to convert them to dBASE III PLUS. The dBASE III PLUS .MEM file will be about 25 percent larger than the dBASE II .MEM file, primarily because dBASE III PLUS stores numbers with more digits of accuracy. *Note:* Colons embedded in memory variable names will be converted to underscore characters.

CONVERTING CUSTOM SCREEN FILES

Option 5 from the dCONVERT menu allows you to convert dBASE II custom screen files (.FMT) to dBASE III PLUS. Colons embedded in field names will be replaced by underscore characters to match field names in the dBASE III PLUS database.

CONVERTING COMMAND FILES

dCONVERT can even convert dBASE II command files (.PRG or .CMD) to dBASE III PLUS, but with limited accuracy. The converted programs will have the commands SET HEADING OFF and SET SAFETY OFF near the top of the program. These options remove headings from LIST and DISPLAY commands, and disable the dBASE III PLUS prompts which ask for permission before overwriting files. This is done to make the dBASE III PLUS program perform as closely as possible to the original dBASE II program. Of course, you can remove these new lines to take advantage of the headings and safety features.

In some situations, dCONVERT will be unable to make an appropriate change. In this case dCONVERT will display a warning message on the screen and continue converting the rest of the command file. The converted command file will have notes, beginning with the characters *!!, that inform you of those sections of the program that may require further attention.

Some dBASE II commands, such as RESET, SET HEADING TO, SET DATE, SET RAW, and TEST, have no dBASE III PLUS equivalent. dCONVERT will eliminate these and inform you of the change with a screen message. If your command file needs a capability that is not available in dBASE III PLUS, you'll have to figure out how to perform a similar task. For example, dBASE III PLUS does not support the SET LINKAGE command. However, the SET RELATION command performs a similar task, so you can set up the relationship between the two files in a different manner.

Generally speaking, dCONVERT does an excellent job of converting dBASE II programs to dBASE III PLUS. The problems it cannot solve are few and far between.

CHAPTER 1 EXERCISES: UNDERSTANDING DATABASES

1. With paper and pencil, list the fields you might use to store information from your check register in a database.

2. On the same piece of paper, write down the number of records and the number of fields contained in the table shown in Figure E.1.

Bristlecone pine	Slow growth	Dense, bushy	Hardy
Knobcone pine	Rapid growth	Open, irregular	Hardy
Foxtail pine	Very slow	Open, irregular	Hardy
Jack pine	Moderate	Open, irregular	Hardy
Calabrian pine	Rapid	Dense, symmetrical	Warm climate
Lacebark pine	Slow	Shrubby, picturesque	Hardy
Beach pine	Moderate	Pyramidal, irregular	Humid climate
Pinion nut pine	Slow	Flat-crowned	Hardy

Figure E.1

CHAPTER 2 EXERCISES: BUILDING A DATABASE

1. Start dBASE III PLUS on your computer, and scroll through all the options on the main (Assistant) menu.

2. Leave the menu to access the dot prompt, then return to the Assistant menu.

3. View the help screen for the *Copy file* option on the *Tools* pull-down menu, then return to the Assistant menu.

4. Create the "check register" database with the structure shown in Figure E.2, using the tips below as a guide:

    • Assign the name CHECKS to the database, unless your instructor has instructed you to use some other file name.

    • Don't be intimidated by the Numeric and Date data types; you'll need them in later chapter exercises. When specifying the type of each field, type **N** for the Numeric fields, and **D** for the Date field.

    • When you've finished creating the database structure and pressed ◄┘ to confirm, type **N** when the screen asks if you want to "*Input data records now.*"

```
Field      Field Name    Type        Width     Dec
1          CHECKNO       Numeric        4        0
2          DATE          Date           8
3          DESCRIPT      Character     38
4          AMOUNT        Numeric        9        2
```

Figure E.2

5. Open the database you created in step 4, and use the *Append* option from the *Update* pull-down menu to add the transactions shown in Figure E.3. Use these tips to help:

    • When typing in numbers, type them exactly as shown in the figure.

- When typing in dates, you don't need to type the slashes. For example, to type in the date 12/01/90, you would type 120190. To enter 1/1/91, you'd type 010191. If you type in a date incorrectly, you'll hear a beep and see the message "Invalid date. (press SPACE)." If that happens, press the Space bar and try entering the date again.

- When you finish typing in all transactions, press ↵ in the last (blank) record to save your work and return to the Assistant menu.

```
CHECKNO DATE     DESCRIPT                      AMOUNT
      0 12/01/90 Deposit (starting balance)   2500.00
   1001 12/10/90 Dr. Robbins                    100.00
   1002 12/10/90 Avco Corporation                50.00
   1003 12/10/90 Firefighter's Assoc.            50.00
   1004 12/12/90 Kids R' Us                      37.87
      0 12/15/90 Deposit                       1000.00
   1005 12/15/90 Apt Properties (rent)          800.00
   1006 12/16/90 Abalone Restaurant              47.50
   1007 12/17/90 SDG&E (utilities)               75.00
   1008 12/20/90 NWSD Water District             65.00
   1009 12/20/90 Kids R' Us                     150.00
   1010 12/21/90 DR. LIM                         50.00
```

Figure E.3

6. View the contents of your database on the screen using the *List* option from the **R***etrieve* pull-down menu.

7. Try listing only the check numbers and amounts on your screen now.

8. If you have a printer, use the *List* option from the **R***etrieve* pull-down menu to print a copy of the entire database. (Don't worry if the printed copy does not appear right away; keep reading below.)

9. Some laser printers do not eject a printed page from the printer until the page is completely filled. If you completed step 8 above, and need to eject the page from the printer,

try the following steps:

- Leave the Assistant to access the dot prompt.

- At the dot prompt type **EJECT** and then press ←┘. (This command ejects the page from the printer; there is no equivalent option on the Assistant menu.)

- Type **ASSIST** and press ←┘ to return to the Assistant menu.

10. Exit dBASE III PLUS now to return to the DOS prompt. (If your instructor has provided you with a disk, don't forget to take the disk with you when you leave the computer.)

CHAPTER 3 EXERCISES: SEARCHING THE DATABASE

1. Start dBASE III PLUS and access the Assistant menu. If you have not yet created the check register database from the Chapter 2 exercises, complete all those steps now.

2. Open (*Set Up*) the CHECKS database that you created in the Chapter 2 exercises.

3. Using the *List* option from the *Retrieve* menu, list only the checks written to Kids R' Us (that is, DESCRIPT = Kids). You should see checks 1004 and 1009 listed.

4. Using a the *List* option from the *Retrieve* menu, list only the deposits (that is, CHECKNO = 0). You should see two deposits listed.

5. Using the same menu options, list only the checks, not the deposits (that is, CHECKNO < > 0). You should see checks 1001 to 1010 listed, without any deposits.

6. Using the same menu commands, list all transactions that are greater than, or equal to $1,000.00 (that is, AMOUNT > = 1000). You should see the two deposits listed.

7. Using the *List* option from the *Retrieve* menu again, construct a field list that contains only the DATE, DESCRIPT, and AMOUNT fields, then display transactions from December 10th (for example, DATE = 12/10/90). You should see three checks listed from 12/10/90.

8. Use the *List* option from the *Retrieve* pull-down menu to display all transactions that took place between December 15th and December 20th inclusive. (Hint: date is greater than or equal to 12/15/90 *and* date is less than or equal to 12/20/90.) You should see one deposit, and checks 1005 through 1009 listed.

9. Go to the dot prompt and enter a **LIST** command to display only checks that have the letters "SD" embedded in the DESCRIPT field. You should see two checks listed.

10. At the dot prompt, enter a **LIST** command that displays checks written for rent or utilities. (Hint: list for "rent" embedded in description, *or* "util" embedded in description.)

11. At the dot prompt, enter a command that will display checks written to doctors (that is, the DESCRIPT field begins with DR.). Notice, however, that Dr. (lowercase) is used in one record and DR. (uppercase) is used in another. You should see two records written to doctors.

12. Quit dBASE III PLUS to return to the DOS prompt.

CHAPTER 4 EXERCISES: SORTING THE DATABASE

1. Start dBASE III PLUS, and open your CHECKS database file.

2. Using the *Sort* option on the *Organize* pull-down menu, create a copy of the database that is sorted by the DESCRIPT field. Name the sorted copy of the file TRANSACT.

3. Open the TRANSACT database.

4. Using the *List* option from the *Retrieve* menu, construct a field list that will display fields in the order DESCRIPT, AMOUNT, DATE, then execute the command to view the results. Notice that the descriptions are in alphabetical order, and the record numbers are in ascending order.

5. Reopen your original CHECKS database, and note that if you list all of its records, they are still in their original order because the sorted records are stored in a separate database.

6. Use the *Index* option on the *Organize* pull-down menu to create an index based on the DESCRIPT field in the CHECKS database. Name the index file DESCRIPT.

7. Using the *List* option on the *Retrieve* menu, construct a field list that will display fields in the order DESCRIPT, CHECKNO, DATE, AMOUNT, then execute the command. Notice that the descriptions are in alphabetical order, but the record numbers are in random order. That's because an index file is now controlling the sort order.

8. Use the *Append* option on the *Update* menu to add these two transactions to the database:

1011	12/21/90	Aardvark Designs	88.50
1012	12/22/90	Visa	95.00

9. List the records again, and notice where the new transactions are listed.

10. List the records in their original order. (Hint: reopen the database without the index, then list all its records.)

11. Quit dBASE III PLUS. (If you are curious about doing sorts-within-sorts with this database, you might want to peek at the section titled *Complex Sorts* beginning on page 342.)

CHAPTER 5 EXERCISES: EDITING AND MODIFYING DATABASES

1. Start dBASE III PLUS and open the CHECKS database file with the DESCRIPT index file.

2. Use the *Locate* option on the *Position* pull-down menu to move to the record written to Apt Properties (that is, DESCRIPT equals "Apt").

3. Use the *Edit* option on the *Update* menu to view that record.

4. Change the word *Apt* to *Adept*.

5. Save your change, and return to the Assistant menu.

6. Use the BROWSE screen to change DR. LIM to Dr. Lim.

7. Stay in the BROWSE screen, and mark the record that contains check 1012 (written to Visa) for deletion.

8. Save your changes and return to the Assistant menu.

9. List all the records to verify that check #1012 is marked for deletion.

10. Pack the database, then list the records again to verify that check #1012 has been deleted.

11. Leave the Assistant menu, and switch to the dot prompt.

12. Enter a command to mark all the deposits (records with 0 in the CHECKNO field) for deletion.

13. From the dot prompt, list all the deleted records (both deposits should be listed).

14. Recall the deleted records with a single command at the dot prompt.

15. List all the records (from the dot prompt) to verify that no more records are marked for deletion.

16. Use the ASSIST command to leave the dot prompt and return to the Assistant menu.

17. Modify the structure of the database to change the width of the DESCRIPT field to 30.

18. Reopen the database without the index, and list all the records to review your modified database with the transactions in their original order. Then quit dBASE.

CHAPTER 6 EXERCISES: CREATING AND PRINTING FORMATTED REPORTS

1. Open the CHECKS database without any index. (You won't be adding, changing, or deleting records in this exercise, so you need not worry about corrupting the index.)

2. Go to the report generator, and assign the file name REGISTER to the report along the way.

3. In the report generator, assign the page title *Check Register* to the report.

4. Change the *Page eject before printing* option to No, and the *Page eject after printing* option to Yes.

5. Set up the report format as shown in Figure E.4 using the tips below as your guide:

   - In the bottom of Figure E.4, 9999 represents the position of the CHECKNO field, mm/dd/yy represents the DATE field, the X's represent the DESCRIPT field, and ######.## represents the AMOUNT field.

   - Add an extra space to the width of each field (that is, make the CHECKNO field five spaces wide, the DATE field 9 spaces wide, and so forth.

   - dBASE will attempt to total the Numeric fields automatically. For the time being, change the *Total this column* option to No when placing the CHECKNO and AMOUNT fields on the report.

6. Save the completed report format and return to the Assistant menu.

7. Display a copy of the report on your screen.

8. If you have a printer available, print a copy of the report.

9. Use the report format to list only checks (no deposits) on either the screen or printer.

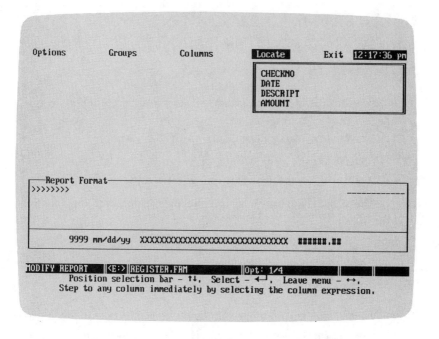

Figure E.4

10. Go to the dot prompt, and open the CHECKS database with the DESCRIPT index.

11. Print a copy of the REGISTER report from the dot prompt.

12. Quit dBASE.

CHAPTER 7 EXERCISES: DESIGNING CUSTOM SCREEN DISPLAYS

1. Open the CHECKS database without the index file.

2. Create a custom format file like the one shown in Figure E.5, using the tips below as your guide:

   - Select the *Format* option from the *Create* pull-down menu to get started.

   - When prompted, assign the file name EDITCHEX to the format file.

   - Place all the fields on the report format, then push them down with the ^N key to make room for the box at the top.

   - Where the figure shows <Your Name Here>, type in your own name.

   - The sample form shown in the figure does not use any modified picture templates or picture functions.

   - Remember that when you edit records, the Insert mode determines whether new text you type into a field is inserted into the existing text, or replaces existing text. The Insert mode works the same way with text (not field templates) on the Screen Painter. Pressing Ins turns the Insert mode on and off.

3. When the form is designed to your liking, save it and return to the Assistant menu.

4. From the Assistant menu, activate the custom form with the *Format for Screen* option from the *Set Up* menu.

5. Use the *Edit* option on the *Update* menu to view your database through the form, and scroll through some records with the PgUp and PgDn keys.

6. Quit dBASE.

```
 Set Up          Modify             Options          Exit  12:21:08 pm
┌──────────────────────────────────────────────────────────────────────┐
│  Electronic Check Register            Created by <Your Name Here>      │
└──────────────────────────────────────────────────────────────────────┘

 Check Number    9999    (Enter 0 for deposits and other credits)

 Date            99/99/99

 Description     XXXXXXXXXXXXXXXXXXXXXXXXXXXX

 Amount          999999.99

┌────────────────┬─────────────────┬────────────────┬─────────────────────────┐
│ Move Cursor    │ Change Record   │ Delete         │ Done                    │
│      Up        │                 │                │                         │
│ Left   Right   │ Next:    PgDn   │ Character: Del │ Save changes: Ctrl-End  │
│      Down      │ Previous: PgUp  │ Field:  Ctrl-Y │ Abandon changes:   Esc  │
│ arrow keys     │                 │ Record: Ctrl-U │                         │
└────────────────┴─────────────────┴────────────────┴─────────────────────────┘
 MODIFY SCREEN   ||<E:>||EDITCHEX.SCR           ||Pg 01 Row 20 Col 00||
        Enter text.  Drag field or box under cursor with ←┘.  F10 for menu.
                       Screen field definition blackboard
```

Figure E.5

CHAPTER 8 EXERCISES: MANAGING NUMBERS AND DATES

1. Start dBASE, and open the CHECKS database without an index file.

2. Use the *Sum* option on the *Retrieve* pull-down menu to sum the AMOUNT field for all the deposits (that is, records with CHECKNO equal to zero).

3. Use the *Sum* option on the *Retrieve* pull-down menu to sum the AMOUNT field for all the checks (that is, records with CHECKNO greater than zero).

4. Use the *Sum* option on the *Retrieve* pull-down menu to sum the AMOUNT field for checks written on 12/21/90.

5. Use the *Count* feature on the *Retrieve* pull-down menu to count how many checks have been written. Exclude the deposits from the count.

6. Using the *Report* option on the *Modify* pull-down menu as your starting point, bring the REGISTER.FRM report that you created in the Chapter 6 exercises back onto the screen for modification.

7. Select LOCATE from the menu at the top, and AMOUNT from the pull-down menu that appears.

8. Change the *Total this column* option from No to Yes.

9. Save your change and return to the Assistant menu.

10. Print the report on the screen, and notice that the entire AMOUNT column is now totaled at the bottom of the report.

11. There's just one little problem with this report; it produces a true total, not a balance. There are two different possible solutions to this problem: either store deposits and checks in separate fields, so that they can be summed separately; or enter checks and any other withdrawals as negative numbers into the database. For the current example, let's use

the second approach. To save you some time, I'll show you how to change each check entry to a negative number with a single *Replace* command. Follow these steps:

a. Select *Replace* from the *Update* pull-down menu.

b. Select AMOUNT as the field to replace.

c. Type – 1*AMOUNT as the numeric expression. (This means – 1 times AMOUNT, which converts the number from a positive to a negative.)

d. Press ⏎.

e. Press →.

f. Select *Build a search condition*.

g. Select CHECKNO.

h. Select >.

i. Type 0 (zero) and press ⏎.

j. Select *No more conditions*.

k. Select *Execute the command*.

12. Press any key to return to the Assistant menu.

13. Print the REGISTER.FRM report again, and notice that it now shows the proper balance.

14. At the dot prompt, display the current system date.

15. If necessary, correct that date using the RUN command.

16. Display records of checks written on a Wednesday from the CHECKS database.

17. Use the *Sum* option on the *Retrieve* pull-down menu to sum the checks written between 12/10/90 and 12/15/90; exclude the deposits from the calculation. (That is, date is greater than or equal to 12/10/90, *and* date is less than or equal to 12/15/90, *and* check number is greater than zero.)

18. Quit dBASE.

CHAPTER 9 EXERCISES: MANAGING MULTIPLE DATA FILES

1. Start dBASE III PLUS.

2. If your instructor has not already provided you with a copy of the ORDERS.DBF database on disk, create a database named ORDERS with the structure shown in Figure E.6. Then add the sample data shown in Figure E.7 to that database.

```
Field   Field Name  Type        Width   Dec
   1    NAME        Character      15
   2    ADDRESS     Character      20
   3    CITY        Character      15
   4    STATE       Character       2
   5    ZIP         Character       5
   6    PRODCODE    Character       5
   7    QTY         Numeric         3
   8    TAXRATE     Numeric         4     2
   9    FULFILLED   Logical         1
```

Figure E.6

3. Create an index file that uses UPPER(PRODCODE) as the index key for the ORDERS database, and assign the name ORDERS to that index file.

4. If your instructor has not already provided you with a copy of the PRODUCTS.DBF database on disk, create a database named PRODUCTS with the structure shown in Figure E.8. Then add the sample data shown in Figure E.9 to that database.

5. Create an index file that uses UPPER(PRODCODE) as the index key for the PRODUCTS database, and name that index file PRODUCTS.

6. Create a view with the file name ORDLINK that will link the ORDERS database and the index file into the PRODUCTS

NAME	ADDRESS	CITY	STATE	ZIP	PRODCODE	QTY	TAXRATE	FULFILLED
Jimmy Jones	1234 Arrow Rd.	Cucamonga	CA	91123	FZ001	1	0.07	.F.
Wilma Whetstone	453 Pebbles St.	Los Angeles	CA	92023	BL001	1	0.07	.T.
Flip Remark	2701 Broad St.	Hatboro	PA	27091	FZ001	1	0.00	.T.
Russ T. Hinge	P.O. Box 3384	Tampa	FL	54321	BL001	1	0.00	.T.
Elsie Bovine	3701 Ashton Rd.	Nashville	TN	37207	BL001	2	0.00	.T.
Annie Bannani	P.O. Box 227	Tulsa	OK	74043	AP001	2	0.07	.T.
Dana Pointe	197 Charleston Ave.	Goleta	CA	93117	AP001	2	0.07	.T.
Rollo Royce	275 Fremont St.	Reno	NE	89501	AP001	1	0.00	.T.
Skip T. Maloo	2121 Early Way	New Orleans	LA	70122	AP001	1	0.00	.T.
Sandy Eggo	2920 Flawless Ave.	Eulen	TX	76039	FZ001	1	0.00	.F.

Figure E.7

database and the index file based on the expression UPPER(PRODCODE). The relation chain must be ORDERS.DBF—>PRODUCTS.DBF.

7. Create a report format based on the ORDLINK view to print the report shown in Figure E.10, using the tips below as a guide:

   • Assign the name ORDTOTAL to the report.

- The *Group on expression* is **UPPER(PRODCODE) + ":
  " + PRODUCTS—>PRODNAME**, and the group
  heading is **Product:** followed by a single blank space.

- The third column contains the following expression:
  PRODUCTS—>PRICE, with a width of 9 and 2
  decimal places. The column is not totaled.

- The fourth column contains the following expression:
  QTY*PRODUCTS—>PRICE, with a width of 9
  and 2 decimal places.

- The fifth column contains the following expression:
  TAXRATE*PRODUCTS—>PRICE with a width of
  8 and 2 decimal places.

- The sixth column contains the following expression:
  (1 + TAXRATE)*(QTY*PRODUCTS—>PRICE)
  with a width of 9 and 2 decimal places.

- The seventh column shows the contents of the FUL-
  FILLED field.

```
Field   Field Name  Type        Width   Dec
    1   PRODCODE    Character       5
    2   PRODNAME    Character      30
    3   PRICE       Numeric         9     2
```

Figure E.8

```
PRODCODE PRODNAME                             PRICE
AP001    Adventures in Pac Land              34.95
BL001    Blazing Lasers                      49.95
DE001    Dungeon Explorer                    49.95
FZ001    Fantasy Zone                        49.95
ME001    Mean 18                             34.95
ML001    Monster Lair                        79.95
OD001    Ordyne                              24.95
```

Figure E.9

Page No.   1

                        Order Summary

```
** Product: AP001: Adventures in Pac Land
  Annie Bannani      2     34.95       69.90       0.00       69.90 .T.
  Rollo Royce        1     34.95       34.95       0.00       34.95 .T.
  Dana Pointe        2     34.95       69.90       2.45       74.79 .T.
  Skip T. Maloo      1     34.95       34.95       0.00       34.95 .T.
** Subtotal **
                     6                209.70       2.45      214.59

** Product: BL001: Blazing Lasers
  Russ T. Hinge      1     49.95       49.95       0.00       49.95 .T.
  Elsie Bovine       1     49.95       49.95       0.00       49.95 .T.
  Wilma Whetstone    1     49.95       49.95       3.50       53.45 .T.
** Subtotal **
                     3                149.85       3.50      153.35

** Product: FZ001: Fantasy Zone
  Flip Remark        1     49.95       49.95       0.00       49.95 .F.
  Jimmy Jones        1     49.95       49.95       3.50       53.45 .F.
  Sandy Eggo         1     49.95       49.95       0.00       49.95 .F.
** Subtotal **
                     3                149.85       3.50      153.35
*** Total ***
                    12                509.40       9.44      521.29
```

Figure E.10

8. Print a copy of the report when you've completed and saved the report format.

CHAPTER 10 EXERCISES: FILE MAINTENANCE AND PERFORMANCE

1. Copy the ORDTOTAL report format that you created in the previous chapter exercise (ORDTOTAL.FRM) to a file named ORDSUMM.FRM.

2. Modify the ORDSUMM.FRM report format, so that the *Summary report only* option on the **Groups** pull-down menu (in the report generator) is set to Yes. Save the modified report, and print a copy of it. (Tip: Remember to open the ORDLINK view before modifying the report format and printing the report.)

3. With the ORDLINK view still open, create a query named ORDSENT that displays only orders that have been fulfilled (for example, FULFILLED is true).

4. Print a copy of the ORDTOTAL report with the ORDSENT query active.

5. Close the ORDSENT query.

6. Quit dBASE III PLUS.

CHAPTER 11 EXERCISES: UNDERSTANDING MEMORY VARIABLES

1. At the dot prompt, enter a command to calculate 6.5% sales tax on a $279.00 purchase. (Hint: .065 times 279.)

2. Enter a command to add 6.5% sales tax to $749.63. (Hint: 1.065 times 749.63.)

3. Repeat the above exercise, but this time have the answer rounded to two decimal places.

4. Store your name in a memory variable named MYNAME.

5. Enter a command that shows the word *Hello* followed by a blank space and the contents of the MYNAME memory variable.

6. Calculate the cube root of 54345.3215 using a command at the dot prompt.

7. Calculate the square root of 5,184 using a command at the dot prompt.

8. Store the number 0.065 in a memory variable named SALES-TAX, and the value 249.95 in a memory variable named PURCHASE.

9. Enter a command that puts the value stored in PURCHASE, increased by the value stored in SALESTAX, in a memory variable named TOTSALE (that is, total sale equals purchase plus sales tax times purchase).

10. Display all the memory variables that you've created so far.

11. Display the contents of the TOTSALE variable rounded to two decimal places.

CHAPTER 12 EXERCISES: CREATING COMMAND FILES

1. These chapter exercises assume that you have completed the Chapter 9 exercises. If you have not, please do so before proceeding with these exercises.

2. Create a command file that will print labels from the ORDERS database that you created in Chapter 9, using the tips below as a guide:

    - Assign the name ORDLABEL to the command file.

    - Use the Mailing Labels Program shown on page 237 as a model for creating your own command file.

    - Instead of starting the ORDLABEL command file with GO TOP, start it with **USE ORDERS INDEX ORDERS** so that it will open the ORDERS database and index file for you.

    - Place the command **SET TALK OFF** in the command file so that it will set the TALK feature off for you automatically. Place this command on its own line, above the DO WHILE .NOT. EOF( ) command.

    - The ORDERS database does not have fields named FNAME and LNAME. The first **?** command should just print the field named NAME.

    - The ORDERS database only allows two characters in the STATE field, so to put some blank space printed between the STATE and ZIP codes, use the command:

        ```
        ? TRIM(CITY) + ", " + STATE + "   " + ZIP
        ```

      to print the third line of the label.

    - Place the command **SET TALK ON** near the bottom of the command file (below the ENDDO command, but above the RETURN command), so that it automatically sets the TALK feature back on when it's done.

3. After completing and saving the ORDLABEL command file, run it to "print" the labels on your screen.

CHAPTER 13 EXERCISES: MAKING DECISIONS

1. Modify the ORDLABEL program that you created in the Chapter 12 exercises so that it will do the following:

   - Ask the user whether or not to send labels to the printer.

   - If the user answers yes, have the program display the message "Prepare printer then press any key" and wait for a keypress.

   - When the user presses a key, the program turns the printer on and prints the labels.

   - When the labels have all been printed, the printer ejects the page (with the EJECT command), then turns off the printer.

   To help you with this task, the *italicized* text below shows the "logic" of the commands to do this job, and where they should appear in relation to commands that are already in the command file. However, you have to convert the italicized text to proper dBASE commands for the program to work properly:

   ```
   * * * * * * * * * * * * * * * * * Mailing Labels Program.
   USE ORDERS INDEX ORDERS
   SET TALK OFF
   ```
   Accept Send labels to printer? (Y/N) to Answer
   If uppercase of answer is Y
   Show "Prepare Printer, then press any key" and Wait for keypress
   Set the printer on
   End of "if" clause

   ```
   DO WHILE .NOT. EOF()
       ...
   ```

The bottom of the command file should look like this:

```
ENDDO
EJECT
SET PRINT OFF
SET TALK ON
RETURN
```

2. After making your changes, run the command file to test them.

3. Modify the ORDLABEL command file once again, so that it only prints labels for records that have .F. in the FULFILLED field. To do so, you'll need to add two commands: **IF .NOT. FULFILLED** and **ENDIF**. Be careful to place these commands in exactly the right places!

4. Save and test your modified command file. It should print only three labels, corresponding to the three records in ORDERS.DBF that have .F. in the FULFILLED field.

5. Quit dBASE III PLUS.

CHAPTER 14 EXERCISES: DESIGNING AND DEVELOPING PROGRAMS

1. In these exercises, we'll use the CHECKS.DBF database from Chapter 2 exercises, REGISTER.FRM report format from the Chapter 6 exercises, and EDITCHEX screen format file from the Chapter 7 exercises. If you have not completed those exercises, do so before proceeding.

2. Figure E.11 shows the pseudocode "program" for a command file that displays a menu for managing the check register. Using that pseudocode as your guide, write the program using proper dBASE syntax with the MODIFY COMMAND editor. Here are some tips:

   - Name the command file CHECKS (that is, use the command **MODIFY COMMAND CHECKS** to start creating the command file).

   - Use the pseudocode example on page 264, and the command file on page 265, as an example to work from.

   - Text shown in *italics* is pseudocode, and must be translated to dBASE.

   - Text shown in **boldface** is already in proper dBASE syntax, and need not be modified.

   - If you don't have a printer connected to your computer, leave the TO PRINT command off the end of the REPORT FORM command.

   - The SET FORMAT command simply activates the EDITCHEX screen before APPEND is executed, so that the custom screen will be shown while user is entering records.

3. After you create your program, run it to test it out. If you encounter obvious errors that are easy to fix, go ahead and fix

them now. Otherwise, wait until you've read Chapter 15 ("Debugging Techniques"), which will help you locate and fix errors.

4. Quit dBASE III PLUS when you've finished experimenting with your completed program.

```
*************************************************** Checks.PRG
*----------------------- Program to manage a check register.
*-- (Assumes all credits are positive, all debits negative.)
Set dBASE talk off
Use the CHECKS database
Set menu choice to 0
Repeat the Main Menu until option 4 is selected
     Clear the screen
     Display the Main Menu like this:

               Electronic Check Register

               1. Add new transactions
               2. Edit existing transactions
               3. Print transactions
               4. Exit the check register

     Ask which option is desired
     If option 1 selected,
          SET FORMAT TO EditChex
          APPEND
     If option 2 selected
          BROWSE
     If option 3 selected
          ***** Show message.
          CLEAR
          ? "Working -- Please wait a moment..."
          ***** Make sure deposits are positive...
          REPLACE ALL Amount WITH ABS(Amount)
          ***** ...and debits are all negative.
          REPLACE ALL Amount WITH -1*Amount FOR CheckNo > 0
          ***** The above commands assume that ALL debits are
          ***** numbered greater than 0.  So bank charges,
          ***** penalties, etc. should be assigned a
          ***** CHECKNO value of 1 or higher when entered
          ***** into the database.
          ********************** Now print the report.
          CLEAR
          REPORT FORM REGISTER TO PRINT
          ***** Remove the command below if two pages are ejected.
          EJECT
Redisplay main menu (unless option 4 was selected)
Exit the check register program
```

Figure E.11

CHAPTER 15 EXERCISES: DEBUGGING TECHNIQUES

1. Figure E.12 shows a sample command file that has some intentional bugs in it. Your teacher may have already provided you with a copy of this program, named BUGGY.PRG. If he or she has not, create that command file, exactly as shown in the figure, and name it BUGGY (that is, enter the command **MODIFY COMMAND BUGGY** to get started in creating the command file).

2. Here are some tips to help you with debugging:

```
*************************** Program with some intentional
*************************** bugs for you to find and fix.
SET TAK OFF
Countit = 1
DO WHILE Counter <= 10
    ? Counter
    Counter = Counter + 1
ENNDO
? "All done."
? "No bugs -- good job!
```

Figure E.12

- A *"syntax error"* or *"Unrecognized command verb"* error means that there is something wrong with the spelling or wording of the command. Use the alphabetical listing of dBASE commands and functions on pages 382–398 to look up proper spelling and syntax of commands.

- A *"variable not found"* message means that a requested memory variable does not exist. When this error occurs, select *Suspend,* then use **DISPLAY MEMORY** to determine what variables do exist (and remember to RESUME the program before fixing the error).

- An *"unterminated string"* error means that there is a " missing from the end of a string of characters (text).

3. When fully debugged, the program should show this on your screen when you run it:

```
1
2
3
4
5
6
7
8
9
10
All done, no bugs.
Good job!
```

CHAPTER 16 EXERCISES: A COMPLETE MAILING SYSTEM

1. Your instructor may assign some exercises that reflect the concepts covered in Chapter 16. Depending on the duration and focus of your course, your instructor might assign any of the following exercises:

    a. Design and build your own custom dBASE application using the techniques presented in Chapter 16.

    b. Design and build your own custom dBASE application using the applications generator, discussed in Appendix B.

    c. Use and study examples of other dBASE applications.

2. If you are serious about becoming a dBASE programmer, we suggest that you "graduate" to a more advanced book that focuses on the dBASE III PLUS language and programming techniques. I might recommend my own *dBASE III PLUS Programmer's Reference Guide,* also published by SYBEX. That book covers everything you need to know to become an accomplished dBASE programmer.

CHAPTER 17 EXERCISES: SOME USEFUL TIPS

1. If you have not completed the Chapter 2 exercises and created the CHECKS.DBF database, do so now and be sure to add the sample data.

2. Open the CHECKS database that you created in Chapter 2, and add a Memo field named REMARKS. Make it the last field in the database. (Hint: Pages 90–93 describe how to modify a database structure.)

3. Use the *Goto Record* option on the **Position** pull-down menu to move to the first record in CHECKS.

4. Use the *Edit* option on the *Update* pull-down menu to edit the first record in the database.

5. Add the following text to the REMARKS field, but let dBASE break the lines naturally. That is, press ⏎ only to end paragraphs—press ⏎ twice to end the first paragraph (to add the extra blank line between the paragraphs), and press ⏎ once to end the second paragraph.

   > This is the first record entered into the CHECKS.DBF database, and represents the starting balance when we switched over to the electronic register.

   > This memo field appears only in commands that specify REMARKS as a field to display, and in custom reports that use it in a column.

6. Using the *List* option from the **Retrieve** pull-down menu, construct a LIST command that displays the CHECKNO and REMARKS fields, then execute that command. (Optionally, enter a LIST command at the dot prompt that displays the CHECKNO and REMARKS fields.)

7. Create an index file named BACKWARD for the CHECKS database that displays records in descending order by check number. List the records to verify your index.

8. Re-create the BACKWARD index, but this time have it display the records in descending order by date. (Hint: the index expression is **CTOD("12/31/99") – DATE**. CTOD is the dBASE Character-To-Date function which converts a character string to a dBASE date.) List the records to verify your index. You might also want to try entering the dot prompt command **LIST DATE,CTOD("12/31/99") – DATE** to get some insight into why this works. Basically, every date is actually an integer, so subtracting an early date from a later date produces the number of days between the two dates; so later dates become "smaller than" earlier dates when subtracted from some date in the future, for example 12/31/99. Hence, the index ends up showing the dates in latest-to-earliest order.

9. Re-create the BACKWARD index one more time, this time sorting into descending order by date, and in descending check number order within each date. You then enter the command **LIST DATE,CHECKNO,DESCRIPT, AMOUNT** to verify your sort order. (The index expression is **STR(CTOD("12/31/99") – DATE,4) + STR (9999 – CHECKNO,4)**.)

INDEX

D

Selections from The SYBEX Library

DATABASES

The ABC's of dBASE III PLUS
Robert Cowart
264pp. Ref. 379-1

The most efficient way to get beginners up and running with dBASE. Every 'how' and 'why' of database management is demonstrated through tutorials and practical dBASE III PLUS applications.

The ABC's of dBASE IV 1.1
Robert Cowart
350pp, Ref. 632-4

The latest version of dBASE IV is featured in this hands-on introduction. It assumes no previous experience with computers or database management, and uses easy-to-follow lessons to introduce the concepts, build basic skills, and set up some practical applications. Includes report writing and Query by Example.

The ABC's of FoxPro 2
(Second Edition)
Scott D. Palmer
308pp; Ref. 877-7

This fast, friendly introduction to database management is now in a new edition for version 2. Concise tutorials show you how to use essential FoxPro features and commands, while hot tips give you special pointers for avoiding pitfalls. Covers everything from simple customer files to multi-file databases.

The ABC's of Paradox 3.5
(Second Edition)
Charles Siegel
334pp, Ref. 785-1

This easy-to-follow, hands-on tutorial is a must for beginning users of Paradox 3.0 and 3.5. Even if you've never used a computer before, you'll be doing useful work in just a few short lessons. A clear introduction to database management and valuable business examples make this a "right-to-work" guide for the practical-minded.

The ABC's of Q & A 4
Trudi Reisner
232pp; Ref. 824-6

A popular introduction to Q & A 4, packed with step-by-step tutorials for beginners. Learn to create databases, use the word processor, print out reports, and more. Easy instructions incorporate practical business applications. With special coverage of the Intelligent Assistant.

dBASE Instant Reference
SYBEX Prompter Series
Alan Simpson
471pp. Ref. 484-4

Comprehensive information at a glance: a brief explanation of syntax and usage for every dBASE command, with step-by-step instructions and exact keystroke sequences. Commands are grouped by function in twenty precise categories.

dBASE III PLUS Programmer's
Reference Guide
SYBEX Ready Reference Series
Alan Simpson
1056pp. Ref. 508-5

Programmers will save untold hours and effort using this comprehensive, well-organized dBASE encyclopedia. Complete technical details on commands and functions, plus scores of often-needed algorithms.

Advanced Techniques in dBASE III PLUS
Alan Simpson

454pp. Ref. 369-4

A full course in database design and structured programming, with routines for inventory control, accounts receivable, system management, and integrated databases.

dBASE IV 1.1 Programmer's Desktop Reference
Alan Simpson

1050pp. Ref. 539-5

This comprehensive seven-part reference is a must for dBASE programmers. It offers full details on every command and function, as well as practical techniques and algorithms for achieving specific programming goals. Fully cross-referenced and indexed by command, function, and topic.

dBASE IV 1.1 Programmer's Instant Reference (Second Edition)
Alan Simpson

555pp, Ref. 764-9

Enjoy fast, easy access to information often hidden in cumbersome documentation. This handy pocket-sized reference presents information on each command and function in the dBASE IV programming language. Commands are grouped according to their purpose, so readers can locate the correct command for any task—quickly and easily.

dBASE IV User's Instant Reference (Second Edition)
Alan Simpson

356pp, Ref. 786-X

Completely revised to cover the new 1.1 version of dBASE IV, this handy reference guide presents information on every dBASE operation a user can perform. Exact keystroke sequences are presented, and complex tasks are explained step-by-step. It's a great way for newer users to look up the basics, while more experienced users will find it a fast way to locate information on specialized tasks.

Mastering DataEase
Susan Harmon

531pp. Ref. 689-8

A thorough, hands-on introduction to database management with DataEase, stressing skills for on-the-job productivity. Build a sample inventory management system, while mastering quick reporting, custom form design, multi-file applications, using Data Query Language, and system maintenance.

Mastering dBASE III PLUS: A Structured Approach
Carl Townsend

342pp. Ref. 372-4

In-depth treatment of structured programming for custom dBASE solutions. An ideal study and reference guide for applications developers, new and experienced users with an interest in efficient programming.

Mastering dBASE IV 1.1 Programming
Carl Townsend

546pp. Ref. 782-9

An in-depth introduction especially for applications developers, and for experienced dBASE users seeking programming skills. This up-to-date new edition covers 1.1 basics, structured programming and database design, and specific techniques for business application programming—with examples for general ledger and invoicing.

Mastering FoxPro 2 (Second Edition)
Charles Siegel

650pp; Ref. 808-4

This highly readable hands-on guide now covers FoxPro version 2.0, with its graphical interface and other powerful new features. Part I is a practical introduction to business database management. Part II adds macros, custom menus, and other special features. Part III is a concise introduction to structured programming with FoxPro 2.0 development language.

Mastering Paradox 3.5
Alan Simpson
650pp, Ref. 677-4

This indispensable, in-depth guide has again been updated for the latest Paradox release, offering the same comprehensive, hands-on treatment featured in highly praised previous editions. It covers everything from database basics to PAL programming—including complex queries and reports, and multi-table applications.

Mastering Q&A 4
Alan R. Neibauer
500pp. Ref. 735-5

This hands-on guide is now covering the latest Q&A release. Tutorials and sample applications illustrate every aspect of using Q&A: treating and manipulating data bases, printing reports, multi-file applications and look-up tables, and integrating Q&A with Lotus 1-2-3; plus networking, macros, and programming the IA. Special sections for word processing and generating form letters and labels.

Paradox 3.5 User's Instant Reference
Loy Anderson
Cary Jensen
186pp. Ref. 766-5

Quick access to concise information on every feature of Paradox 3.0 and 3.5. Entries are organized by function, and provide exact keystrokes, command options, instructions for common tasks, and thorough cross-references. Topics include creating and working with tables; forms; reports; queries; crosstabs; graphs; tools; scripts and PAL; networking; and SQL.

Understanding dBASE III
Alan Simpson
300pp. Ref. 267-1

dBASE commands and concepts are illustrated throughout with practical, business oriented examples—for mailing list handling, accounts receivable, and inventory design. Contains scores of tips and techniques for maximizing efficiency and meeting special needs.

Understanding dBASE III PLUS
Alan Simpson
415pp. Ref. 349-X

A solid sourcebook of training and ongoing support. Everything from creating a first database to command file programming is presented in working examples, with tips and techniques you won't find anywhere else.

Understanding dBASE IV 1.1
Alan Simpson
900pp, Ref. 633-2

Simpson's outstanding introduction to dBASE—brought up to date for version 1.1—uses tutorials and practical examples to build effective, and increasingly sophisticated, database management skills. Advanced topics include custom reporting, managing multiple databases, and designing custom applications.

Understanding Oracle
James T. Perry
Joseph G. Lateer
634pp. Ref. 534-4

A comprehensive guide to the Oracle database management system for administrators, users, and applications developers. Covers everything in Version 5 from database basics to multi-user systems, performance, and development tools including SQL*Forms, SQL*Report, and SQL*Calc. Includes Fast Track speed notes.

Understanding Professional File
Gerry Litton
463pp. Re. 669-3

Build practical data management skills in an orderly fashion with this complete step-by-step tutorial—from creating a simple database to building customized business applications.

Understanding R:BASE 3.1
Alan Simpson
Ron Dragushan
656pp. Ref. 727-4

The definitive introduction to database management with R:BASE—now in an up-to-date new edition for release 3.1. Easy-to-follow tutorials for everything from designing a first table to editing data, searching, sorting, reporting, multi-table applications, macros, and programming. With a complete sample application for accounts receivable.

Understanding SQL
Martin Gruber
400pp. Ref. 644-8

This comprehensive tutorial in Structured Query Language (SQL) is suitable for beginners, and for SQL users wishing to increase their skills. From basic principles to complex SQL applications, the text builds fluency and confidence using concise hands-on lessons and easy-to-follow examples.

Up & Running with Clipper 5.01
Richard Frankel
158pp; Ref. 693-6

Start programming your own database applications in just 20 time-coded steps. No step takes longer than an hour to complete, and most take just 15 or 30 minutes. Learn to create and modify source code, customize reports, debug your programs, run database applications on local networks, and more. Covers versions 5.0 and 5.01.

Up & Running with dBASE III PLUS
Robert Cowart
140pp; Ref. 886-6

Now you can learn dBASE III PLUS in just 20 easy steps. This streamlined tutorial is designed for the reader who may be new to databases or to dBASE, but who does have fundamental computer skills. Each step covers an essential dBASE III PLUS function, and is designed to take less than an hour to complete; many take no more than 15 minutes.

Up & Running with Q&A 4
Alan Simpson
140pp. Ref. 719-3

A concise tutorial and software overview in 20 "steps" (lessons of 15 to 60 minutes each). Perfect for evaluating the software, or getting a basic grasp of its features. Learn to create databases, use the word processor, print out reports, and more. Includes coverage of the Intelligent Assistant.

OPERATING SYSTEMS

The ABC's of DOS 4
Alan R. Miller
275pp. Ref. 583-2

This step-by-step introduction to using DOS 4 is written especially for beginners. Filled with simple examples, *The ABC's of DOS 4* covers the basics of hardware, software, disks, the system editor EDLIN, DOS commands, and more.

The ABC's of DOS 5
Alan Miller
267pp. Ref. 770-3

This straightforward guide will haven even first-time computer users working comfortably with DOS 5 in no time. Step-by-step lessons lead users from switching on the PC, through exploring the DOS Shell, working with directories and files, using essential commands, customizing the system, and trouble shooting. Includes a tear-out quick reference card and function ·key template.

ABC's of MS-DOS (Second Edition)
Alan R. Miller
233pp. Ref. 493-3

This handy guide to MS-DOS is all many PC users need to manage their computer files, organize floppy and hard disks, use EDLIN, and keep their computers organized. Additional information is given about utilities like Sidekick, and there is a DOS command and program summary. The second edition is fully updated for Version 3.3.

SYBEX Computer Books
are different.

Here is why . . .

At SYBEX, each book is designed with you in mind. Every manuscript is carefully selected and supervised by our editors, who are themselves computer experts. We publish the best authors, whose technical expertise is matched by an ability to write clearly and to communicate effectively. Programs are thoroughly tested for accuracy by our technical staff. Our computerized production department goes to great lengths to make sure that each book is well-designed.

In the pursuit of timeliness, SYBEX has achieved many publishing firsts. SYBEX was among the first to integrate personal computers used by authors and staff into the publishing process. SYBEX was the first to publish books on the CP/M operating system, microprocessor interfacing techniques, word processing, and many more topics.

Expertise in computers and dedication to the highest quality product have made SYBEX a world leader in computer book publishing. Translated into fourteen languages, SYBEX books have helped millions of people around the world to get the most from their computers. We hope we have helped you, too.

For a complete catalog of our publications:

SYBEX, Inc. 2021 Challenger Drive, #100, Alameda, CA 94501
Tel: (415) 523-8233/(800) 227-2346 Telex: 336311
Fax: (415) 523-2373

SYBEX®

TO JOIN THE SYBEX MAILING LIST OR ORDER BOOKS
PLEASE COMPLETE THIS FORM

NAME _____ COMPANY _____

STREET _____ CITY _____

STATE _____ ZIP _____

☐ PLEASE MAIL ME MORE INFORMATION ABOUT **SYBEX** TITLES

ORDER FORM (There is no obligation to order)

PLEASE SEND ME THE FOLLOWING:

TITLE	QTY	PRICE
_____	____	____
_____	____	____
_____	____	____
_____	____	____

TOTAL BOOK ORDER ____ $____

CUSTOMER SIGNATURE _____

SHIPPING AND HANDLING PLEASE ADD $2.00 PER BOOK VIA UPS _____

FOR OVERSEAS SURFACE ADD $5.25 PER BOOK PLUS $4.40 REGISTRATION FEE _____

FOR OVERSEAS AIRMAIL ADD $18.25 PER BOOK PLUS $4.40 REGISTRATION FEE _____

CALIFORNIA RESIDENTS PLEASE ADD APPLICABLE SALES TAX _____

TOTAL AMOUNT PAYABLE _____

☐ CHECK ENCLOSED ☐ VISA
☐ MASTERCARD ☐ AMERICAN EXPRESS

ACCOUNT NUMBER _____

EXPIR. DATE _____ DAYTIME PHONE _____

CHECK AREA OF COMPUTER INTEREST:

☐ BUSINESS SOFTWARE

☐ TECHNICAL PROGRAMMING

☐ OTHER: _____

THE FACTOR THAT WAS MOST IMPORTANT IN YOUR SELECTION:

☐ THE SYBEX NAME

☐ QUALITY

☐ PRICE

☐ EXTRA FEATURES

☐ COMPREHENSIVENESS

☐ CLEAR WRITING

☐ OTHER _____

OTHER COMPUTER TITLES YOU WOULD LIKE TO SEE IN PRINT:

_____

_____

OCCUPATION

☐ PROGRAMMER ☐ TEACHER

☐ SENIOR EXECUTIVE ☐ HOMEMAKER

☐ COMPUTER CONSULTANT ☐ RETIRED

☐ SUPERVISOR ☐ STUDENT

☐ MIDDLE MANAGEMENT ☐ OTHER:

☐ ENGINEER/TECHNICAL _____

☐ CLERICAL/SERVICE

☐ BUSINESS OWNER/SELF EMPLOYED

CHECK YOUR LEVEL OF COMPUTER USE

☐ NEW TO COMPUTERS

☐ INFREQUENT COMPUTER USER

☐ FREQUENT USER OF ONE SOFTWARE

  PACKAGE:

  NAME _____

☐ FREQUENT USER OF MANY SOFTWARE

  PACKAGES

☐ PROFESSIONAL PROGRAMMER

OTHER COMMENTS:

_____

_____

_____

_____

_____

_____

_____

PLEASE FOLD, SEAL, AND MAIL TO SYBEX

SYBEX, INC.
2021 CHALLENGER DR. #100
ALAMEDA, CALIFORNIA USA
94501

SEAL